Edwin Arlington Robinson

Edwin Arlington Robinson at the time of *Collected Poems*

Edwin Arlington Robinson

Emery Neff

NEW YORK / RUSSELL & RUSSELL

This is
WANDA'S BOOK

Acknowledgments

I BEGAN this book out of admiration for Robinson as a man and as a poet. I am completing it with gratitude to his relatives and friends, who have told me much not hitherto set down in writing, and to scholars who have generously given me access to unpublished information.

Mrs. William Nivison, the poet's niece, was my guide in the town of Gardiner, and, together with her sister, Mrs. Harold Wright Holt, read and corrected in manuscript the portions of my book concerned with his life in Maine. Professor and Mrs. Daniel Gregory Mason, Mr. and Mrs. Ridgely Torrence, the late Mr. Louis V. Ledoux and Mrs. Ledoux, Mr. and Mrs. James E. Fraser, and Mrs. Lewis M. Isaacs, long friends of Robinson, were my hosts on several delightful occasions and gave me intimate impressions of his personality and manner of working. Mr. Fraser permitted me to read those pages of his unpublished autobiography relating to Robinson. Mrs. Isaacs, by her generous gift of manuscripts and letters to the New York Public Library, permitted me to discover the date of the composition of "The Man Against the Sky." Mr. Torrence, Mrs. Isaacs, and Professor Mason did me the great favor of reading my entire manuscript and removing errors of fact and interpretation. For those that may remain, the responsibility is wholly mine.

To Miss Margaret Perry I owe illuminating reminiscences of Robinson's friendship with her parents, Thomas Sergeant Perry and Lilla Cabot Perry, and permission to quote from one of his letters to Lilla Cabot Perry. Mrs. Edward MacDowell, to whom I owe the privilege of meeting the poet at the MacDowell Colony, drew from her rich recollections. Dr. Carl Van Doren, who had a large share in establishing Robinson's reputation, has supplied important biographical details. For intimate glimpses of Robinson as a Harvard undergraduate, I am indebted to Professor Robert Morss Lovett. To have met these faithful friends of the poet has been a great privilege.

The aid of scholars hastened the preparation of this study by many months. Professor Lawrance Thompson advised and guided from the outset, put at my disposition unpublished letters in the Princeton University Library, and concerning various matters secured the opinion of Mr. Robert Frost, whose biography he is engaged in writing. Professor Denham Sutcliffe, with the consent of Professor William Jackson and of the Harvard University Press, allowed me to read his typescript of Robinson's letters to Harry de Forest Smith, the most important source of information concerning the poet's early life and work, almost a year before their publication. He and his mother, Mrs. S. E. Champney, were my hosts and richly informed guides during my visit to the Kennebec Valley. My colleague Mr. Joseph Doyle, who is writing a critical biography of George Edward Woodberry, not only aided me with his knowledge of the literary scene when Robinson began to write but also introduced me to Robinson's friends Mr. and Mrs. Louis V. Ledoux, Mr. L. V. Pulsifer, and Mr. Harold Pulsifer. Through his kindness I also had the pleasure of stimulating discussion with Mr. Thomas Riggs, Jr., who is preparing a study of Trumbull Stickney. Professor Robert Lee Wolff helped me greatly toward an understanding of Harvard in the nineties and went to the trouble of copying for me useful excerpts from newspapers.

I am much indebted to Professor Perry Miller for informing me concerning the large collection of unpublished Robinson letters in the Harvard Library and to Professor William Jackson for granting me permission to quote from letters to James Barstow, Craven Langstroth Betts, Mrs. Mabel Dodge (Luhan), John Drinkwater, John Hays Gardiner, Richard Watson Gilder, Arthur R. Gledhill, Louis V. Ledoux, Percy Mackaye, Mr. and Mrs. William Vaughn Moody, Edward G. Moore, and Josephine Preston Peabody; also from letters by Peter Duffield and Professor Bliss Perry concerning the manuscript of "Captain Craig," from a letter by Richard Watson Gilder to Robert Underwood Johnson, and from a biographical note by Ridgely Torrence. Miss C. E. Jakeman of the Houghton Library and Miss Nora E. Cordingly and Mr. John L. Sweeney of the Poetry Room of the Widener Library were exceedingly helpful in directing me to valuable documents. Mr. Robert W. Hill and Mr. Karl Küp very obligingly gave me access to the Isaacs Collection of Robinsoniana at the New York Public Library while it was being catalogued. To Mr. Howard G. Schmitt I owe the opportunity to read two of Robinson's letters to Arthur R. Gledhill and permission to quote briefly from one of them. I thank

Mrs. George W. Latham for the privilege of quoting from Robinson's letters to her husband, Professor Latham.

The editors of the American Men of Letters Series, Professors Joseph Wood Krutch, Mark Van Doren and Lionel Trilling and Miss Margaret Marshall, have aided me in many ways. I am exceedingly grateful to Miss Marshall and Professor Trilling for detailed criticism of my manuscript.

For the large outlines of Robinson's life and for the record of his characteristic sayings, I am indebted to Mr. Hermann Hagedorn's biography. It has not been possible to indicate departures from his version of events; but those departures have been based upon documents, often inaccessible to him, or upon reliable word-of-mouth authority. Mr. Charles Beecher Hogan's *Bibliography of Edwin Arlington Robinson* has spared me more hours of search for information concerning the poet's publications and their critical reception than I can well imagine.

Acknowledgment is gratefully made to The Macmillan Company for permission to quote from Robinson's poems contained in the volumes *Captain Craig, The Man Against the Sky, Merlin, The Three Taverns, Avon's Harvest, Roman Bartholow, The Man Who Died Twice, Dionysus in Doubt, Tristram, Cavender's House, The Glory of the Nightingales, Nicodemus, Amaranth,* and *King Jasper:* from *Edwin Arlington Robinson: A Biography*, by Hermann Hagedorn: from *Music in My Time, and Other Reminiscences*, by Daniel Gregory Mason: and from *Selected Letters of Edwin Arlington Robinson.* Acknowledgment is gratefully made to Charles Scribner's Sons for permission to quote from Robinson's poems contained in the volumes *The Children of the Night* and *The Town*

Acknowledgments

Down the River: to the Harvard University Press for permission to quote from *Untriangulated Stars: Letters of Edwin Arlington Robinson to Harry de Forest Smith,* edited by Denham Sutcliffe: to the New York Public Library for the privilege of quoting from a record by Lewis M. Issaacs of a conversation with Robinson about Alfred H. Louis.

E. N.

New York
April 1948

Contents

Introduction

EDWIN ARLINGTON ROBINSON is the outstanding poet between Emily Dickinson and the
poetic revival immediately before the First World
War. In itself, this might be a pallid distinction, for the
'nineties and the opening years of the twentieth century
were among the least fruitful decades in American verse.
But Robinson's distinction is more positive. With Robert
Frost, he shares the foremost place in the first half of this
century, and he will remain beside Frost among the greatest
American poets. The pages to follow give grounds for my
belief that he has written the most impressive poem in
American letters: a poem that will bear comparison with
the great English odes. The slowness with which Robinson,
severe in his demands upon the reader, won recognition
suggests that his full stature may not be apparent for a
considerable time to come.

Robinson's verse is rooted firmly in our soil and character. With the exception of three Arthurian poems written
late, its themes are almost wholly American; and its humor
is unmistakably New England. But its American quality is
not of the flamboyant sort attractive to European seekers

and exploiters of novelty. His fresh and original observation of life flows into traditional verse forms, and his idiomatic language shuns slang and the merely picturesque. In a time of unbridled, sometimes fantastic, experimentation Robinson, as Frost observes, "stayed content with the old-fashioned way to be new." Through that way he speaks to other peoples—a Frenchman is among his best critics—and will speak to other times.

Robinson's steadfast devotion to writing during long years of neglect—the critics accepted him at forty-seven, the general public at fifty-eight—is one of the heroic chapters in American biography. With standards as exacting as Flaubert's, he had no private income, and could not count upon the literary sophistication of an old nation. Unfitted to gain a living by other means, he was thrown back repeatedly upon the one talent which apparently it was starvation to show. Despair he kept at bay by almost superhuman patience. In 1916 John Gould Fletcher was impressed with his "lonely integrity in defeat—an attitude, so far as I could see at that date, utterly alien to most Americans, or to the popular conception of Americans." The means of his ultimate victory shed light on the problem of the fastidious and scrupulous author in a democracy.

Edwin Arlington Robinson

Father and Sons

EDWARD ROBINSON, ship's carpenter turned general storekeeper in the hamlet of Head Tide, Maine, was ready to retire as he passed fifty, hale and hearty. Buying and selling timber lands, he had accumulated eighty thousand dollars, which would maintain his household well if invested in the industries of the Kennebec River town of Gardiner, twelve miles away, where his sons could have better schooling. The removal of the family was delayed by the birth of a third son on December 22, 1869. The child, who almost cost his mother's life, was unchristened six months later, when she was convalescent at the seashore. One of the summer visitors, concerned over his nameless state, suggested a choice by lot. The name Edwin came out. Mrs. Robinson rewarded the woman from Arlington, Massachusetts, responsible for the idea by adding Arlington. Thus casually the name Edwin Robinson received a touch of distinction.

In September the family went to Gardiner, where the future poet was to spend all but two of the next twenty-seven years. A town of just under 4,500 inhabitants, it was admirably located for manufacture and trade at the junction of the rapid Cobbossee, a source of power for lumber, paper, and textile mills, with the deep tidal Kennebec, which harbored seagoing ships. Maine's manufactured products, after doubling in value during the Civil War decade, continued to grow in the 'seventies and 'eighties, and Edward Robinson drew substantial profits from local factories and banks. The westward expansion of the nation offered good returns from farm mortgages. He became a leading citizen: alderman, councilman, member of the school board, bank director.

The ambition of the hale elderly man extended to the future of his sons, which, after the fashion of most fathers in those days, he planned for them. Admiring a philanthropic neighbor who was a physician, he decided upon a medical career for his studious eldest son, Dean. Herman, eight years younger, handsome, active, popular, was obviously cut out for the more important career of business. Edwin, the latecomer, four years Herman's junior, shy, not robust or notably studious, presented a problem. One would have to wait to see what he could do.

Vivid among Edwin's early memories was one of himself alone on a high stool in a store while his parents did errands. Women came up and tried to make him talk. He remained stubbornly silent. Finally one said: "I know why that little boy doesn't talk. He hasn't any tongue." He stuck his tongue out as far as he could, but wouldn't speak. Taciturnity, beyond the measure allowed the proverbial Down-Easter, attended him throughout life, often to his acute embarrassment. But he liked to hear others talk and followed their actions with keen eyes.

By the age of five he realized, from experience with assertive playmates, that he was "never going to be able to

elbow [his] way to the Trough of Life." The tactlessness
and callousness of adults made him interpret the Scriptural
"Suffer little children" as a command to endure. At home,
in spite of comforts and care, he felt he didn't belong.
While he rocked in a chair much too big for him, he
sometimes wondered why he had ever been born. But his
was a reading family—his mother had been a teacher—and
learning to read at five opened a world for which he
seemed to have been made. The child of six, sitting on the
kitchen floor, read aloud to his parents the strongly
rhythmic lines of Poe's "Raven." Noting how well the
boy remembered, Edward Robinson would quote a line
from Campbell's "Lochiel's Warning" and ask him to
go on. Perhaps there was a touch of atavism here, for his
mother's people, the Palmers, were descended from a sister
of the Colonial poetess Anne Bradstreet, "the Tenth Muse."
Reading had terrors as well as delights. Dean's medical
books, with their horrible illustrations, convinced him that
he had "lock-jaw, lupus, leprosy, cancer, elephantiasis,
Bright's disease and falling of the womb, all at once."

Since Dean was twelve years older and Herman too
active and domineering, Edwin sought playmates outside
his home. Across the street lived a Jordan boy and girl
whose father mysteriously came and went, a sea captain
who told thrilling stories of whales and sharks. The village-
like neighborhood of comfortable frame houses scattered
among lawns and gardens about a spacious Common and
a cemetery was safe for small children's roaming. The
Robinson house and barn stood in two acres of garden and
orchard, with the ravine of a rivulet which could be
dammed to make a pool. Now and then came a long buggy
ride through hemlock forests and meadows to Grand-

father Palmer's farm. Edwin liked to hear old farmers talk; they were gentle and leisurely, and told droll stories. Even the prayer meetings at the Congregational church, where his mother took him, were not always tedious. Queer-looking people said funny things in their prayers.

Fog horns and factory whistles were familiar long before Edwin was big enough to be allowed to explore the part of Gardiner from which they sounded. A boy had to go down a steep hill, wonderful for coasting, and cross busy Water Street, full of wagons and buggies, before he could get to the wharves and watch floating logs being pushed into the mouth of the Cobbossee for the sawmills, or ice cut and stored in big houses along the shore. In the spring, tugs brought up great four-masters, last of sailing ships that once ruled the seas, to take Kennebec ice, famed for its crystal purity, to New Orleans or to India. Twice a day tides brought the tang of the sea. Steamers arrived from Boston to take on finished lumber, cloth, or shoes. A passenger boat went down between the thickly wooded banks of the river to its mouth, where the Robinsons, like many other Gardiner families, had an island summer cottage. Sawdust and chemical dyes from the Cobbossee were killing the fish, but there was good swimming from docks free of shipping. About a mile down the Kennebec lay Oaklands, built by the Gardiners, who had given the town its name, of dark granite in the Tudor style, with battlements and twisted chimneys. It was occupied only in summer; its 300 acres were free to visitors at other times. Or the Cobbossee, once more a dashing stream above the mill dams, could be explored through woods and fields to its source six miles away in beautiful Lake Cobbossee, famed for bass fishing. "The Cataract of Lodore," full of words that tried to catch the ever-changing wonder of water, was one of Edwin's favorite poems in the thick volume of Bryant's *Library of Poetry and Song*.

At ten, he was collecting words. With Gus and Alice Jordan he made a game of seeing who could find the biggest: long Bible names like Melchizedek and Nebuchadnezzar, words from Shakespeare that sounded grand even though you didn't know what they meant. At eleven he was writing verses. Opposite the foot of his bed he hung an engraved likeness of Poe.

Growing too fast, he found it hard to keep up with the other boys in coasting, swimming, punting rafts, trying to ride logs like rivermen. Before the end of the day he was "tuckered," though he wouldn't own up. Lying awake well into the night, he wondered if the shin bones of the rest of the boys ached as much as his did. He enjoyed rainy spells when he could sit and read.

At school, his thoughts often strayed out of the window. Once a teacher, irritated at his persistent inattention, stole behind him and struck with the side of her hand a sharp blow underneath an ear that had already been giving him pain. The ear troubled him more and more, for there was neglected mastoid infection.

At the end of his thirteenth year he entered high school, choosing on his father's advice the "scientific" course recently introduced as an alternative to the traditional classical curriculum by a business community in revolt against the "uselessness" of Greek. This meant shutting the door to college, since most colleges required the classics; but the boy unconsciously accepted as a truism his father's frequent declaration that college did no one any good. Chemistry, mathematics, typing, and stenography, the backbone of this course, proved boring. Latin, however, aroused in him a lively interest incomprehensible to most of his classmates. Greek would have been still more to his liking, as he discovered with immense regret when he was out of high school. In the upper classes Latin and English became increasingly attractive. Milton's minor poems led him to the sonorous lines of *Paradise Lost*.

At sixteen he tried turning an assigned translation of Cicero's oration against Catiline into blank verse, which unexpectedly proved to be more difficult than the rhymed forms in which he had been writing. He found the possibilities of its structure and music so fascinating that he could not stop until he had versified the entire oration. The result "may not have been poetry and probably wasn't," Robinson recalled in the years of his fame, "but many portions of it had music and rhythm and an unmistakable presence of what is nowadays called 'punch'—for which Cicero may possibly deserve some credit. It was written and rewritten with a prodigality of time that only youth can afford, with an elaborately calculated variation of the caesura, and with a far more laborious devotion than ever was expended on anything that I was supposed to be studying." He was indignant to find himself conditioned at the end of this year while classmates with much less ability but more even attention to assignments were passed. Fortunately the new principal, finding the standards of the high school too low, persuaded the school board to add a year to the curriculum. Edwin reveled in the *Aeneid*, reading ahead of the class from sheer delight in the poetry.

At length he had found friends who saw nothing odd in his tastes. Harry Smith, son of a ship's caulker and small farmer, planned to specialize in the classics at Bowdoin;

Arthur Gledhill intended to follow his father into the Congregational ministry. A third, Ed Moore, a lover of nature, was hesitating about entering his father's plumbing business. After Smith, a class ahead, was graduated, Gledhill, Moore, and Robinson formed a League of Three, proudly announced by a triangular badge with the figure 3 engraved inside. As recompense for their extra year, they asked and obtained the privilege of spending study hours outside the schoolroom. Choosing the belfry in order to be unobserved, they smoked pipes and plastered the beams with chewing tobacco. To heat the laboratory one night after school, Gledhill and Robinson burned a settee. When the janitor's son "blew" on them, they denied guilt. For years the incident weighed on Edwin's conscience.

The League of Three decided that the graduation of the class of '88 was an occasion for special festivities. Under their leadership its twelve members (seven of them girls) solicited a fund of four hundred dollars, which they spent on sawdust- or hay-rides, and dances and suppers with a brass band.

Edwin enjoyed the fun and comradeship the more because shadows were gathering at his home. Dean had come back the year before, a despairing man at twenty-nine. His medical interest lay in research, but he had yielded to his father's predilection for the active life by taking a country practice on the seacoast. Exposure in winter calls had induced neuralgia, stilled with morphine until he had fallen victim to the habit. His father, near seventy and yielding to old age, now lay for hours on the parlor sofa, his head on his devoted wife's lap. Herman, in his sanguine early twenties and working in a bank where the family had an interest, was advising his parent to shift into investments, like Western real estate, which offered quicker returns. Both parents looked to Herman to follow in his father's footsteps. Edwin suffered when he compared Herman's easy success with the appalling defeat of the brilliant, gentle Dean. He himself had often taken Herman's leavings, done dull chores while his handsome brother drove off in his buggy to shine before the girls. It was not an attractive prospect—his father aging, his mother self-effacing, his businessman brother growing in importance.

But in Gardiner High, Edwin was accepted as a leading spirit. His class went out in a blaze of glory, with Commencement exercises held under the ample roof of the Colosseum skating rink. Gledhill addressed the audience in Greek. Robinson produced the class poem, a skit on feminine foibles.

Then everything for him appeared to stop. Moore entered his father's business. Other friends made their choice of college or of a job. Robinson once more felt himself outside of the normal course of things. The desire for college had come in his junior year, when it seemed too late, with prerequisites to make up and his father more convinced than ever, by Dean's plight, of the perils of higher education. For business Edwin had no taste, in spite of encouragement from parents and friends. He temporized by requesting another year at high school, to study Horace and Milton with his favorite teacher, "Lizzie" Austin, and by taking odd jobs, such as timekeeping for the Oakland Ice Company.

His ambition to live by writing he was ashamed to avow, as he might have done in Europe where authorship was a recognized career. "There's no money in it," would have been the obvious and final reply, even though in nearby

Bowdoin *Uncle Tom's Cabin* and some of Longfellow's poems had been written, and Hawthorne had studied. His reading of the lives of poets freed him from any illusion that material success necessarily accompanied fame. Fortunately, with Herman managing his father's affairs, the family did not need help. He had time to consider.

Robinson had already asked himself, when he was translating Cicero, what his verse was worth by professional standards. "L'Allegro" and "Il Penseroso," written in Milton's early twenties, he admitted to be far beyond his own reach in his seventeenth year. But he had read that the English mind, nourished by a rich national culture, had the opportunity to mature five or ten years earlier than the American. Did his verse show promise as American writing? He ventured to ask the only Gardiner poet he knew, the homeopathic doctor Alanson Schumann, who lived on the same street.

Dr. Schumann returned his verses with the frank statement that Win Robinson was already a better poet than he. The middle-aged bachelor and the high school student became friends in the fellowship of their craft. One day when he dropped in at the doctor's office in the bank building where Herman worked, Robinson found him elated over straightening out a line of verse that had baffled him for two years. Evidently the pains that Edwin himself had bestowed on the Catiline oration had been nothing out of the ordinary.

Schumann had caught zeal for versifying from his high school teacher, Miss Caroline Swan, one of the early Radcliffe graduates. Schumann and the Probate Judge, Henry Webster, met with her weekly to read poetry and criticize each other's verse. The high school student, admitted as a fourth, found to his embarrassment—for he knew no modern language—that their chief models were French. Some fifteen years earlier, Théodore de Banville's *Petit traité de versification française* had started a vogue for mediaeval French verse forms in England. Gosse, Symons, Dobson, Lang, Henley, Stevenson, and Swinburne played charmingly with triolets, rondeaux, ballades, and villanelles, and of late Francophile writers of American magazine verse like Brander Matthews and Clinton Scollard. Miss Swan would read aloud a poem by Villon, Charles d'Orléans, or Passerat, and then translate line by line, explaining structure and verbal felicities. Afterwards one or another of the group would read his own verse, to be criticized by the rest.

The complex French forms provided admirable exercise in verse-making, for they required subtler and more structural use of the refrain than the British popular ballad, and their demands upon rhyme were more severe in English because of the ban on identical rhymes. Yet effort must be so concealed that the result seems spontaneous. The tunes of the ballade and the villanelle began to haunt the student's memory, and words and sentences sprang to wed themselves to their movement.

Edwin Robinson had his own contribution to make to the weekly meetings: a theory of the language and word order of poetry. Ever since he had begun to read the poets he had disliked departure from the language of prose and of daily speech, inversion or twisting of the natural grammatical order. His own taste demanded the reforms advocated by Wordsworth at the beginning of the century. Wordsworth had seemed to triumph over eighteenth-century periphrasis and Latinisms, yet by the time of his death Tennyson's imitation and elaboration of the early Keats' fondness for the quaint and strange was about to culminate in Pre-Raphaelite exploitation of the charms of obsolescent verbiage. Tennyson and the Pre-Raphaelites dominated American taste of the 'eighties, when Robinson began to write; but he found support for his own instinct for the direct and the contemporary in Bryant's Introduction to *The Library of Poetry and Song*, the anthology designed for family use which had opened to him the wide realms of English and American poetry. The dean of American poets, writing in 1870, praised Wordsworth for the "impulse which brought the poets back . . . to a certain fearless simplicity." But he deplored a recent tendency to relapse. Poets were striving to excite admiration by "striking novelties of expression," by "luxuriance of poetic imagery and of epithet." Bryant rebuked their apostasy by reasserting his own faith: "The elements of poetry lie in natural objects, in the vicissitudes of human life, in the emotions of the human heart, and in the relations of man to man. He who can present them in combinations and lights which at once affect the mind with a deep sense of their truth and beauty is the poet for his own age and the ages that succeed it. It is no disparagement either to his skill or his power that he finds them near at hand."

Bryant's credo had become Robinson's. The mature members of Miss Swan's group found the shy high school student tenacious in defense of his verse, though he welcomed criticism. When he became famous, he described with zest in *The Colophon* how he proceeded to create his style: "In those days time had no special significance for a certain juvenile and incorrigible fisher of words who thought nothing of fishing two weeks to catch a stanza, or even a line, that he would not throw back into a squirming sea of language where there was every word but the one he wanted. There were strange and iridescent and impossible words that would seize the bait and swallow the hook and all but drag the excited angler in after them, but like that famous catch of Hiawatha's, they were generally not the fish he wanted. He wanted fish that were smooth and shining and subtle, and very much alive, and not too strange; and presently, after long patience and many rejections, they began to bite."

He had been meeting with his verse-writing friends for two years or more, when in June 1889 he bade reluctant farewell to Gardiner High School and decided upon the precarious profession of letters. Dr. Schumann, let into the "grisly secret," approved. "He told me once," Robinson recalled, "that I should have to write poetry or starve, and that I might do both—although he did not believe that I should starve, or not exactly." Gardiner people, who observed the doctor sitting on a bench in the Common to avoid patients while pursuing a poetic idea, might have pointed to his ruined practice as a commentary.

In an unheated upstairs room, the apprentice to poetry read, meditated, and wrote, when he was not doing errands or chores about the yard, or helping to while away his father's time. Edward Robinson, like so many men of action, had limited interior resources as his strength failed, and needed company for cards or checkers. It was a dull life for a young man of twenty. "Sometimes a week or ten days goes by without my seeing one of the boys or girls (I believe I never saw much of *them*, anyway) unless I happen to run across one of them down street in the afternoon for a minute or two," he wrote to Gledhill in the summer of 1890. "I never was much of a light in company, but it hardly suits me to become a genuine eremite." The news of Gledhill's engagement to marry, received just as he came back from Herman's wedding dinner the year before, had made him keenly aware that something set him apart. Could he have met young women easily, like Gledhill, instead of worshiping them from afar, had he been a hunter and camper like Joe Barstow, or skilled with his hands in a town of carpenters and mechanics, he might have escaped qualms of conscience about being a "parasite" at home, as he feared his father thought him, though there was no word of reproach.

Nostalgia for the years of school comradeship went deep. It might have been an old "grad" of thrice his years who implored Gledhill not to forget: "Sometimes when you are strolling around the campus after twilight, alone [Gledhill was at St. Lawrence] . . . you may think of the fellow down east who never seemed to amount to much in school (or anywhere else) but who was proud to believe he was not altogether a nincompoop. He never had a great many friends, this fellow, but those he did have he has never forgotten, and never will. He could forgive a petty insult or injury very easily, but somehow or other he could never forget a favor, however small."

In search of variety and pocket money, he joined surveyors mapping the Kennebec. He got fifty dollars for the month's labor, but would have preferred to read Virgil; there was "something to life outside of business." A weekend visit with Harry Smith at Bowdoin rekindled his desire for college. Since knowing Miss Swan, he had felt the need of modern languages and literature as a basis for his poetry. Harvard admitted special students. But how persuade his father to give money for a year there, and how convince the rest of the family that he was not indispensable at home? Even Dr. Schumann shared the popular impression, encouraged by newspaper stories, that Harvard students wasted time in riotous living. While he hesitated, neighbors kept asking innocently, "Well, now, Robinson, what do you intend to do?" The well-meant inquiry made him boil with repressed rage.

He apologized to Smith for filling his letters with comments on books. There was "little else to write about, situated as I am." Accounts of his reading reveal critical judgments much less advanced and sure than his conception of what his own poetry must be. Superlatives were indiscriminate. Keats' sonnets are "the greatest in the English language." Bret Harte's "Outcasts of Poker Flat" not only surpasses Kipling but is "the best short story" in English. William Black's romance, *Macleod of Dare*, is "a great novel." Condemnation of Daudet's *Sapho* (by hearsay) as pornography and praise of the sentimental *John Halifax, Gentleman* for its "realism" consort strangely with relish for Byron's *Don Juan*. But Robinson's letters also revealed the direction of his mature judgment. He was steeped in the poetry of Matthew Arnold and Robert Browning, and preferred Kipling's verse to his prose.

What distinguishes his opinions from those of the usual bookish twenty-one-year-old is interest in literary technique and especially curiosity as to the ways and means of the profession of letters. In a translation by John Jay Chapman of the Fourth Canto of the *Inferno* in *terza rima* he finds the meter "a little shaky" and identical rhymes too frequent. Character analysis seems more profound in *A Pair of Blue Eyes* than in *The Mayor of Casterbridge* or *The Return of the Native*. On finding nothing available for stationery but some old-style foolscap, he remarks that this is "the kind of paper most of the famous novels and histories have been written upon," and in observing how little of it he can cover in an hour is in awe of the "stamina," the "bull-dog persistence and enthusiasm" which created books as long as *The Newcomes* and *Our Mutual Friend*. The discovery of Hardy by way of *The Mayor of Casterbridge* was a "revelation." He had never supposed that "a writer of such power could achieve so little popularity (in the general sense of the word)" while such trash as Wilkie Collins' *Heart and Science* was widely known. The answer was found a month later in Carlyle's *Sartor Resartus:* "The introduction states that he had a most doleful experience in finding a publisher; this seems to be the case with nearly all great literary efforts." To his friend Smith, Robinson proceeds to quote in full Carlyle's solution of the problem by rejecting conventional standards of living: "The Fraction of Life can be increased in value not so much by increasing your Numerator as by lessening your Denominator."

He recommended that Smith read Arnold's poem, "The Future," "once or twice for enthusiasm," if he were to be assigned a speaking part in the Bowdoin Commencement exercises. Survey of world history had suggested to Arnold, the son of a historian, that the present trend to industrialism and commercialism might be temporary, even though our minds, confused as the cries which we hear

> . . . say that repose has fled
> For ever the course of the river of Time,
> That cities will crowd to its edge
> In a blacker, incessanter line;

> That the din will be more on its banks,
> Denser the trade on its stream,
>
> .   .   .   .
>
> That never will those on its breast
> See an ennobling sight,
> Drink of the feeling of quiet again.

How vividly this passage called up the exploitation of the
Kennebec since the seventeenth century! Arnold, seeing
history steadily and seeing it whole, went on:

> But what was before us we knew not,
> And we know not what shall succeed.

Perhaps the river of Time will acquire "a solemn peace"
as it widens to approach the ocean of Eternity, and bring
to the soul of man

> Murmurs and scents of the infinite sea.

Meditating on the meaning of individual lives, Robinson
quoted approvingly to Smith from FitzGerald's version of
the *Rubáiyát* the quatrain suggesting that the Creator will
spare from Hell "the luckless Pots he marred in making."
In this letter of March 10, 1891, thus appears what was to
be a major theme of Robinson's verse, the problem of
individual responsibility for failure, no doubt pressed upon
him by his brother Dean's disaster and fatalism. How long
before this he had discarded the Hell of popular religion
is not known. Although his father was not a churchgoer,
Robinson had attended with his mother the Congregational
church, whose creed was Unitarian. Science in high school,
at a time when the Darwinian controversy was still much
in the American air, may have started his drift away.
Finding the "rather grim philosophy" of Omar "rather

attractive" was a stage through which many thoughtful youths have passed in their rebound from inherited creeds; but Robinson had not known life so easy as to be satisfied with the Persian's sugar coating of Epicureanism. The creedless spirituality of *Sartor Resartus*, reinforced by Carlyle's "half diabolical humor," impressed him more, although he later discovered that he was far from understanding it. Carlyle and Omar, in their positive and negative fashions, alienated him from a Puritan tradition that had scarcely absorbed Darwin's challenge to a literally inspired Bible. But the alienation from popular religion would have been greater in most towns of the Middle West and South.

Robinson had informed Gardiner citizens of his doubt of conventional judgments of the living and the dead in his first published poem, the sonnet "Thalia," which appeared in the local *Reporter Monthly* for March 29, 1890. Two months later, the same newspaper had printed his blank-verse translation of the galley race in Book V of the *Aeneid*. He never chose to reprint these early exercises; but a sonnet version of Horace's verses to Leuconoë, enclosed in a letter to Smith of May 21, 1891, not only entered, in revised form, his first volume but also survived the scrutiny of his maturity to remain in his *Collected Poems*.

The invitation to watch Smith graduate from Bowdoin made him "feel queer." In declining he explained: "I have a vague idea that I am trying to define an exit from a school as a dividing point in a life. Mine was thus divided three years ago, but it seems to linger about the old gash, which somehow is rather slow in healing." In contrast to the "excruciatingly active and practical individuals" about him, he found altogether too much of his time occupied by "memories and ruminations."

Taking pity on his younger brother's unhappiness, Herman, happily married to a beautiful wife, intervened to urge his Harvard plea upon their father. Even the influence of the favorite son might scarcely have availed, had it not been supported by Edwin's physical condition. On Dr. Schumann's advice, he had gone to Boston for medical examination, and had been told that a necrosis had destroyed the drum of his ear and infected the bones. Worse might follow, if he did not have periodic treatments at the Massachusetts General Hospital. The necessity for these journeys weakened the objection to his more prolonged absence from home.

Permission gained, he confessed to Smith in June that he could never have been satisfied to give up the "idea of a further literary knowledge." Thomas Hood had warned that the struggle to live by the pen was "at best a sorry game," but "I suppose I shall have to try it or else live the rest of my days in a state of general dissatisfaction." He would be content to make ends meet by working for a publishing house or a good newspaper.

Smith's return to Gardiner for summer vacations had been a great boon. An indulged only child, Smith had a brusque manner and was subject to moods, but his hunger for learning was as great as Robinson's. His ambitions were the scholar's, not the writer's; he read widely and had stimulating opinions. Robinson envied his knowledge of Greek. Their favorite place of meeting, a grove of trees they called their "bower" behind the Smith house less than a mile out of town, seemed infinitely remote from the house where Edward Robinson was slowly dying and Dean

Robinson in a state possibly worse. But during this summer the spiritual hunger one sees in the eyes of Edward Robinson's portrait at Head Tide brought the first meeting of the minds of father and youngest son. Nearing death, the old man became interested in spiritualism, and the poet was too much aware of mystery in the universe not to join wholeheartedly in trials of levitation. In his horse's strange excitement as he drove one night past a cemetery he read the possibility of instinctive communion with the dead.

Smith's departure in September, to teach at Rockland, threw Robinson into a gloom which made him aware of the abnormal state of his mind: "The truth is, I have lived in Gardiner for nearly twenty-two years and, metaphorically speaking, hardly been out of the yard. Now this is not right; the process tends to widen one's thoughts, or rather sympathies, to an unwholesome extent. . . . Solitude (in the broad sense of the word) tends to magnify one's ideas of individuality; it sharpens his sympathy with failure where fate has been abused and self demoralized; it renders a man suspicious of the whole natural plan and leads him to wonder whether the invisible powers are a fortuitous issue of unguided cosmos, or the cosmos itself." In calmer moments he still doubted the popular idea that every man is the architect of his own fortune: "I sometimes have a clambering idea that there is another architect behind ourselves." Fortunately, a mere fortnight away was Harvard, with "new forms and faces."

New Forms and Faces

A BARE half-hour remained before the closing of registration, and Robinson was not yet admitted to Harvard College. His request for advanced courses in literature might conceal the design of a short cut to the A.B. degree. A representative of the English Department had to be consulted. Noting that the applicant came with uneven marks from a high school whose curriculum had only recently been stiffened, Mr. Lathrop played safe by conditioning him in English composition and by adding Anglo-Saxon for "discipline" to his elections of Shakespeare and Nineteenth-Century Prose Writers. German was postponed until after a year's grounding in French.

Rusty from two years without regular study, Robinson approached his first examinations with fear exaggerated by anxiety over his ear, which had to be syringed daily. Anglo-Saxon was "hellish" and the advanced courses in literature were not what he had anticipated. The celebrated scholar Francis Child, old and hard of hearing, made Shakespeare an almost purely linguistic study, in which obsolete words were hunted down and difficult passages interpreted. Young Lewis Gates approached nineteenth-century prose through history and biography. "If the questions were to be of an essentially aesthetic character," Robinson complained to Smith, "I should have little to fear as to the result." Only in English composition (unfortunately taught by mass methods) and in French did he feel reasonably safe. If he were "fired," he planned to conceal failure from his "dear friends" in Gardiner by taking a job in Boston until the end of the academic year. Fortunately this precarious subterfuge was not necessary. By dropping Anglo-Saxon he surmounted the examinations in early November, and began to breathe easily.

"I feel as if I had always been here, and as if I should always like to stay here," he informed Gledhill, adding that he envied the freshmen with four years of college ahead instead of his own eight months. He confided to Smith the intention of "a strong attempt to get in with the *literati* of Harvard" by sending verse to undergraduate publications. *The Harvard Advocate*, whose fiction he admired, promptly printed "The Ballade of the White Ship" and "Villanelle of Change." He aimed higher by sending a sonnet, "Thomas Hood," to *The Harvard Monthly*, an almost exclusively literary journal, one of whose editors, a junior named William Vaughn Moody, had made the professional columns of the November *Scribner's* with the poem "Dolorosa."

The *Monthly* was slow to respond. Meanwhile the staff of the *Advocate* invited him to attend one of the meetings at which they criticized contributions sent in or collected from English courses. Charles Macomb Flandrau, then an undergraduate, was to describe reminiscently in *The Diary of a Freshman* a typical meeting, when the *Advocate* secretary read manuscripts aloud amid parodies and witticisms from the group, which after voting consumed beer, crackers, and cheese before an open fire. Robinson, after months of loneliness, came full of anticipation, but was struck dumb by the liveliness of their talk. He went away convinced that they thought him a dolt. The memory of the humiliation rankled, as every hurt rankled with Robinson.

He tried more general society by attending a Thanksgiving party given by his faculty adviser, Professor Sumichrast of the French Department. There he met a young English law student who knew Andrew Lang; but the buzz of the crowd tortured his partial deafness, and he was glad of an opportunity to slip away with a young woman to the professor's library, where they talked for an hour, chiefly of French novels. "She thinks they are shocking in their immorality and hopes I will not read them," he reported to Smith with subtle humor. ". . . Her simplicity and innocence, or mine, was startling. I do not think she was trying to seduce me, however; her eyes were too large and earnest. I do not remember her name, but she was apparently growing quite fond of me when I left her."

A week later there was a student caller at Robinson's lodgings, remote from the College Yard but convenient to the Massachusetts General Hospital. He introduced himself as Robert Morss Lovett, editor-in-chief of the *Monthly*. The editorial board, he said, had decided after much discussion that they could not use "Thomas Hood," but wanted him to offer other contributions. Lovett added that the *Monthly* rarely accepted anything by a first-year man. The rejection was conveyed so courteously that the hypersensitive newcomer was not hurt. Indeed he felt "honored" that a senior, "perhaps the leading spirit of Harvard outside of athletics," should have gone so far out of his way to look up a first-year man, and a Special at that. Such was Harvard equality, he boasted to his Bowdoin correspondent; the common reproach that it had less college spirit than other schools was a tribute to its maturity.

The acquaintance with Lovett, so auspiciously begun, and with Lovett's poet friend Moody did not ripen in these undergraduate years beyond respectful regard. None of Robinson's poems was accepted by the *Monthly*, whose poetry columns he was not far wrong in thinking a monopoly of its editors. During that academic year 1891-92, three-quarters of its verse was written by Moody, Hugh McCulloch, Philip Savage, Trumbull Stickney, and Samuel Duffield of the editorial staff, Moody appearing in almost every number. The contributions of Moody and McCulloch show why they must necessarily have been cool to Robinson's offerings, in spite of Lovett's efforts in his behalf. McCulloch wrote long poems on Greek themes in the *Endymion* couplet. Moody took his subjects chiefly from the Middle Ages, following the manner of William Morris (in "How the Mead Slave Was Set Free"), that of Keats' "La Belle Dame" (in "The Amber-Witch"), Browning's (in "Angelle"), and that of Tennyson's "Idylls" (in "The Lady of the Fountain"). Both reveled in archaisms and followed Stevenson's then potent advice to play the sedulous ape to many masters, Moody with much skill in the control of form. How could either like the plainness and contemporaneity toward which Robinson was striving? Only Trumbull Stickney, who had just entered college at seventeen, showed promise of an individual style; he was already experimenting with assonances and rhyme schemes.

In the midst of this imitative late Romanticism, five sonnets in good classical style by a young instructor in philosophy, George Santayana, stood out sharply, giving Robinson an indirect taste of Leopardi. That Santayana's verse, the best in America in the early 'nineties, should attract almost no attention, while Moody's "Dolorosa," full of Browning echoes, interested the poetry editor of *Scribner's,* was no good omen for Robinson's professional future.

The *Monthly's* prose came from more hands and was more mature. There was stimulating criticism of men of letters: of Dumas *fils* by Jefferson B. Fletcher, of Paul Bourget by Norman Hapgood, of Whitman by McCulloch and Dickinson S. Miller, of Amiel and Mark Pattison by Lovett, of Ibsen by Hutchins Hapgood. Lovett's broad editorial sympathies encouraged social topics: "The Place of Mysticism in Modern Life," "Social Stages," "What is a Philistine?" (by Santayana); and serious consideration of educational problems, such as the inroads of German scholarship, the effect on Harvard of its recent transformation from a New England college into a national university. There were brief reviews of books, including Howells' *Criticism and Fiction,* Norton's translation of *The Divine Comedy,* Royce's *Spirit of Modern Philosophy,* and Hardy's *Tess of the D'Urbervilles.* The course of Robinson's development if he had been accepted into this more traveled and sophisticated group now, instead of becoming intimate with some of its members eight years later, is worth speculating upon.

Although disappointed in not gaining entrance into these established literary groups—the serious fringe of those undergraduates from old Harvard families and private schools, the activities of whose clubs, never mentioned in his letters, formed the staple of fiction about Harvard life —Robinson began to find congenial spirits through casual meetings. Harvard was still small, with 1,500 enrolled in the college and fewer than 400 more in the graduate and professional schools; but President Eliot's policy was attracting students from all over the country and encouraging an association of graduate and undergraduate students of which Robinson, older than most first-year men, took advantage. In the cheap and noisy dining room incongruously situated under the stained glass and the grave Puritan portraits of Memorial Hall, he found a junior, George Latham, who was later to be Professor of English at McGill University. Latham felt the power of Robinson's "arresting eyes," and admired the taste with which he clothed his tall, well-proportioned figure. "Anybody would take a second look at him. In some ways Richard Cory is a portrait of his creator." Enthusiasm for Arnold's verse— then usually neglected for Tennyson, Browning, and the Pre-Raphaelites—was a bond between them. Latham's moods, shifting from expansive idealism to taciturnity and aloofness, intrigued Robinson as a complex problem in character. One of Sumichrast's parties threw him with G. L. Tryon, whom he understood better because of their common Maine origin. Tryon was impressed by the somewhat formal precision of Robinson's speech, which shunned colloquialisms (Dr. Schumann, by calling attention to slovenly pronunciations like "noozpaper," had made him as self-conscious in conversation as in writing).

In a crowded restaurant in Harvard Square Robinson was put at a table where a tall, heavy-set youth was talking to a single auditor. Contrary to his usual habit, Robinson interrupted with an objection. The talker, who loved argument, admitted him to the discussion, and after the meal invited him to his room, where they conversed well into the night. Mowry Saben was in revolt against established opinion and social convention. The revolt had come out of severe but illuminating experience. The son of a mathematician, he had exasperated his father by showing promise in every study but mathematics. When what seemed mere perversity proved to be sheer incapacity, the outraged parent blindly retaliated with repressive discipline that drove the son to a nervous breakdown, which an attempted cure aggravated into general physical collapse. When Saben wished to enter Harvard, his physician had warned that any excess might kill him. Dreading a pallid existence more than death, Saben had ventured forbidden foods, tobacco, alcohol even to drunkenness—and to his surprise had flourished. He was now the voluble preacher of a self-discovered gospel that the road of excess leads to the palace of wisdom, a gospel which may account for Robinson's drawing from the college library this year a copy of Blake's poems.

George Burnham, a slight, fair-haired law student of twenty-four as quiet as Saben was emphatic, attracted Robinson because he, too, had been the victim of misunderstanding between father and son. Of a prosperous New England family like Saben and Robinson, he had run off to the West at seventeen because his father hurt his youthful pride. He had been farm hand, bartender, hotel worker in New Mexico. One winter he had wandered north to Wyoming and, finding no work there, proceeded on foot toward Butte, Montana. Misdirected, he had spent a bitterly cold night warding off deadly drowsiness by kicking the trunk of a tree. By daylight he managed to stagger back to the town he had left, his feet so badly frozen that they had to be amputated. The narrow escape from death had taught him stoicism and the resolve to make up for the years of educational opportunity thrown away in adolescent revolt.

Saben, the hedonist, led excursions of the student group into Boston for the theater, followed by convivial pipes and beers preliminary to explorations of the city's night life. Robinson could not resist satisfying his artistic curiosity as a detached spectator of what the average sensual man called pleasure, though he paid dearly by haunting images of disgust and pity. But the theater was unalloyed delight, whether the curtain rose on *Dr. Jekyll and Mr. Hyde,* Tennyson's *The Foresters,* or a Sothern and Marlowe performance of Shakespeare.

With the second term, he saw the social advantages of living near Harvard Yard. Invited to Saben's room to celebrate the end of midyear examinations, he found himself in a party so noisy that the landlady called the police. He was alarmed when Saben was summoned for faculty discipline, for although he felt sure Saben would not reveal the names of his guests, he knew that students had been expelled recently for playing poker in the dormitories. Low marks settled Saben's fate of suspension, Robinson thought. Saben took to a life of ease, smoking over books he charged to his father, and borrowing theater money from friends. Robinson, the student of character, marveled at his nonchalance.

Latham admired Robinson's sure choice of subjects and his cavalier treatment of them when they disappointed. After a term's trial, he knew he had chosen two courses unwisely. Shakespeare, promising the richest literary experience in English, was so presented as to be a waste of his time, he told his faculty adviser. With indifference he received a condition in the subject. An editorial in *The Harvard Monthly* for January of this year had attacked the course as the outstanding example of the mistaken policy of giving English literature before the seventeenth century over to philology: "Explanation, comment, emendation abound, but of Shakespeare as anything more than an ingenious writer of prolepses and transposer of adjectives there is almost no mention. . . . Of Shakespeare as an artist, as an expression of an age and a life, as a force in literature and civilization, there is absolutely no consideration at Harvard." Although Robinson had the good mark of B plus in English composition, his ire was roused because themes were graded erratically by instructors who were little more than boys: "If there is any course where the best instruction should be received, it is in the department of English composition." Fortunately nineteenth-century prose was in the hands of a teacher with taste. Lewis Gates was indulgent toward what he called Robinson's "impressionistic" attitude toward the course, which varied from boredom with Jeffrey, Sydney Smith, and George Eliot and indifference toward Gates' favorites, Newman and the Tractarians, to enthusiasm for Jane Austen and Thackeray. Finding in Thackeray "the ideal student of human nature," never tempted to Dickens' exaggerations, he made a labor of love out of a long essay on *Pendennis,* and was delighted when Gates marked it A. French was taught by the completely bilingual Sumichrast and Marcou in a way that roused his admiration. After a mere six lessons in grammar, students were set to reading.

By March he could read readily and in May could enjoy a student performance of *Le Bourgeois Gentilhomme*, with a businessman as the butt of ridicule. He drew from the college library Henry James' *French Poets and Novelists* and a translation of six tales by Coppée, with an Introduction by Brander Matthews extolling the French *conte* as an art form.

One day in May, Latham startled him with a question out of the blue: "I can't see what this life of ours amounts to, anyway. What's the object of it?" He was set to wondering once more whether his own life had a plan; and, if so, why that plan had not brought him directly from high school to Harvard, where his tastes and interests could freely expand. In view of how environment could warp, conventional judgments of individuals must often be unjust. "Sometimes," he wrote to Smith, "I think that Hell may not be such a bad place after all. . . . Think of the company." One might sit there "upon a red-hot boulder and read Daudet and Zola." He planned a satiric sonnet about a man never touched by temptation, "a good wholesome white-haired man who never told a lie or drank Maine whiskey." The sonnet directed him toward a positive and serious treatment of the same theme of the possible error of conventional judgments. People scorned as "churls and sluggards" might be triumphant in the eyes of God. Might he himself, whose ways were looked at so doubtfully by his neighbors, triumph, even in the eyes of men? For his mother's sake he hoped so; but his father was too near the grave ever to see his vindication. And had he himself refrained from calling others "churls and sluggards"? From these musings issued the sonnet "Supremacy," published in *The Harvard Advocate* for June 16, 1892. Saben warmed the author's heart by calling it a great poem.

This was still far from justifying his way of life to his father. A month later, Edward Robinson died.

There was now no obstacle to his return to Harvard. The first year had been explorative; the second would be for study. Robinson knew the reputation of courses and could make his own choice. There would be the deferred German, French composition and literature, English literature of the eighteenth century, psychology and philosophy to probe into man's mind and destiny, and Charles Eliot Norton on ancient art, a very popular course but apparently the real thing. Robinson took lodgings with a family that wanted quiet, at 1716 Cambridge Street, not far from the Yard.

Before he could settle down to work, however, he must face the long-dreaded operation on his ear, which might disclose that necrosis had gone beyond the small bones. "If it has, I may hear a trumpet blow a little sooner than I would ordinarily—that's all." The result was encouraging. He was back from the hospital in the third week in October, with one healthy small bone left, and half the anvil. In February, severe pain in the lungs brought up images of cancer or lupus, but proved to be only shingles, soon gone. The tension of his nerves, which had been almost unbearable in the last weeks of his father's illness, was relaxed as his mind and senses found abundant nourishment at Harvard and in Boston.

Professor Norton's opening remark, "Gentlemen, this is a sad sight," directed at the five hundred students crowded into his lecture room, struck the right note with Robinson. His lectures were "magnificent." They related Greek art to Greek history, and took side "swipes" at Chauncey Depew's after-dinner speeches or the World's Fair at Chicago. Ruskin called Norton his "first tutor," Robinson reported to Smith. "I suppose there is no doubt he is by all odds the greatest man in America, and I am beginning to realize what a privilege it is to sit within six feet of him three times a week." He was keenly conscious of the odds against which the bent, white-haired teacher with the gentle voice was striving. His lectures were for those who "have a fondness for the better things of life, which I sometimes think may be a misfortune. . . . Wholesome, healthy ignorance and indifference is a thing to be envied."

Another Harvard giant, Josiah Royce, was a disappointment in psychology and philosophy, and German script, a strain on the eyes, led to little rewarding literature. But Robinson was proud of a high mark for another long paper in English, and found French opening up a fascinating literature and civilization.

Buying imported paper-bound books in foreign tongues led to the "refined vice" of looking over "samples of crushed morocco in all colors and grades" for permanent bindings. Schoenhof's bookstore was a revelation: "You are used so well that you wonder [where] the difference comes in between foreign and American shopkeepers." Among his purchases were *Faust*, Voltaire's prose fiction, the comedies of Beaumarchais, *Madame Bovary*, *Manon Lescaut*, stories by Coppée, Daudet, and Mendès, and Gautier's *Le Capitaine Fracasse* (probably because of Henry James' praise). Glimpses of French newspapers made him think American dailies "a disgrace to civilization."

Seeking an American equivalent of the British weeklies,

he subscribed to *The Nation*, foreseeing difficulties for himself after having been reared on *The New York Tribune*. But soon he was regretting that he had not sent directly to England for *The Athenaeum* or *The Spectator*, since *The Nation* was only their "feeble imitation," with book reviews of ludicrous pedantry. In calling it "elegantly dry" he hit off capitally the weakness of the "genteel tradition" which was trying to offset the crudities of the Gilded Age. *The Critic* was no better: "I cannot understand why it is that Americans cannot publish a decent review. I read the Specker [*Spectator*] the other day and it made me sorry for my country." Lowell's *Biglow Papers*, disliked hitherto because of their spurious New England dialect, he now enjoyed for their satire on American chauvinism and "Anglo-Saxondum's idee . . . thet every man doos jest wut he damn pleases." Lowell, Professor Norton, Ruskin, Arnold, and the French were agreed that there were standards of taste. He enjoyed Henry B. Fuller's *The Cliff Dwellers*, a Chicago novel recommended by Norton, for its satire on "the unhealthy American rush." Latham, amused at his having remained a staunch Maine Republican, made him read Lodge's biography of Alexander Hamilton, a genuinely aristocratic conservative. A mind so inhospitable to abstract thought that it got little from Royce was being drawn by the widening and refining of its literary acquaintance toward an examination of political and economic principles. The movement was scarcely conscious, and exceedingly gradual.

Robinson published no verse this year, and apparently composed none. But he was reading two contemporaries, Meredith and Kipling, who were to influence his writing for good and for ill. *Diana of the Crossways,* "full of philosophy and sharp sayings," encouraged him to think that the brilliant remarks which occurred to him too late for the give-and-take of conversation might be put down on paper. *Barrack-Room Ballads* were in refreshing contrast to the backward-looking elegance of Dobson's *At the Sign of the Lyre.* "Danny Deever," "Gunga Din," "The Ballad of the Bolivar," "Mandalay," proved that the so-called scum of the earth, speaking their own racy language with no prettifying, could be the stuff of poetry. What vigor in the rhythm: "Seven men from all the world." What amplitude and freedom in the swing down "The Long Trail," which reminded him of the "old and plain" popular poetry commended by Shakespeare in *Twelfth Night.*

More poignantly poetic was a story from Kipling's new volume *Many Inventions.* Interpreting a motto from Emerson, Robinson's favorite American poet—

> When half-gods go,
> The gods arrive—

Kipling had created a myth about divine beings who were willing to relinquish cloudless immortality for the fuller and deeper, though ephemeral, existence of human tears, laughter, and love. Here was the answer to Latham's disturbing question, What is the object of life? Sweated labor, suffering, loss of our dearest, consciousness of our own inevitable end, were the sole road to the highest joy and beauty. Courage to endure, to extract wisdom and beauty from endurance, was the chief virtue for man. The central figure in "The Children of the Zodiac" is thus taught to be a poet. Poetry's function is to cast radiance over life by means of unflinching realism, through acceptance of the mystery of suffering. In the same volume was still more enlightenment on the origin of true art. " 'The Finest Story in the World' " is the ironic tale of a London bank clerk who is proud to exhibit his verse—of the utmost triteness—but who throws aside as worthless the prose passages that come to him in his dreams, though by some miracle of atavistic memory these fragments gradually reveal the authentic experiences of an ancient galley slave. Robinson was only twenty-three when he drank in this mature wisdom about the meaning of life and art and about the unconscious character of the creative impulse.

After he had heard in December Walter Damrosch's orchestra play Beethoven's *Eroica* Symphony, Grieg's *Aus Holbergs Zeit,* and a selection from *Tannhäuser,* "Pop" concerts became as frequent a goal of his Boston visits as the theater. But his tastes remained catholic, including light opera (with Lillian Russell) as well as the *Fingal's Cave* Overture, *Lady Windermere's Fan* as well as *Twelfth Night.* After the play or the concert there was convivial conversation, most often at the Old Elm restaurant just off Boston Common. While his companions drank deep, he would sip stout or try the flavor of some cordial. He liked "the Bohemian atmosphere and the smoke," which he had enjoyed reading about in *Pendennis,* but (he assured Smith) there was no danger of his "ever becoming a drunkard unless by circumstances of a most untoward nature." Sometimes he sat on the Common "to watch the people. People are rather interesting after all, if you don't have to talk with them."

For the congenial few his appetite remained almost insatiable. Saben, allowed to return by a relenting faculty, was the chief talker at the Corncob Club—including Latham, Burnham, Tryon, Joseph Ford, Walter Hubbell, and a Boston freshman, William Butler—which discussed whatever students include under the fascinating term "life." There was sufficient clash of opinion. Saben and Burnham, attacking Christianity, met firm opposition in Tryon, who was to enter the Episcopal ministry, and in Hubbell, a Swedenborgian. Robinson took a middle ground, defending Robert Ingersoll's attacks on popular religion yet insisting that there was mystery at the heart of things. He was frankly perplexed by the flouting of morals by men of unquestionable genius, like François Villon. In literary matters the club inclined toward innovation, turning away from the popular Tennyson and the Pre-Raphaelites to admire Arnold and Whitman. Robinson was still less conventional, praising the neglected Crabbe for his honest portrayal of village life, and Kipling. He preferred listening to talking, but his patience was not unlimited. He was bored when Saben, arriving drunk, monopolized a Corncob session by reading Ingersoll, Omar, Coppée, and Gray's *Elegy*. On another occasion, when Saben and Crapo had argued in his room for five hours, he drove them out.

Although he told Maine stories, some so salty as to perplex the free-living Saben, who did not understand the artistic impulse which sets a chaste man to studying every aspect of human nature, he gave no hint of the sorrows left behind in Gardiner. Saben, catching tones of melancholy, attributed them to anxiety about his health. With quiet determination the young poet was looking outward, storing his mind and senses with ideas and impressions against the day when he must again depend upon the resources of his inner life.

Two years of college was all he could ask from the

dwindling family capital. Indeed, disquieting news from home plagued his conscience with the old question of a "job." But that must wait, he decided, until authorship had had its trial. His home would harbor him meanwhile. At Schoenhof's, he bought books, mostly in French, for models and companions. As he took his final examinations in June 1893, he let Smith know what Harvard had meant to him. "I have seen things that I could not possibly see at another place, and have a different conception of what is good and bad in life."

Oh for a Poet—

ROBINSON returned to Gardiner to find more of the family money gone than he had feared. Twenty years of almost uninterrupted prosperity for the nation ended in that summer of 1893, as industrial depression joined the depression in agriculture which had grown steadily worse since 1887. The July newspapers told of railroad and commercial bankruptcies, strikes, bank failures, deaths of moneyed men from heart failure or suicide. Prices and wages kept falling, and there seemed no market for anything. During the following twelve months the unemployed rose to four millions. While "Coxey's army" marched on Washington, tramps knocked at Gardiner doors, mills shut down, and fewer ships came up the Kennebec.

Almost half of Edward Robinson's savings disappeared in the collapse of St. Louis real estate. Herman, blaming partners and himself for the loss, was trying to drown despair in drink. That such losses could result from a national catastrophe and not from individual dishonesty or incompetence was beyond the comprehension of Northern Americans, accustomed to automatic expansion of the national economy. Edwin Robinson was filled with pity to see his brisk and buoyant brother losing faith in himself, as Dean had. Dean, at thirty-six, was like an old man, worn down by a habit which he had come to regard as fate. Their mother, never strong, had failed physically since her husband's death, and Herman's wife, Emma, with her small children, had moved into the house.

From the conflagration of his father's dreams, Edwin, who had been least counted on, must save what he could. His mother, unaware of the direction of his ambition, feared for him as much as for her other sons, so much the dreamer he appeared. But his sister-in-law, sensing in him something extraordinary, kept assuring her: "God will take care of him." More than once in the family councils was it proposed that he go into business: this and that prominent citizen was set before him as an example. There were moments when he was so worried by family finances that he was tempted to abandon writing for money-making. But he reflected: "I am perfectly helpless in what the world calls business." He maintained the passive resistance of tactful silence, having a vent in letters to Smith and Gledhill for his lack of reverence for some of the successful men. Dr. Schumann sustained him with a "Ballade of the Law" whose refrain ran: "He sells his soul for a paltry fee."

Worse than anxiety about money was inability to read. Trouble with German print had been a disregarded warning that he needed glasses. Early in July, when newspapers were full of the business panic, the panic thought seized him that he was going blind. A visit to an oculist was reassuring; but even with glasses, for the next six months he could not read more than ten minutes at a time without discomfort. During these months he was utterly miserable, deprived of escape through books from the unhappy here and now, worried lest his eyes never recover enough to permit him to write, and temperamentally incapable of enjoying physically active pursuits like searching with Smith in the marine deposits near Iron Mine Hill, which the great English geologist Lyell had thought worth a journey. Smith's companionship and a visit from Butler helped fill the vacuum of the summer, but the autumn, with Smith gone, was intolerably boring: "To live week after week without a soul to speak to on any congenial topic is hell to a man of my nature." Fortunately, Harvard had revealed that he was not "so hopelessly different from the world" as he had thought. Letters to Harvard friends and weekly correspondence with Smith kept him from eating his heart out until he could go to Cambridge for a fortnight after Thanksgiving, and there make Smith acquainted with Butler, Tryon, Saben, and the rest. Butler seemed a little changed by having gone into his father's department-store business: "I wonder where I got this warm hatred for anything pertaining to business? The word itself almost nauseates me, sometimes."

"They fail, and they alone, who have not striven." Robinson had recalled the verse from Thomas Bailey Aldrich when in late September his eyes permitted him to write intermittently for three or four hours daily. Blindness was not going to make his one talent useless, after all. The upstairs room where his chilled fingers had so often written letters to Smith and Gledhill was converted into a study by the addition of a heat register and a bookcase. If there was no money in verse, there was admittedly some in prose fiction; and his uncle Edward Proby Fox, employed by the

Riverside Press, could put his manuscripts into the hands of the editor of *The Atlantic Monthly*.

Robinson aspired to write, not the American short story (he detested the very name), but something more artistic, after the manner of the French *conte*, which he called the "sketch." "Fiction is more consciously an art in France than anywhere else," he had read in Brander Matthews' Introduction to *Ten Tales by François Coppée*. ". . . From the men who are writing in France we may gain much. From the British fiction of this last quarter of the nineteenth century little can be learned by any one—less by us Americans in whom the English tradition is still dominant." Matthews stressed French supremacy in form and construction, the rigorous suppression of nonessentials. The *conte* could be written in prose or in verse. Coppée had succeeded with both. His subjects were "some incident of daily occurrence made significant by his interpretation . . . some character commonplace enough, but made finer by conflict with evil or victory over self . . . the humble, the forgotten, the unknown; and it is the feelings and struggles of these that he tells us, with no maudlin sentimentality, and with no dead set at our sensibilities." Though his stories had not the "sharpness" of Maupassant or the "brilliancy" of Daudet, they were remarkable for "sympathy, poetry, and a power of suggesting pictures." The counsel of another reliable critic, Henry James, went in the same direction, with stress on Daudet: a direction congenial to Robinson because it bordered on poetry, yet allowed for the range of daily experience in Gardiner. He grasped at materials close at hand in his first subjects: "The selfishness of self-denial," "The philosophic enmity of two brothers who were not born for the same purpose."

He became frank to his friends concerning his ambitions and his ideals of craftsmanship. "This itch for authorship is worse than the devil and about spoils a man for anything else," he wrote Gledhill in late October. ". . . Writing has been my dream ever since I was old enough to lay a plan for an air-castle. Now for the first time I have something like a favorable opportunity and this winter I shall make a beginning. If I make a failure of it, and the chances are about ten to one that I shall, my life will be a disappointment and a failure." With admirable detachment he put the problem of his qualifications and his audience before Smith a week later. "I think I have a little originality, but have I the genius for selection that is the one requisite of a literary man next to an easy flow of language? —not necessarily rapid, but easy in effect. I could never make a rapid writer; I am too fussy. . . . I demand a certain something in the arrangement of words, and more in their selection, that I find in very few of our writers today. The question is—will it be found in what I write? and if it is, will the public care anything about it? I do not wholly believe in art for art's sake, but I do not believe that anything is good literature where art is wholly sacrificed to the subject-matter." For matter, he would not lack. It lay about him everywhere in the neglected richness of American life, of which only Europeans seemed aware. Concerning Dvořák's *New World* Symphony he lamented: "The chief use of America in the aesthetic world seems to be to furnish material and suggestions for others to take advantage of." There was "poetry in all types of humanity —even in lawyers and horse-jockeys—if we are willing to search it out."

To broaden and sharpen his observation of humanity,

he read as much as his returning power of sight would permit. Sir John Lubbock's discussion of the "Hundred Best Books" in world literature saddened him by revealing lost opportunities; he felt constrained to believe in immortality, so unfair the disparity in individual opportunity seemed. Coppée's *Toute une jeunesse* revealed intriguing differences between the youth of a French writer and that of an American. *L'Idée de Jean Têterol*, by Cherbuliez, brought peasant parvenus and decadent aristocrats amusingly and instructively into conflict. An absorbing discovery of these months among the books he had brought from Cambridge was Daudet, a writer very like Dickens, but with much stricter art. Daudet's dedication of *Jack*, "This book of pity, indignation and irony is dedicated to Gustave Flaubert, my friend and master," promised the qualities Robinson most desired for his own work; and did not disappoint. By showing how poverty and harsh manual labor could brutalize a youth with poetic gifts, it should open men's eyes, he thought, to the cruelties of life and widen their sympathies. In the contrapuntal theme of men utterly without talent who were slaves to the urge to create in literature and the other arts, failures who might have succeeded as mechanics or artisans, Robinson first encountered an ambiguous matter for pity and ironic humor which was to hold his attention throughout life. He recommended the book to Latham in spite of its "bad ending," since his friend was "above such foolish criticisms as that." He was attracted by the strange character of William Cowper, a man of "almost pathetic sincerity" revealed in *The Task*, a poem which would endure for its "true art in homely things," such as the story of the woodcutter and his dog. Most of all, "wonderful human effect" had its "synonym" in Shakespeare. Robinson was "thunderstruck" by *Measure for Measure*, "a comedy of the flesh and a tragedy of the soul." He urged upon Harry Smith, who unaccountably had no liking for Shakespeare, a course of reading beginning curiously with *Troilus and Cressida*, which revealed his wisdom and breadth, and proceeding by way of his narrowest but still highly entertaining work, *Timon of Athens*.

Yet when Smith complimented him on his insight into human nature he confessed: "Even the happy mortals we term ordinary or commonplace act out their own mental tragedies and live a far deeper and wider life than we are inclined to believe possible in the light of our prejudices . . . but I must acknowledge the dismal truth that the majority of mankind interest me only as studies. They are 'a little queer,' like the Quaker's wife." Much as he would like to make friends with everyone, his vanity forbade. There were wrinkles in his forehead, but none about his mouth, "because I think more than some people, and do my laughing in my gray matter instead of upon my face."

He read slowly, his eye vigilant for skill, noting the *mot juste* as Kipling's python "seemed to *pour* himself along the ground," and preferring Rossetti's translation of Villon's "Ballade of Dead Ladies" to Payne's because of its greater freedom from archaisms. How much labor, he exclaimed, Daudet must have put into compressing *Tartarin de Tarascon*, whose reader forgets that it is a "microscopic narrative," so well does the author make "every sentence count."

In spite of the handicap of weak eyes, he could announce in early March that five sketches would be ready for Smith's criticism in Easter vacation. They might have advanced more rapidly, if poems had not got in the way of his "more serious work" by insisting on being written. Old French forms went singing through his head, obliging him to set down in February a villanelle, "The House on the Hill." There were also sonnets.

To keep his hand in against the return to poetry he now felt inevitable, he proposed to Smith a joint version of Sophocles' *Antigone*. Smith was to provide a prose translation preserving the Greek spirit. Robinson would put the speeches into blank verse and would learn the Greek alphabet in order to seek English equivalents for the varied meters of the choruses. His ignorance of the language might have the advantage of saving him from slavish literalness. As for the rest, he added, pride in self-knowledge overcoming his usual understatement: "I have something of the Hellenic spirit in me, and have a pretty good conception of what the word means. I may lack some of 'the serene and childlike joy in life' but I have the spirit of wise moderation and love of classical completeness which, I suppose, is more marked in the later poets of Pericles' time than in the Homeric period." Smith agreeing, Robinson got himself ready by reading Moulton's *Ancient Greek Drama, Samson Agonistes*, and *Atalanta in Calydon*. Swinburne seemed "hollow" after Milton.

Conditions for writing were not so favorable as he had anticipated. With Herman away all day on business and Dean's health shattered, the women of the household had to call on him for chores, from picking fruit, trimming trees, and splitting firewood to shoveling snow, four feet deep in February. These interruptions, the noise of his nieces' playing—and when they were asleep in the adjoining room he could not use his typewriter—his mother's objection to his smoking in the house, made him regret the Harvard den in which he did what he pleased, when he pleased. "This feeling of dependence is hell," he told Smith. "You, who are making a living, cannot conceive how cutting it is for a man of twenty-four to depend on his mother for every cent he has and every mouthful he swallows." There was loneliness, too, to fight against, as he confessed to Latham: "The people of Gardiner are good people enough but they are not companions for me any more than I am of them. We have nothing in common as regards personal tastes and ideals," like admiration for Arnold's verse. His fate was "as monotonous as the brook, which is eternally running below my window." The announcement that Brahms' Second Symphony was to be played brought acute nostalgia for Boston. A "persistent presentiment" that his ear might be the death of him before he could go to live in a city was part of his "pleasure-destroying fatalism."

In late January came the welcome opportunity to tutor in French a young woman, five years out of high school, who was preparing for Wellesley. An outburst of poetry and progress with his sketches followed, as his affections became involved. There was apparently an informal engagement. But late in April the tutoring was broken off abruptly, just as a book sent by Butler arrived: Hardy's *Life's Little Ironies*. Not long before Butler had given him *Ships That Pass in the Night*. He must be a mind-reader, Robinson remarked in confessing to Smith "a horrible dose of blues."

Commencement at Harvard lay ahead, offering momentary release. There he would meet again "men to talk with whose goddess is not engrossed on a silver dollar—men whose literature is not newspapers." The prospect was darkened by the thought that before long all of his friends would be graduated, scattered inaccessibly over the vast American geography or in Europe. Even before Commencement, Saben would be off to Oxford. *The Atlantic Monthly* was considering three of his sketches, but he was not sanguine about their reception. "I am one of those unfortunate devils who must have a little encouragement before they can put their heart in what they do," he told Smith. Without letters from friends, he would be "in hell."

Smith's reply dealt the heaviest blow of this devastating spring. It announced his engagement to be married. Until this moment, Robinson had not fully realized how much he had been leaning on him. Their intimacy could no longer be the same, he responded in an agony that opened every window into his soul; when they smoked together another person would be invisibly present. For the past six months he had felt Smith withdrawing. Not that he blamed him. "I have always looked upon a bachelor as only half of a man. . . . I have always believed in love, and shall always believe in it." By finding his mate, Smith had achieved maturity: "but somehow I, with my crotchets and childish sensibilities, cannot put away the old things." Before he went to Harvard, in the years when his life was "a kind of hell from which there seemed to be no release," Smith had been everything to him. Now his Harvard friends were soon to scatter, and Smith had won a mate while he had failed. "I am not (now) engaged to be married, I am not happy, and the world and the future look so dark and gloomy that I look mostly into the past. . . . The world frightens me; my one talent is ever laughing at me." Even if he should partially succeed, he saw himself "living alone in some city—Boston, most likely—with a friend or two to drop in upon me once in a while and a few faithful correspondents." He begged to be excused from witnessing Smith's wedding.

He fled his sorrow by writing of things remote from his experience, a dramatic monologue, "The Night Before," full of "battle . . . murder and sudden death." After two weeks he had recovered sufficiently to apologize to Smith. The outburst had been part of a general sense of failure to achieve some sort of independence. "My pride is almost unnatural and sometimes I wonder if it is not killing me by inches." Even this was not the worst. Something else had the power to make him really disagreeable and gloomy, something he hesitated to confide to paper, but would tell Smith when he came to Gardiner for the summer.

The sketches were returned by *The Atlantic Monthly*, with a comment from the editor, Horace Scudder, which was a slight balm to his wounds: "These sketches seem to me not without some claim to notice. They show restraint and an effort at telling something worth while." His uncle, Mr. Fox, passed on an encouraging word from an aged proofreader, that editors could be badly mistaken. Lowell, for instance, had refused for the *Atlantic* Howells' *Sketches of Venetian Life*. Robinson assured Latham that there was no danger of the rejection driving him to "the Chatterton act."

On the eve of his going to see Tryon and Ford graduate, came his first commercial acceptance. *The Critic* had taken his sonnet, "Oh for a poet—for a beacon bright," probably one of the two composed under the stress of his disappointment in love, which seemed to point to success in writing as his only chance of happiness. Even in literature, he felt appallingly apart and alone, as he considered current poetry. The poets who had found inspiration in American life, its potentialities and problems—Bryant, Emerson, Longfellow, Lowell, Lanier, Dickinson, Whitman—had died during his youth, some very recently. The aftermath of the Civil War had seemed too crass for their successors— Bayard Taylor, Richard Henry Stoddard, George Henry Boker, Thomas Bailey Aldrich—whose verse sought refuge in ideal beauty of the past or of other climes and lands. The verse Robinson read in the magazines belonged to the private world of its authors, a world of pallid dreams and tepid emotions. Its characteristic form was the sonnet, which even in expressing trifles offered a challenge to skill and taste. The state of American poetry resembled that of English poetry a century before, when Cowper complained that the successors of Pope made it "a mere mechanic art," and Blake rebuked the Muses for forsaking the land:

> How have you left the ancient love
> That bards of old enjoy'd in you!
> The languid strings do scarcely move,
> The sound is forced, the notes are few.

The indignation he felt at the American musician for neglecting native melodies until a foreigner took up their idiom for his *New World* Symphony flared in Robinson once more as he prayed for a genuine poet, who would put to flight the "little sonnet men," mechanical contrivers of "songs without souls." Why was the age "barren," a "changeless glimmer of dead gray," when man and nature, the eternal subjects of poetry, remained:

> Here are the men, the women, and the flowers,
> The seasons, and the sunset, as before.

With irony, Robinson had used a sonnet, packed with meaning, to rebuke vacuous sonneteers. It brought him no money, only a year's subscription to *The Critic,* which printed it in the issue of November 24, 1894. "The House on the Hill," in which Robinson had answered his own cry by treating impressively a contemporary local tragedy— the forsaking of the East for the broader lands and wider opportunities of the West—could find welcome in no commercial periodical. Eager to see it in print on any terms, he was presenting it gratis to *The Globe,* a flimsy New York quarterly whose editor, William Thorne, was a friend of a Gardiner author, Kate Vannah. There was no word from *The Dial,* which had been holding a sonnet on Poe since April. Not a penny for a year's work.

Returning from Commencement, he had the companionship of Smith for the last summer before the latter's marriage, and could unburden the mysterious secret weighing on his mind. He admired his friend as "far stronger and less visionary" than he, with wider interests embracing the political and economic thinking of Goldwin Smith as well as the verse of Andrew Lang. During this summer when for two nights his ear "ran like a brook," he found relief in composing a prose "study in darkness," called "The Black Path."

This "morbid period" of gloom about his family and himself was arrested in late September by the thought: "if things are bound to go to the devil anyway, the best thing for me to do is to let them go." Glancing through British stories in *The Yellow Book,* he didn't think his own a waste of time. He planned to double their number during the winter. But poetry got in their way more imperiously than ever. The worst of it was that he could give himself no credit for anything good. It came from outside himself. He explained to Gledhill that he could no more "help making" the Poe sonnet, for instance, than he could "help feeling." A series of Tavern Songs began to plan itself, and the *Antigone* exercise went on, being about one third done when *The Globe* carried "The House on the Hill." Seeing the villanelle in print dissatisfied him with two stanzas. He wondered if Horace's counsel to keep verse unpublished for nine years shouldn't be taken literally. He was amused at Dr. Schumann's turning out one love poem after another, unaware that love poetry, "to be good, must be very good."

With Herman following the painfully familiar course of Dean toward ineffectualness and the family money slipping away as the economic depression reached its height, he found it impossible to hold rigidly to his resolution to let things take their fated course. His anxiety came out in irritation at trifles, at having to gather the apples he enjoyed eating, even at the play of his three nieces, who innocent of misfortune kept running by his study door, seeming to shake the whole house. To cool his temper, he would take his hat and walk down to Water Street. By Thanksgiving, he was looking "at everything through blue glasses—everything but literature. . . . I have confidence in myself regarding that that is hardly natural to me."

Sometimes his very confidence in his writing brought him up against the dreadful thought of what it would mean if this, too, failed. The Christmas of 1894 was the "sorriest" he had spent: "Christmas has an effect upon me which I cannot describe—something like that of the first hand-organs in the spring—makes me feel hollow and vaguely conscious of wasted time, or as I prefer to call it,

lost time." His friends were getting settled professionally,
passing him in the race of life. He pleaded with Smith to
postpone marriage, so as to grant him one more summer.
Smith was the last intimate within call. "When he goes, I
shall be alone except for letters."

Pegging away at the *Antigone* kept him close to Smith's
mind. There was need to consult him on aesthetic problems: How near to the original could a translation keep
without ceasing to be poetry? Was the messenger's first
scene with Creon intentional mixing of humor with tragedy? Familiarity with Sophocles—he had recently read
Oedipus at Colonus in translation—tempted him to try what
Arnold called the "grand style" in his own verse. He had
long admired the grand manner of scattered passages in
Emerson:

> The sun set, but set not his hope:—
> Stars rose, his faith was earlier up:
> Fixed on the enormous galaxy,
> Deeper and older seemed his eye,
> And matched his sufferance sublime
> The taciturnity of Time.
>
> . . . .
>
> One accent of the Holy Ghost
> The heedless world has never lost.
>
> . . . .
>
> Things are in the saddle
> And ride mankind.
>
> . . . .
>
> He builded better than he knew;—
> The conscious stone to beauty grew.
>
> . . . .
>
> So nigh is grandeur to our dust,
>
> . . . .

O tenderly the haughty day
Fills his blue urn with fire.

In December, Robinson composed an experimental quatrain: "As long as Fame's imperious music rings"; in January he boldly created a chorus on the legendary fate of King Aegeus, the subject of lost dramas by Sophocles and Euripides. In majesty and compassion, this "Chorus of Old Men in 'Ægeus' " was not unworthy of the Greek tragedians. It was the earliest of his verse to go into his *Collected Poems* without a single verbal alteration.

He was acquiring a collection of rejection slips. Even "Aaron Stark," a fruit of his admiration for Molière, failed to interest *The Chap-Book*. But he had a recurring dream of a paid acceptance. At length in February 1895 he could announce his first "blood money," seven dollars from *Lippincott's Magazine* for the Poe sonnet.

Prose fiction, which he planned to collect in a book of 350 to 400 pages, went forward slowly—sometimes an hour for a dozen words—and its audience was problematical: "The short story as a work of art has never taken a great hold on this country, as the standard set in the leading magazines will easily show." But he was "radiant" to find that he could "do anything, in [his] own way" that he undertook, and his mind was bulging with good material. "My worst and most persistent enemy, though, is a constant inclination to write poetry. Sometimes I am afraid the damned stuff will kill what little ability I have." The prose volume should be ready for market by the fall of 1895, he told Gledhill, adding: "I have so many things to contend with outside my regular work that that is really the smallest part of the strain that comes on my poor gray matter."

Smith's marriage loomed ahead in June as the seal of his isolation. Seeing Ford over a week end at Exeter, where his friend was well established in teaching and about to leave for France with an invitation to call on the novelist Paul Bourget, only increased his discouragement. He envied the prospect of Ford's taking a "little glass" with "Daudet and the rest of them." Smith, too, was looking ahead to Europe after the next year as a graduate student at Harvard. As ambitious as they, Robinson feared he had not sufficient physical strength, even if he were to have opportunities. This summer of 1895, with his ear "going like the devil," he was surer than ever that he would not live to be older than thirty or thirty-five. Yet he was just as sure he would do something before he died, he wrote Gledhill in August, that would make his friends remember him, something more lasting than becoming a "Prominent Citizen."

He believed, and with justice, that he had already done something rather big, the "Chorus of Old Men," and persistent rejection slips did not shake his faith that he had struck an original vein in "Aaron Stark." His pride came out in disparagement of popular taste. How could Americans take *Munsey's Magazine* seriously? Book lists of the leading publishers made him "tremble for humanity." Critics and editors were encouraging mediocrity and overlooking excellent work. Payne in *The Dial* discussed new poetry with "patronizing ease"; *The Critic* was flippant, Hamilton Wright Mabie of *The Chap-Book* unspeakably flat. *The Atlantic Monthly*, so "expeditiously conservative" that it kept his own manuscripts less than forty-eight hours, ran true to form in giving "half a line of faint praise" to George Moore's *Esther Waters*, a greater novel than any in America since Hawthorne. To turn from the much-applauded *Manxman* of Hall Caine to Hawthorne's *Blithedale Romance* was to enter another world. Hawthorne's superiority came largely from "an amount of brain racking and tinkering of which the modern ink spiller has no conception." Think of the five years spent over *The Marble Faun*.

Hawthorne, and the best contemporary work in France and England, kept the pride of the twenty-five-year-old apprentice within bounds. In spite of eyes that made him pay dearly for every page, he had read more widely this second year out of Harvard than the first. *Fromont jeune et Risler aîné* fortified his conviction that Daudet was "the greatest artist in fiction now living—and his art never crowds out his humanity." His study of jealousy, *La petite paroisse*, used the method of implication, arranging incidents so that the reader would discover their significance for himself. Although still hesitating to read Daudet's *Sapho* because of its pornographic reputation, he defended Ibsen, whose constructive skill he was to draw upon for long poems, and tasted Zola and the Goncourts in a book of specimens of difficult French that Smith sent him.

Happy to perceive, by dint of careful reading, "literary touches and other individualities of style," he pronounced it better to take foreign literature in translation than "to slop through it after the manner of the bright young ladies who read French a little, German a little, sing a little, play the piano a little, and do nothing at all with anything like completeness." If he had the rearing of a girl he would insist on her doing one thing well, "if that thing were only to take good care of her eyebrows." "A fairly intelligent girl's opinions of *Esther Waters*, *The Mayor of Caster-*

bridge, and 'The Children of the Zodiac' may take me a long way into her inner chambers."

He savored the "old nutty flavor" of Montaigne by browsing slowly, and warned Latham that "to read Meredith in a hurry is to drink Pommery from the bottle, more than that, it is . . . rank injustice to a man who works like the devil with his pen." He recalled his own struggles with *The Egoist* and with *Diana of the Crossways,* which has "the damnedest opening chapter in the world." Quoting Henry James as saying that to do justice to Daudet one must read him at least twice, he found this true also of Hardy. *Far from the Madding Crowd* modernized Shakespearean comedy and mingled it successfully with tragedy. *Jude the Obscure,* just appearing in *Harper's Magazine* as *Hearts Insurgent,* told the somber truth about life. He paid tribute to Hardy in a sonnet accepted by *The Critic* early in May. (It appeared in the November 23rd number with a false apologetic note from the editors: "Written before the appearance of *Hearts Insurgent,*" so great was the hue and cry against the novel's supposed indecency.) The opening of *The Mill on the Floss,* describing the sufferings of a brother and sister because their father, with the best intentions in the world, gives to each the upbringing and education suited to the other, carried him along for a hundred pages before he realized the strain on his eyes. Applauding *Esther Waters, Une Vie,* and Tolstoi, Robinson observed that his "love for romance, pure and simple," was almost gone.

The so-called "roughness" of Kipling's verse, he explained to Latham, was really as subtle art as *The Idylls of the King:* "When the 'seven men' on the Bolivar saw 'some damned liner's lights go by like a grand hotel' they were all poets; they were the same when they were 'rolling down the Ratcliffe Road, drunk and raising Cain.'" A set of Wordsworth, Smith's gift, revealed another poet who, he rightly surmised, would henceforth be "part of [his] life." Apparently he had known only the shorter poems in anthologies. Now he began with *The Excursion* and proceeded slowly to *The Prelude* and *The Recluse.* Wordsworth's verse was "clear and wholesome, not to say magnificent," and the ode on "Intimations of Immortality" was worth "all the rest of his work put together." In due time the ode would inspire Robinson to a great ode of his own. Opening the Bible one day casually to Matthew and Mark, he discovered what his generation, which had rejected dogma, had been losing by not knowing the King James version as "mere literature." In order to have an entirely human picture of the founder of Christianity, he sent for Renan's *Life of Jesus.* The Old Testament, which was to furnish magnificent similes for his ode, he planned to read during the summer, but the reading was delayed for years.

Smith's departure in the fall of 1895 for graduate study at Harvard was a new tie to the University, which he called "the object of almost the only patriotism" he possessed. Robinson urged his friend to take time from his classical studies to hear Norton, the "only one of the great sort" there. The need of discussing their *Antigone* translation and Butler's offer of a room brought him to Boston for the first time in sixteen months. To Gledhill he described the fortnight's visit as depressing, since the varied activities of his friends made him feel that he must soon play some part in the world or else "go to the wall." He added almost casually: "If a volume of my verse reaches you some time during the next twelve months . . ."

He had capitulated to his natural inclination to poetry after a two years' struggle with prose that found no publisher, while unexpectedly his verse had better fortune, slight though that was. "I am making all sorts of poems nowadays," he announced to Smith on November tenth, "and dare not stop for fear I might realize what a damned fool I am." The "pull" of his poems slackened their correspondence. The labor was even harder than with prose: "I never had such a damned time in life with anything as with some of those verses which ought to go like bees and things and which want to go like camels. It is hunting for hours after one word and then not getting it that plays the devil with a man's gray matter and makes him half ready to doubt the kindness of the Scheme." At this rate his volume would kill him by the time it saw print.

The first mention of "Tilbury Town" is in a letter of December 14, 1895, announcing the creation of "John Evereldown" and "Luke Havergal." The name Tilbury, to recur so frequently as the locale of Robinson's poems, presumably comes from the tilbury, a smart two-wheeled open carriage of those days. A new Gardiner acquaintance, a middle-aged man named Jones, who defended Zola for "the truth and sincerity that lies at the bottom of his nastiness," was apparently the inspirer of Robinson's sonnet on that much-debated author (and not *L'Assommoir*, as he thought late in life, for a letter reveals that he did not read the novel until a year later). Reading was a luxury his eyes, strained by steady composition, seldom permitted; for diversion he turned to his violin.

The news of Latham's engagement to marry, coming late in 1895, had set him meditating once more on the disadvantages and advantages of single life. "A man by himself, because of the inevitable self-examination he is subjected to, becomes, nine times in ten, distressingly conceited or abnormally the other way. My own case is a queer mixture of both. . . . Before I went to Harvard I was as near to being a damned fool as a man can be and live." The College had "worked wonders" in drawing him out of himself. Nevertheless, Henry James' story, "The Lesson of the Master," which he read in early February 1896 and pronounced a work of genius, stressed the disadvantages of marriage for a man of letters. In the young writer Paul Overt, James' central character, there was uncanny likeness to Robinson's own temperament and problems. Overt is represented as pained and perplexed by the falling off of the fiction of Henry St. George, who once produced works of the highest quality. The Master is obviously writing too fast, diluting himself. The two authors become acquainted. St. George, struck by the promise of Overt's first book, in a burst of frankness confesses the deterioration of his own work and warns against its cause: a wife who insists on his financial and social success for their children's sake. No woman, he insists, especially none from the comfortable classes, can comprehend or sympathize with an artist's striving for perfection. Overt, convinced, runs away from England to escape a general's daughter whom he loves, and in Switzerland takes two years of seclusion to produce a book better than his first. Returning to London he finds that St. George has lost his wife and is about to marry the general's daughter. Has he been tricked? With bitterness of heart he seeks out the Master, who hints that he has won the girl to keep her from ruining Overt. He himself is beyond further ruin, since he has vowed he will write no more. Does he keep the vow? James does not say. He adds, however, that if the Master fails to keep it, and resumes work of his best quality, Overt, though convinced of his treachery, will be the very first to praise it, "which is perhaps a proof that the Master was essentially right and that Nature had dedicated him to intellectual, not to personal passion."

These concluding words of James may have been for Robinson the ultimate stroke of genius, revealing him to himself as a thoroughly normal male of the rare species, artist. He could thus understand why Smith's engagement, threatening to sever their intellectual companionship, had unexpectedly hurt more than his own disappointment in love, devastating as that had been. James knew the capacity of "the complicated artistic soul" for "disinterested disappointment." "Do you know I have a theory that Browning's life-long happiness with his wife is all humbug?" he wrote Smith two years later. "The man's life was in his art, but he was big enough to make the world think otherwise." A repeated phrase, "the false gods," in "The Lesson of the Master," lingered in Robinson's memory, to give him the title of a poem in middle life. The rest of James' counsel he translated into action. The artist, in order to be independent and genuine, must "be able to be poor," to find sufficient reward in his conscience and in the praise of the few, possibly not more than one or two, who know what it is to pursue perfection. The letter praising James' story offered Smith a glimpse of one of these resolutions. The book of verse he was completing probably wouldn't sell, but it contained "steps" toward perfection: "I may never get it, but I can climb and make myself believe that I shall."

By the end of February 1896 a little book of one hundred manuscript pages had accumulated. Christened *The Tavern and The Night Before*, it went off to a publisher. The poet relaxed by examining postage-stamp catalogues, admiring especially the colors of British colonials.

Six weeks with no word. Against the hurt of rejection, he shored himself by reflecting that confidence in his work had become "chronic" and must be accepted with a "kind of optimistic desperation," like the condition of his ear. Three weeks more of anxious waiting, and the poems were back. Adding "The Dead Village" and a sonnet to Verlaine, he sent them off again, confident of readers once the publishing hurdle should be over. "If printed lines are worth anything, they are bound to be picked up sometime; and then if some poor devil of a man or woman feels better for anything I have said, I shall have no fault to find with the scheme or anything in it." He had designed the poems to suggest "something wiser than hatred and something better than despair." But financially the prospect was bleak; possibly on the distant horizon two or three hundred dollars a year: "You don't know what it is to be twenty-six years old, and still a little child so far as a prospect of worldly independence goes." While awaiting response from the publisher, he revised the completed *Antigone* and read his sonnet, "The Clerks," in the *Boston Evening Transcript* for June 4, 1896.

He was seeing almost no one outside his home: Dr. Schumann now and then, Smith's parents, and Jones. Isolation he was coming to accept as an instrument of fate, obliging him to meditate and keeping his ideals unsullied.

He found satisfaction in people's not inviting him "to the damned times they have. . . . Dancing—that is, formal dancing, is to my mind a deliberate sacrifice of man's native dignity." Dancing for joy after victory in a college game was quite different. He quoted R. L. Stevenson: "To know what you prefer instead of saying Amen to what the world tells you you ought to prefer, is to have kept your soul alive."

A second rejection of the poems, coming in the summer, made him re-examine their quality. The "Tavern Songs" he doomed to the wastebasket, but the rest seemed good. "I was unable to foresee oblivion for the poems," Robinson later recalled, when they were popularly accepted, "although I could foresee a long and obscure journey for them before they should have more than a small number of friends. Fortunately, a few really responsive and intelligent readers were all that I should expect or require for some years to come, but I wanted those readers badly, and knew well enough I was going to have them." It was worth spending his own money to distribute his verse to the best judges of poetry he knew. Through his uncle he learned that the Riverside Press could produce for fifty-two dollars three hundred and twelve paper-bound copies of the reduced volume of forty-four short pieces, renamed *The Torrent and The Night Before.* Negotiations were secret, for he intended the booklet as a surprise for his mother.

Thus modestly, in form and prospects, was issued the most distinguished first volume by an American poet. Its qualities are those rare in youth: wisdom and wide sympathy, urbanity, detachment, evenness of quality, avoidance of sentimentality, sparseness in figures of speech, use of models without echoes. Intellect and taste keep youthful passion and challenge within bounds.

The American scene promised in "Oh for a poet—" appears in "The House on the Hill," "The Dead Village," "John Evereldown," "Aaron Stark," "The Wilderness," and "The Clerks." Evereldown, Robinson has revealed, was a composite of two local characters. "Aaron Stark" freshens the agelong theme of the miser by giving him "eyes like little dollars in the dark." The theme of Whitman's "O Pioneers" takes on finished artistry and tragic grandeur in "The Wilderness," where restless explorers, held up by the rigors of winter, are torn between the yearning to return to the love and comforts of home and the inexorable passion for wandering which sends them to their doom. "The Clerks" is a triumph of the poetry of the seeming commonplace, a poetry whose masters are the strangely assorted Wordsworth, Baudelaire, and Leopardi. Men we have all seen "shop-worn" by years of monotonous employment become symbols of the triumph of time, one of the supreme themes of poetry.

Robinson records his struggles against doubt and discouragement as he carved this verse out of his immediate environment. "Dear Friends" is a subtly barbed plea for tolerance of the sedentary and contemplative habits that produced it. "On the Night of a Friend's Wedding" reveals fear lest the few who have confidence in its worth may fail him. In the "Ballade of Broken Flutes," addressed to Dr. Schumann, the seeming impossibility of his dream "to command new life" into "the shrunken clay" of poetry, neglected by his generation, produces a momentary resolve to abandon it for that generation's pursuit of money. But a sonnet, "The master and the slave go hand in hand," confesses inescapable the "mission of his bondage" to seek "the perfect word."

Acceptance of the world as a theme for art proved less difficult than its acceptance as a place for meaningful living. That its sensual and material satisfactions, ending in the grave, could not outweigh life's pain and sorrows, if it did not also contain, however dimly, "Light" which points beyond, is the theme of "The Children of the Night." Light does not flood in from the traditional and material conceptions of popular revealed religion. Glimmers come to those, and those only, who have faced the uttermost challenge of doubt and darkness and been cleansed by suffering. Its full splendor is reserved beyond the grave:

> Never until our souls are strong enough
> To plunge into the crater of the Scheme,

shall we know how much of it our frailty and cowardice have hidden ("Two Sonnets"). Precisely because life is horrible, it must have meaning. Stated baldly, here is the central vision of life which Robinson was to clothe in the majesty of his mature style in "The Man Against the Sky."

Already, however, he had clothed the vision with symbols, suggesting spiritual truths too great for the finite intellect, in a poem which creates its own atmosphere, "Luke Havergal." To trace literary ancestry, to derive "Luke Havergal" from Poe's "Raven" (with Rossetti's variant in "The Blessed Damozel") and Emerson's "Brahma," would not explain its superiority to these predecessors, its perfect fusion of philosophic symbolism with human passion. Beside it "The Raven" seems rhetorical posturing, "The Blessed Damozel" mere picture, "Brahma" dry speculation. Robinson's humorous self-depreciation, "my un-comfortable abstraction called 'Luke Havergal,' " probably refers to the discomfiture of readers searching for a baldly stated idea. The octave of the second of "Two Sonnets" utters precisely that idea, but Robinson was too much an artist to put such language into a voice "out of a grave," which must say cryptically:

> The dark will end the dark, if anything:—
> God slays Himself with every leaf that flies,
> And hell is more than half of paradise.

The identity of the voice is shrouded, though its reading of Havergal's thoughts suggests either the lost loved one or Havergal communing with himself. The poet doubtless preferred Theodore Roosevelt's admission: "I am not sure that I understand 'Luke Havergal,' but I am entirely sure I like it," to any facile plucking of the heart out of its mystery. Desperately passionate, it would seem to spring from some desolating loss in Robinson's life. The lover's desolation pierces even through the quiet imperious in-sistence of the voice beyond life upon relinquishment of earthly ties and trusting acceptance of "the western gate," which will unriddle all riddles. Flying leaves startle with the touch of a vanished hand and whisper with a voice that is still. A gate opening to the west where glooms are gathering toward the early autumn dark while human passion vainly yearns for dawn in eastern skies—such sym-bols clash in the paradoxically "fiery night" in the lover's eyes. The name Luke Havergal, with its dying fall and associated rhymes and assonances (Robinson had a fine ear for proper names) sets the tone from the first line, and repeated words, phrases and refrains, a legacy of his apprenticeship to intricate French forms, build up to the final irresistible imperative.

The companion piece, placed immediately after "Luke Havergal" as a counterpoise of classical to romantic art and as a pagan pronouncement on the vanity of earthly greatness, is the "Chorus of Old Men in 'Ægeus.' " The aged men sing as they contemplate the shattered corpse of the Athenian king, who has thrown himself from a cliff on seeing the black sails of the ship—the sails that his son Theseus, intoxicated by triumph over the Minotaur and winning Ariadne, has forgotten to change to white as a signal of his safe return. Their song has Sophoclean skill in legendary allusion, Sophoclean irony and compassion. Robinson leaned on Matthew Arnold for the trimeters,

> Out of the flare of life,
> Out of the whirl of years,
> Into the mist they go,
> Into the mist of death,

but the majestic alternation of hexameters and pentameters was his own voice:

Better his end had been as the end of a cloudless day,
Bright, by the word of Zeus, with a golden star,
Wrought of a golden fame, and flung to the central sky
To gleam on a stormless tomb forevermore.

.   .   .   .

But the fates are ever the fates, and a crown is ever a crown.

The pentameter line,

Bright, by the word of Zeus, with a golden star,

has a poised rhythm of joy which Robinson, for all his later mastery of blank verse, was never to catch again. But later the King James version of the Scriptures would enrich his "grand style," which had its impulse from Emerson, Arnold, and Sophocles. Other young Harvard poets were soon to treat Greek themes after the manner of the Greek dramatists—Trumbull Stickney with *Prometheus Pyrphoros* (1900), William Vaughn Moody with *The Fire Bringer* (1904) and George Cabot Lodge with *Herakles* (1908). All read Greek, indeed Stickney took the Doctor's degree in the language and literature at the University of Paris; but none produced a chorus so close to the Hellenic spirit.

Keats, reaching toward maturity, had repudiated "Miltonic inversions," Latinisms, Grecisms, insisting that "English must be kept up." Robinson, in reaction against the archaizing exaggerators of Keats' early manner, was maintaining, by example, that contemporary English must be kept up in verse. He was also sticking as closely as he could to the word order of prose and speech, disdaining the lazy practice of doing violence to syntax in order to meet the demands of meter and rhyme. Unlike Whitman, who had the same modernizing goal, he accepted traditional verse forms for their well-tested advantages. By dint of labor he succeeded in making natural and seemingly effortless word order fit those forms. The result had been a quickening of movement, an octave or sestet of a sonnet formed of a single sentence, as in "The Altar," and a simplicity concealing art, as in the opening quatrain of "The Clerks," where every word is a monosyllable save one, and that one among the commonest in the language. Rhymes seem to come unsought. Even triple rhyme, which Swinburne had been using with virtuosity but with little

intellectual content, Robinson had conquered as the medium of subtle thought—thought moreover expressed in the
simplest words:

> But cursed him for the ways he had
> To make me see
> My envy of the praise he had
> For praising me.

Such stanzas—unaccountably, it would seem—demand the
second reading Robinson thought every good craftsman
deserved. Not for nothing had he studied the labors of
prose masters: Hawthorne, George Moore, Daudet, Maupassant, Flaubert.

Wordsworth's simplicity serves the eye primarily, Robinson's the ear. In "Credo" and in "The Dead Village"
music is used together with the Light as a synonym of the
spiritual world, recalling Emerson's

> Or Music pours on mortals
> Its beautiful disdain.

The sonnets to his literary enthusiasms—Hunt, Hardy,
Arnold, Crabbe, Zola, Verlaine—have each a tone suited
to the personality invoked. The tune of the villanelle,
suffusing desolation with beauty, helps keep "The House
on the Hill" from sentimentality. Robinson's style of inevitable statement is richer in sound than Emerson's or
Arnold's: the miser Stark is "Glad for the murmur of his
hard renown." Assonance and alliteration are subtle:

> Song sloughs away the sin to find redress
> In art's complete remembrance.

From Tennyson and from the old French forms he had
learned the power of refrain, of repetition, of pauses as

eloquent as words. His alteration of the punctuation of "Luke Havergal" through successive printings was to show his unending search for exact timing. The changes of pace in "The Wilderness" serve admirably the changes of mood from the opening dactyls and anapests to the split rhythm of the final line: "And the long fall wind on the lake."

For a young author, Robinson is notably economical in figures and in descriptive epithets. Each is reserved for telling effect. Metaphor and simile combine unforgettably in the final lines of "On the Night of a Friend's Wedding":

> As if the time were come, or almost come,
> For their untenanted mirage of me
> To lose itself and crumble out of sight,
> Like a tall ship that floats above the foam
> A little while, and then breaks utterly.

Landscape is made characteristically American by select detail, reinforced in one instance, "the crimson chill of autumn," by paradox.

Economy is the impression *The Torrent and The Night Before* leaves in the memory. As Robinson said of Voltaire's "Zadig," it is "magnificently small," each short piece crammed with meaning and artistic device. And such variety. "Luke Havergal," "The Chorus of Old Men," "The House on the Hill," "Oh for a poet—," "Aaron Stark," "Dear Friends," "George Crabbe," so individual, and each likely to find permanent place in American literature.

"Dear Friends" will serve as well as any to illustrate the maturity of the artist and his method. This sonnet, opening with a plea for tolerance, leads quietly to

> . . . the games we play
> To fill the frittered minutes of a day,
> Good glasses are to read the spirit through,

so unemphatic that its double-edged truth comes home only on second reading, and to final lines with ironic urbanity worthy of Horace:

> The shame I win for singing is all mine,
> The gold I miss for dreaming is all yours.

A volume so different from the American verse in vogue would have dubious reception, Robinson foresaw. "You won't find much in the way of natural description," he warned Gledhill. "There is very little tinkling water, and there is not a red-bellied robin in the whole collection. When it comes to 'nightingales and roses' I am not 'in it' nor have I the smallest desire to be. I sing, in my own particular manner, of heaven & hell and now and then of natural things (supposing they exist) of a more prosy connotation than those generally admitted into the domain of meter. In short I write whatever I think is appropriate to the subject and let tradition go to the deuce." The title page of the little blue pamphlet bore a challenge in the motto from one of Coppée's plays: *"Qui pourrais-je imiter pour être original?"* and in the dedication "to any man, woman or critic who will cut the edges of it—I have done the top."

The Christmas rush in publishing held back the printing of *The Torrent* far into the autumn of 1896, a decisive autumn in American political and economic life. Industry and finance, fully recovered from the panic of '93, were pressing their advantage over a still depressed agriculture, which had found a brilliant defender in the young William

Jennings Bryan. Robinson, a bit shocked when his friend
Jones called the gold-standard men "robbers," yet amused
at the campaign biographies of McKinley and Hobart, was
an aloof spectator, gladly pocketing two dollars a day as
polling clerk. In amusement he joined the torchlight procession to congratulate a successful local candidate, who
chose to bestow on the embarrassed poet the warmest of
his intoxicated embraces. Nevertheless, he was disappointed
that Bryan did not get more votes, for he was coming to
regard Bryan as "the greatest political figure in America
since Lincoln," even though the immediate need of the
country was for a more "politic" president.

His letters to Smith offer a commentary on the basic
philosophy of his forthcoming poems. The successful local
candidate, "not a bad lot . . . only blind" and an ugly
schoolhouse just erected were object lessons in the "results
of modern materialism." Jones, lending him *Science and
Health*, helped him to see what Carlyle had been driving at
in *Sartor Resartus:* "denial of the existence of matter as
anything but a manifestation of thought. Christianity is
the same thing, and so is illuminated common sense" in
Epictetus, Socrates, and Emerson. In studying philosophical
idealism at Harvard he had only an inkling of the truth,
now fortified by experience, that it was "the one logical
and satisfactory interpretation of life." Pain and disappointment had led to his "acceptance of life" as "a kind of
spiritual exercise (or at least a chance of that) by which
we may, if we will, put ourselves beyond it."

He had desperate need of this faith in a home whose
material basis was slipping away, in which his mother and
sister-in-law, with his brothers broken men, must be sustained by his advice and courage. In November his mother

returned from a Boston visit feeling so ill that Emma Robinson had to be summoned by night from her father's house across the Cobbossee. The doctor diagnosed "black diphtheria," so dreaded in those days before antitoxin that he refused to return to the house. Dean, in the emergency, recalled his medical skill. But Mary Robinson lived only two days more.

Neighbors feared to enter the house. Even the undertaker would come only as far as the door with the coffin, and he could find no one to drive the hearse. In its stead, the sons were able to engage an express wagon. They helped the driver lift the coffin upon it. The minister was the only other person at the grave.

A fortnight later, Robinson summoned courage to write to Smith in Berlin: "Things have been going so like the devil with me for the past two months that nothing short of idealism would have kept me together; and a fortnight ago, to put a finishing touch, my mother died of diphtheria. . . . She has gone ahead and I am glad for her. You see I have come to look on death as a deliverance and an advancement." Reading Barrie's *Margaret Ogilvy* nine weeks later stirred regretful memories. "No man can ever appreciate the debt he owes to his mother. . . . If I had read this little book . . . three or four years before it was written perhaps I should not have to think of some things which I think of now—things that come back to me in spite of my conviction that everything is better as it is and that my mother is to be congratulated. These things sound hard, but they are true." As he cleaned ashes from the cellar, he thought remorsefully of his former resentment of such work while absorbed in writing. Now he was reconciled, even saw that it did him good.

The long-awaited package from the Riverside Press, a few days too late for his mother's eyes, had meant so little that he left it unopened from morning until evening. The blue-bound booklets, not as long or as broad as his hand, seemed "so small and so devilish blue" that they sickened him. Jones and a new acquaintance, Arthur Blair, employed in a local bank, started the return of his confidence by praising "The Chorus of Old Men." In sadness he sat down to what was to have been a labor of love, the sending of inscribed copies to lovers of poetry and to influential editors. Smith received three; others went abroad to Hardy, Swinburne, and Gosse. Among American men of letters addressed were the poets Thomas Bailey Aldrich, Richard Watson Gilder, Edmund Clarence Stedman, Clinton Scollard, Frank Dempster Sherman, and Whitman's friend Horace L. Traubel, the novelists Edward Eggleston and S. Weir Mitchell. Several copies were sent to Harvard: to President Eliot, to Professors Norton, Wendell, Briggs, Hays, and Baker, and to the recent graduates Robert Morss Lovett and Pierre La Rose. Among editors and journalists were H. E. Scudder of *The Atlantic Monthly*, Harry Thurston Peck of *The Bookman*, William Morton Payne of *The Dial*, W. P. Trent of *The Sewanee Review*, and Nathan Haskell Dole. Copies went to *The Critic*, *The Independent*, *The Nation*, and to newspapers as far afield as *The Times-Picayune* and the *Denver Times*.

The responses, though inadequate to the book's quality, were more heartening than hitherto. Gosse praised the sonnets, especially "George Crabbe." "Oh for a poet—" impressed *The Dial*, *The Bookman*, and *The Sewanee Review*. *The Dial* rated the volume "far above the average in thought and expression" and commended its "note of se-

vere restraint . . . so rarely heard in contemporary song."
The Bookman mingled praise and regret: "There is true
fire in his verse, and there are the swing and the singing of
wind and wave and the passion of human emotion in his
lines; but his limitations are vital. His humor is of a grim
sort, and the world is not beautiful to him, but a prison
house. In the night time there is weeping and sorrow, and
joy does not come in the morning." Professor Trent in
The Sewanee Review felt an "indescribable something
called poetry" in "The Children of the Night," "Brown-
ingesque verve" in "The Night Before" and in the author
"knowledge of the technique of his art and an obvious love
for it"; but he deplored the "unnecessary note of flippancy"
in the dedication, the "lack of restraint" in "The Wilderness." With the desire "to encourage Mr. Robinson with
the thought that he has at least one attentive reader," he
proffered advice. The poet "must learn that the impressionistic effect in 'The House on the Hill' is not worth
striving after and that the chaotic effect produced in 'A
Poem for Max Nordau' is distinctly to be avoided." In
The Bookseller, Newsdealer and Stationer Nathan Haskell
Dole was prophetic: "The little volume has only 44 pages,
but I should not wonder if curiosity seekers should in
future times pay high prices for it—especially if Mr.
Robinson goes on in the same free course." The sonnets
were "vital, virile expressions of a wholly modern spirit."

The newspapers were more uniformly favorable than
the periodicals. Chamberlain of the *Boston Evening Transcript* found it "a pleasure to get hold of a man who knows
something on his own account and isn't measuring the
world according to somebody else's system." He added a
personal response to Robinson, inviting him to meet lively

writers at the St. Botolph Club when he came to Boston. The *Denver Times* hailed "one of the books of the year . . . a young man of great accomplishment." (Robinson adorned a clipping for Smith's benefit with a caricature of himself with a hugely swollen head and small body.) Other Western reviews were responsible for a letter from an Oregon man in praise of "The Wilderness" and another from a bank president in Vancouver. Local fame dear to a young writer appeared in the request of the *Bangor Daily Commercial* for his photograph and autobiography.

Harvard was enthusiastic. Barrett Wendell wrote: "Very rarely, I think, does one find such work as yours—where every line that meets the eye proves itself at a glance real literature." Briggs found in *The Torrent* "more interest, and enjoyment of thought and workmanship than . . . in any volume of new verse in a long time." Hays admired the "positively distinct touch . . . unique point of view" and reported Professor George Rice Carpenter of Columbia as "loud in praise." *The Harvard Monthly*, which had refused Robinson's undergraduate verse, gave favorable notice.

Especially intimate were the replies from Edward Eggleston, author of *The Hoosier Schoolmaster*, and Dr. Titus M. Coan. Eggleston's letter began: "I don't thank you for sending me a book, for I get books of poetry until I haven't shelf-room for them. But you have given me a rare sensation: you have sent me a book that I can read, and for that I thank you. I am a very busy man, but you have sent me a book I cannot help reading, and for that I forgive you. I cannot find anybody in my circle who knows you. I find friends of good judgment who on reading your poems wonder and wonder how it is that you are unknown. . . . Let a total stranger hail you with admiration, putting aside all flattering words of which you have no need, for which you have no desire. . . . I have ventured to use some of the expressions of this letter in an interview to be published in February." (It appeared in *The Outlook* for February 6, 1897.) Titus M. Coan sent praise and counsel from his New York Bureau of Revision: "I call it unmistakable poetry—most of it, indeed, of the 'inevitable sort'; and in many of the lines there is a deep and moving music. . . . 'Boston' [referring to Robinson's poem in praise of the city] would not help you much; if you could go to England and stay there!" The letter concluded by inviting him to call when he was in New York.

The literary world beckoned; and Robinson was free to seek it. When his mother's estate was settled, he would have a little money of his own. Europe, where Smith, Saben, Butler, and Ford had gone, was beyond his resources, but not New York. Boston had lost to New York the leadership in American publishing, and shrewd men of letters like William Dean Howells were migrating there. Robinson had plenty of time to consider, for it might be more than a year before the estate would be divided.

In early January Miss Edith Brower, employed in Coan's office, wrote to thank him for what the idealism of *The Torrent*, especially "Two Sonnets," had done to clarify her view of life. As he had hoped, his hard-won insights could help others. Replying to her took him out of himself, gave him a sense of usefulness.

As he read St. John's Gospel a few days later, he found it "entirely different" from what "the popular misinterpretation of Christianity" had led him to expect. Jones broadened his religious horizon farther by reading to him from Oriental sacred books, until he concluded that Christianity was "nothing more than Buddhism humanized" and "Nirvana and Heaven . . . pretty much the same thing." Emerson's essay on "The Oversoul," with its Eastern background, illuminated what had been obscure in the essay on "Compensation."

The consolations of philosophy and of usefulness to others barely brought him through this winter of bereavement; he understood why after Hallam's death Tennyson had been tempted to take chloroform. As the long Maine winter drew to a close, he poured out to his old friend Smith the full story of its anguish and travail in accents of unconscious nobility: "How long do you think a man can live in hell? I think he can live there a good many years— a hundred perhaps, if his bowels keep in decent order—but he isn't going to have a good time. No man can have a very good time—of the right sort, at any rate—until he understands things; and how the devil is a man to understand things in an age like this, when the whole trend of popular thought is in the wrong direction—not only that, but proud of the way it is taking? The age is all right, material progress is all right, Herbert Spencer is all right, hell is all right. These things are temporal necessities, but they are damned uninteresting to one who can get a glimpse of the real light through the clouds of time. It is that glimpse which makes me wish to live and see it out. . . . What I am after is the courage to see and to believe that my present life is the best thing for me, and that every man has it in his power to overcome whatever obstacles may be in his way—even that seeming obstacle we call by the name of Death. I have not said much about my life for the past three years—I mean the past ten—because with all its lack of anything like material hope or pleasure—it was tolerable. With all my long lean face, I never gave up; and I never shall give up; I can't do it; but I can suffer like damnation, which shows there is something wrong about me somewhere. The last three months of my life, however, are quite another thing. If they had come two years ago, or even one, I think they would have finished me. The book has helped me out a little—in fact I was rather bewildered by its reception—but that counts (the praise, I mean) for very little. There are things here at home that are pulling me back, and I've got to look out for them. I can't get away, just now—I don't see how I can for a year—and the result is that all my best strength is required in keeping my thoughts in some kind of rational order. The one great pleasure of my life is the knowledge that my poor mother is out of it. I can't understand—yet—the laws of compensation that make a woman suffer as she did and from so many causes . . . she had endured all [she] could and was ready to die. I had been watching it for a year. If she had not had diphtheria . . . or whatever it was that took her off so hellishly, she would have gone crazy. I am not going crazy, for I see some things she did not see—some things she could not see; but I am going to lose all those pleasures which are said to make up the happiness of this life and I'm glad of it. I'm glad to say I am strong enough to do without them. . . .

"The great scholars of the world are for the most part spiritual imbeciles, and there is where the trouble lies. The willingness 'to be a child again' comes hard—so hard that it will never come to many who are in the world today. That is not what they are here for. 'The world was made in order and the atoms march in time.' * It is a damned queer time for those of us who are here now; but it is all right and we are going to hear it as it is—when the mortal wax gets out of our ears." *The Bookman* for this month of March 1897 printed Robinson's correction of the mistaken idea of his pessimism conveyed by its notice of *The Torrent.* He stated his position with wisdom amazing for his twenty-seven years: "The world is not a 'prison house' but a kind of spiritual kindergarten, where millions of bewildered infants are trying to spell God with the wrong blocks."

Faith and courage met another test during a late March trip to Boston in search of a "respectable imprint" for his poems. "Publishers are mysterious beings to me and I am wondering what the process is by which they are captured," had been his comment on the invitation to meet literary people extended by Chamberlain of the *Transcript.* There was a pleasant luncheon at the St. Botolph Club, with Chamberlain as host, and another at the Colonial Club, where he met Professor Albert S. Hill, his teacher in English Composition at Harvard; but neither resulted in a definite offer to print *The Torrent*, although a publisher whose name seems to have been Lawson held out a faint possibility for the autumn. "To spend four or five years in getting a small book together and have it just fall short 'is a damned tough bullet to chew,'" he admitted, although he knew it was the common lot of authors.

Gardiner offered more companionship this spring. Arthur Blair, the banker, Linville Robbins, a geologist, and Seth Pope, an unemployed teacher, joined with Robin-

* Emerson's "Monadnock."

son to rent a rear room on the third floor above Brown's store on Water Street for the modest sum of two dollars a month. Calling themselves the Quadruped after their several vocations, they met there for social evenings, in which Robinson enjoyed Blair's violin and the mental exercise of combating Robbins' zeal for purely materialistic evolution. During the day the deserted clubroom was available for writing undisturbed by family life.

Laura E. Richards, a daughter of Julia Ward Howe who had written "The Battle Hymn of the Republic," and herself author of light verse and popular children's stories, had been living in Gardiner since 1876, when her husband, a cousin of the Gardiners who had founded the town, was called back from architecture in Boston to help his brothers manage the family paper mills. Even though she had thus been in Gardiner almost as long as the Robinsons, she had heard of the poet only lately; for the Richards, although public-spirited, kept apart from the social life of the town, remaining within their family connections and preserving contact with Boston, New York, and Europe. Now her son Henry, meeting Robinson at the Barstow home soon after his return from Boston, spoke of him enthusiastically. But when she suggested inviting him to call, Henry shook his head, saying that Edwin Robinson was a confirmed recluse. From her son's description, she recognized him on the street: "a slender figure, erect, distinguished, breeding and race in every line of it, dark, glowing eyes, brilliant color." His sending her an inscribed copy of *The Torrent* opened the way for an invitation tactfully inserted in her acknowledgment.

He had to be urged by Schumann to accept. But Mrs. Richards, who had seen her parents welcome distinguished liberal refugees from Europe, knew how to thaw his reserve. There was lively talk of Stevenson, Meredith, and Kipling. Robinson told of his recent discovery of *A Shropshire Lad* in a Boston bookstall for twenty-five cents. Music was another bond, and the eldest Richards daughter played the piano well. A villanelle requested his return on April 23, when he was introduced to a Richards cousin, John Hays Gardiner, a bachelor six years older than he, who taught at Harvard the English Bible as literature, a recent innovation. Between bits of music, Gardiner, who had written on Renan for *The Harvard Monthly* while Robinson was a student, spoke interestingly of books. "I had a good time," Robinson reported to Smith. "I repeat this, because it has been such a devil of a time since I had the last one. That must have been the last sawdust ride. You see I'm still a little boy, though hardly anyone suspects it here in Gardiner. . . . There's a good deal to live for, but a man has to go through hell really to find it out."

Feeling lonely one day in May, he broke his habits to go unannounced to the Richards house, and found two daughters in. They entertained him with music, including a setting of Kipling's "Mandalay," which he regretted being unable to encore for fear of disturbing Mr. Richards, who had a visitor in the next room. He could scarcely reconcile himself to his pleasure with these new acquaintances, so accustomed had he become to generalize his own sad experience: "The only trouble with that family is that they are too abnormally happy and unconscious of the damnation that makes up nine tenths of life. This world is a grind and the sooner we make up our minds to the fact the better it will be for us." The Richards got a glimpse of this feeling when he rebuked their applause of a piece by Tchaikowsky with "How can anyone see anything but heart-break in that?" But a circle in which the arts were as natural as breathing drew him irresistibly. Soon he was spending evenings with Hays Gardiner in his Tudor manor house, Oaklands, in a living room hung with Copleys and Stuarts, where the Colonial atmosphere lingered. Gardiner's staunch friendship would be of inestimable value in the struggles for literary recognition that lay ahead.

By letter, a friendship was springing up with Miss Brower. Her gift of a photograph showed her to be much older than he, and allayed fear of sentimental involvement. He thought her comments on literature clever, and agreed in admiring the style of Pater's *Gaston de Latour,* which she sent him. At twenty-seven, he enjoyed the piquancy of his first correspondence with a woman, whose opinions revealed "the eternal feminine." When she announced a trip to Switzerland for the summer, he replied gallantly that the western world would be lonely and uninteresting without her. Arthur Blair teased him by calling her his great-aunt.

With spring returned the need to write. His hard-won insights into human nature and destiny he compressed into a series of "Octaves," each a single thought in eight lines of unrhymed pentameter: a lapidary form "damnably exacting," he groaned as he toiled in April. The first of these is a frank statement of his purpose in writing:

> To get at the eternal strength of things,
> And fearlessly to make strong songs of it
> Is, in my mind, the mission of that man
> The world would call a poet. He may sing
> But roughly and withal ungraciously;
> But if he touch to life the one right chord

Wherein God's music slumbers, and awake
To truth one drowsed ambition, he sings well.

Another is a prelude to political poems still far distant:

Tumultuously void of a clean scheme
Whereon to build, whereof to formulate,
The legion life that riots in mankind
Goes ever plunging upward, up and down,
Most like some crazy regiment at arms,
Undisciplined of aught but Ignorance,
And ever led resourcelessly along
To brainless carnage by drunk trumpeters.

A fine sonnet, "Calvary," reproached mankind for cowardice centuries long in not putting into practice the precepts of Jesus. "Charles Carville's Eyes," "Cliff Klingenhagen," "Fleming Helphenstine," "Reuben Bright," "Richard Cory"—possibly condensations of sketches that had not sold—peopled Tilbury with a variety of characters, each with hidden springs of action partly revealed by a single gesture, or the pressure of some incident. "Richard Cory," so widely known among Robinson's short poems because it is pellucid in style and thought, has a surprise ending like many of Maupassant's stories, withholding until the final line the contrast between the outward seeming of material success and the hidden canker of despair, between the calm summer night and the desperate deed. In its four quatrains there is no deviation from prose order, and its diction is as unaffected as it is effective: ". . . he *glittered* when he walked." His own sorrow fresh, Robinson began with "The Pity of the Leaves" and "Amaryllis" those intimate expressions of the bereavement and the loneliness of old age which are among his characteristic contributions to poetry.

The flow of creativeness, ceasing momentarily in May, left a sense of latent power: "I am going to write a poem some day—a poem that will live even though it kills me." The new poems, added to those of *The Torrent*, would make a better-balanced volume. While Lawson gave no further sign of interest, temptation came in a letter from Richard Badger & Company of Boston. Mr. Robinson's privately printed volume had impressed these publishers, the letter ran. No doubt he had in manuscript poems of equal merit, which they would be happy to consider. There followed a delicately worded hint that the author might be permitted to share in the expense of publication.

Had the young poet been acquainted with the commercial side of authorship, he would have shunned the Badger imprint as a sign to reviewers and seasoned readers of a probably unpublishable poetaster. But he was desperately eager for an audience, and his admirer William Butler was willing to supply the money. Besides a trade edition of five hundred copies, fifty were to be printed on vellum and bound in vellum, indulging the author's taste for bookmaking as an art. He discarded from *The Torrent* the dramatic monologues "The Night Before" and "For Calderon," another immature piece, and the skit "For Max Nordau," which reviewers and other readers had taken seriously, added the new poems, and called the volume *The Children of the Night*.

To arrive in New York just before its publication in December, which would serve as an introduction to men of letters, was an attractive prospect. He could live on West Sixty-fourth Street with his Harvard friend Burnham, an appealingly unworldly figure since he had given up for moral scruples a lucrative position with a firm of corporation lawyers. He could see Dr. Coan, Miss Brower, and Thorne, could attend meetings of the Authors' Club recently launched under the patronage of Andrew Carnegie, and could meet old acquaintances at the Harvard Club. In cosmopolitan New York, more than in Boston, must lie the American counterpart of the Bohemia of which he had been dreaming ever since he had read *Pendennis, Trilby,* and *Le Capitaine Fracasse.* Somewhere in smoke-filled rooms he would find the brilliant talk and the easy manners of artists and men of letters. To Harry Smith, who had recently passed through New York on his way back from Germany, he announced on November 1 his imminent departure: "I have lived this sort of life about as long as I can and my system—physical, intellectual and spiritual—demands a change. . . . I have an incurable feeling that I am going to do something though I never expect to make much money. If I make a living after a couple of years of brain shrivelling I shall feel that I am doing well. From the *Children* I do not expect much, if anything, in the way of direct remuneration but I shall always feel, even if I starve to death some day, that the book has done a good deal for me. Perhaps the knowledge that I have done a good deal for the book has something to do with this feeling."

Unwittingly he was leaving the town which had helped him succeed as a poet while his cosmopolitan Harvard contemporaries were failing. Years afterward George Santayana, discussing *The Last Puritan* with William Lyon Phelps as one former *Harvard Monthly* contributor to another, was to explain "the fate of a whole string of Harvard poets in the 1880's and 1890's—Sanborn, Philip Savage, Hugh McCulloch, Trumbull Stickney and Cabot

Lodge . . . all these friends of mine, Stickney especially, of whom I was very fond, were visibly killed by the lack of air to breathe. People were very kind and appreciative to them, as they were to me, but the system was deadly and they hadn't any alternative tradition (as I had) to fall back upon; and, of course, they hadn't the strength of a great intellectual hero who can stand alone." Robinson had learned to stand alone because he couldn't leave Gardiner. There he was not in an enfeebled Brahmin tradition overshadowed by European literature, cowed into translations, into medieval and classical scholarship. While others were imitating the classics, ancient and modern, he caught their spirit, as the young Goethe and Leopardi had done, and by it interpreted the life of contemporary America, which had come to despise poetry as something alien to itself, too delicate to touch manly pursuits. "Ever since the youth of R. W. Emerson," Henry Adams observed acutely, "the sense of poetry had weakened like the sense of religion. . . . In America, the male is not only a bad listener but also, for poetry, a distinctly hostile audience; he thinks poorly of poetry and poets, so that the singer has no choice but to appeal to the woman." Robinson, very masculine, chose to write for the male. Unable to flee periodically, like the others, to Europe, especially Paris, to enjoy a society which respected poetry, he faced the necessity of creating verse which the American man would respect for its hard thinking and acceptance of the realities of life. Gardiner, characterized by its historian, J. W. Hanson, as "masculine in the extreme," offered a challenge to his art.

His humor was a bond with his fellow townsmen. When he began to experiment with French forms, he caught up a phrase from conversation, "the perfect boozers live in

Maine," for the refrain of a rondeau, and built a triolet about mock nostalgia for "The mouldering boots of other days." Gardiner was small enough for the affairs of everyone to be common property, yet large enough for a variety of masculine occupation and for considerable literary culture among the women. It had roots in the oldest colonial culture—the mouth of the Kennebec was settled as early as Jamestown—and its commerce kept it in touch with Europe and Asia. After Harvard had given him a certain detachment and acquaintance with the methods of the French realists and naturalists, Robinson began to see the rich materials for poetry lying about him. How Robinson, who seldom left his house, learned so much from Gardiner is one of the mysteries of genius. One is reminded of the poems of Leopardi about his native Recanati, which he saw only from the windows of his ancestral *palazzo*. But poets have quick eyes, and ears preternaturally open to what their families bring home from daily contact with their neighbors. If Robinson had been able to seek ideal urban literary society, as all young poets yearn to do, he would have missed the study of humanity where he had the opportunity to know it best. Remaining at home, he built poetry with materials at hand and created a spiritual interpretation of life to replace a religious tradition grown anemic. There were times when he felt his chilling isolation in Gardiner as Hawthorne his in Salem, times when he lamented almost as loudly as Leopardi had lamented in Recanati. But the town gave originality and strength to his verse. In leaving it now for literary Bohemia, he did not suspect how often his poetry would return for nourishment.

The Pauper

IF ARTHUR BLAIR had not gone back for his
umbrella it never would have happened, Robinson
liked to recall, musing on chance and fate. They had
started for a walk in Gardiner, and Blair decided it looked
like rain. While he searched for the umbrella, Robinson
opened *The Century Magazine* and came upon an attractive quatrain signed Titus M. Coan. The author, he
thought, might be interested in *The Torrent and The
Night Before*. From the inscribed copy sent in care of the
magazine came an invitation to New York, the correspondence with Miss Brower, initiation into Bohemia, and the
central character for his first long poem.

To find that Coan, middle-aged member of the staid
Century Club and son of a prominent clergyman, was the
collector of pornographic photographs crowding the walls
of one room of his apartment intrigued Robinson's sense
of the incongruous in human nature. In this bizarre setting
he met a dignified Nova Scotian in his forties, Craven
Langstroth Betts, proud of his descent from Tory loyalists
who had fled Boston. Betts' enthusiasm for poetry, which
he could recite endlessly, won Robinson's heart. Another

of Coan's friends, Alfred Hyman Louis, was startling at first sight: a diminutive, heavily bearded old Jew of benign aspect, collarless and clad in a filthy frock coat. His voice, musical and resonant, had an indescribable accent of authority. Apparently he had been everywhere and known everybody. He spoke intimately of Ruskin, Meredith, Trollope, and George Eliot, of Burne-Jones and the Rossettis, of Spencer, Huxley, Lewes, and Mill, of Longfellow and Howells, of Kingsley, Maurice, and Louis' schoolfellow Edward White Benson, late Archbishop of Canterbury. His mind ranged easily over international affairs; only the enmity of Gladstone, he hinted darkly, had prevented a political career, prepared for by legal study at the Temple. He looked like a tramp and smelled like a tramp, but he played Chopin divinely and recited his own verse in tones suffused with the sorrow and mystery of human existence. In old Louis, unmistakably, was all that Robinson had come to New York to seek.

The shy young poet was accepted into the Clan, as Coan's friends called themselves. Sometimes a feminine member, the divorced wife of a playwright, Mrs. Henry Guy Carleton, would join it in restaurants and bars, Raganachi's, The Cave, Cavanaugh's, Café des Fantômes, to discuss life and letters. Robinson delighted in the foreign cooking, the wines and cordials, but at first was as tongue-tied as he had been at the humiliating meeting with the staff of *The Harvard Advocate*. With effort he would blurt out some bald statement like "Kipling's verse is better than his prose," then stop short, unable to bring to his lips the qualifications he could so readily have set down on paper, coloring deeply at his apparent transgression of strict truth. After painful silence he might add, "Perhaps I shouldn't have said that." But as he listened enthralled to the nimble wits of the others, absent-mindedly drinking more than he intended, his tongue was loosed, like Joseph Addison's almost two centuries before. With the lengthening of the night he would be talking as brilliantly as the characters he admired in Meredith.

In the first week of December 1897 the publication of *The Children of the Night,* dedicated to the memory of his father and mother, brought an invitation to the Authors' Club, where he shook the hand of Hamlin Garland, grim interpreter of the hardships of the Midwestern farmer. But there, and at the Harvard and the Century Clubs, meeting a variety of people gave him no chance to recover from initial embarrassment. Burnham, living in the same lodging house, was on the other hand slow and meditative, and had likewise found spiritual support in Oriental philosophy and religions, which the two old friends discussed, with long intervals of silence, over glasses of beer.

The impersonality of New York, its remoteness from every sad association of his life, calmed Robinson's nerves, which had been "like the E string of a fiddle" when he left Gardiner. It was a foretaste of the absolute liberation Europe might bring. "For the present I prefer New York to Boston and should prefer London to New York," he wrote Hays Gardiner in January. "I have a queer feeling that I should like to camp for a week at the foot of the Great Pyramid."

He had chosen the readers of *The Torrent,* but *The Children of the Night* sought popular response. Three hundred copies, over half the edition, were sold by February, but reviews, which might draw attention to the volume and give its author reputation, were tardy and sparse. The *Boston Evening Transcript*, which reached the most discriminating readers in the city, printed two notices immediately upon its appearance. The first praised the style as "simple and direct," quoted "Richard Cory" and the Crabbe sonnet entire, and commended the new poet's "deep sympathy for all who suffer and struggle." The second and fuller notice, by the friendly hand of Hays Gardiner, described the salient features of the volume as "a natural realism of method which reminds one of Wordsworth and withal a shrewd and Yankee directness which is like nothing we remember. . . . At his freest Mr. Robinson shows much of that singing quality of verse which expresses almost more than the words themselves." *The Harvard Advocate*, where Robinson's undergraduate verse had appeared, praised the "compression of phrase." Then Boston was silent for eight months, until in September *The Literary World* dismissed the poetry as mere careful workmanship. Chicago offered a single review, highly favorable, in *The Chap-book*. But New York, whose word counted most, gave no sign, except in Thorne's insignificant *Globe*, until June.

The Nation for June 2 gave Robinson much the highest praise among more than twenty poets discussed in a survey, "Recent American Poetry." It found in him "vigor" and "creative imagination" united with skill, and characterized with discernment his manner of working: "He writes of men and women, not of external nature, and uses the latter only as the Greeks did, for a setting, which is the better way. When he deals with books, there is the same power of characterization. . . . And when the young poet . . . turns his lens upon the village street which he knows so well, the result shows the same power of putting a whole life, or a whole generation of lives, into the same narrow compass of fourteen lines." "The Clerks" was quoted entire to illustrate, and also "Luke Havergal" "to show him capable of a lyric flow and of providing something which shall haunt the reader." This review was reprinted two days later in *The Evening Post*, a newspaper with much the same standing in New York as the *Evening Transcript* in Boston. A month later *The Musical Courier*, in its art and drama section, hailed a new poet eschewing "shopworn superfluities" for "frugality of word" and "strenuousness of thought." Nothing "quite so good" had come to the reviewer's attention in "years."

Then New York, too, fell silent. No word from *The Bookman*, which had noticed *The Torrent*, nor from *The Critic* and *The Independent*, the other leaders along with *The Nation* in literary influence. The Badger imprint may have been to blame.

Those critics who had read *The Children of the Night* gave it respectful and often discerning attention. But they were few. Robinson still felt himself writing into the void.

His confidence was unshaken. In January he had begun with twenty-four lines about George Annandale a volume which he called "an entirely new departure." He wrote steadily until lack of money drew him back to Gardiner in May.

Dread of witnessing once more Dean's physical decline and Herman's losing battle with adversity was stilled by the joyous cries of three little girls rushing to their Uncle Win. They were delightful companions for his free moments, especially Ruth, the eldest. Mrs. Richards' daughter Rosalind has described the charming sight of uncle and niece together: "It wasn't just that her hand was in his, all the way down the street, she looking up at him, laughing and talking and frolicking along; it was the way in which he held her hand, and the utter confidence with which she seemed to own him. She sat in his lap while he talked; leaning back against him, in the contented relaxation of childhood." The tug at his heart made him understand what it would mean to renounce marriage for art. His imagination leaped to the greater tragedy of the spinster, with no art to console her, who toiled in a city at some monotonous task, with short vacations among nieces and nephews as the sole outlet for her maternal instinct. In the Quadruped room over Brown's store, looking down upon a Cobbossee mill pond, he blocked out a poem, "The Old Maid."

One day a fantastic funeral procession, led by the Gardiner brass band and Knights of Pythias in full regalia, wound past the Robinson house. E. R. Protheroe, a beloved music teacher who had come to Gardiner twenty years ago to put on an oratorio and liked the townspeople so much that he had stayed, was going to his grave. To see the modest little Welshman escorted with a flourish he would not have dreamed of, amused the poet and yet touched him, for it was the town's original way of doing homage to art, to beauty of character. He was reminded of old Louis, living somehow in a New York garret, who likewise represented the triumph of art and mind. He planned a poem of spiritual victory, to be called ironically "The Pauper." For the gigantic humor of the thing he read Aristophanes and borrowed from Smith Xenophon's account of Socrates. It was a long poem, but it so absorbed him that it was "nearly all written in the rough" before November.

Six months' arduous polishing would finish it; but how

subsist meanwhile? He could not in conscience remain too long at home, where the discouraged Herman could scarcely see the value of what Edwin was doing and showed signs of resentment when his wife turned to his younger brother for advice and counsel. If he ran down to New York for two or three weeks, he warned Betts, he would have to be fed: "I expect to work most of my meals out of the ash cans that spot the landscape o' mornings between Fourth and Eighth Streets. I am told that those on Eighth are the more nourishing on account of the number of grocery shops." In November he accepted Blair's offer of winter shelter in the Maine village of Winthrop, where he had gone to manage a bank.

Meanwhile Hays Gardiner, who during the summer had become something of the confidant and adviser Smith had been before his marriage, had been searching for work that Robinson could do at Harvard. In December he suggested a confidential clerkship for President Eliot. This promised to be monotonous employment that would not draw upon a poet's creative energy. If it slowed up "The Pauper," that might benefit the poem ultimately, Robinson thought. "I am a great believer in Parnassian pickle," he wrote Betts, with oblique admonition of his friend's too facile Muse, "and I think it would be a mighty good thing for all of us if we made more use of it. My ideal method of writing books of verse is to spend a year in getting together the first draft; let it soak six months; work on it another six months; soak it again—ditto; and then fix it up. This would mean one book every three years, which God knows is often enough."

During the Christmas holidays Robinson ran down from Winthrop for an interview in Cambridge. Early in January

1899, he was installed in a pleasant room between the President's office and the imposing chamber in which the faculty met. Looking over applications for admission to the University, his eyes caught the name of a divinity student, Louis Craig Cornish. The juxtaposition of Craig with the name of his New York friend Louis settled that of the chief character in "The Pauper": he would be called Captain Craig.

Robinson admired President Eliot sufficiently to have sent him an inscribed copy of *The Torrent* on December 12, 1896. But Eliot had the indiscretion to ask if he were married, and to comment on his reply: "A great mistake. A young man should marry." Touched to the quick, the author of "The Old Maid" never forgave him. Eliot on his part was probably annoyed by the poet's impracticality, as he had been by Santayana's two years before when he was doubting the wisdom of promoting him to an assistant professorship. His confidential memorandum on Santayana had run: "The withdrawn, contemplative man who takes no part in the every-day work of the institution, or of the world, seems to me a person of very uncertain value. He does not dig ditches, or lay bricks, or write school books; his product is not of the ordinary, useful, though humble kind." Although Eliot could see beyond some worthy citizens in admitting that such a man might conceivably produce "something of the highest utility," the chance seemed too great that it would be "something futile, or even something harmful because unnatural and untimely."

Worse than incompatibility with his employer was Robinson's discovery that even this routine job kept his thoughts from poetry. His was "a single track mind," and he soon regretted bitterly his bartered freedom, precarious though that was. He could do no work on "The Pauper" until March, and then only between eleven and one at night, with resulting insomnia.

The compensation for these frustrated months was friendship. Through their colleague Hays Gardiner he renewed acquaintance with members of the English Department, Barrett Wendell, George Pierce Baker, J. J. Hays, and Lewis Gates, who had been kind to him as an undergraduate. An assistant to Wendell, Daniel Gregory Mason, attracted Robinson by his misfortunes as well as by congenial tastes. Born into a family of musicians who understood in every way the development of his musical talent, Mason had had an initial advantage Robinson missed. Then overstrain in preparation to be a pianist had brought on nervous cramp in the right arm which forbade the piano and made even writing painful. Meanwhile the piano and organ business of Mason & Hamlin had been hurrying since his father's death toward a financial ruin like that of Edward Robinson and his sons, until Mason was glad to earn a living through his secondary interest in literature. The two young men had been at college together without meeting, and Mason had remained to graduate in 1895. Now, as Mason was entering what he was to remember as a "long, dark tunnel of his life," they had strong grounds for fellow feeling.

After the "romantic warmth" of William Vaughn Moody and the "delicate idealism" of Philip Savage—Harvard poets he knew intimately—Mason was disconcerted by the "dry, almost prosaic" quality of Robinson's mind, until he penetrated to the irony beneath. It was the Maine man's eyes that betrayed him: "They gleamed and glowed behind his spectacles, alternately quiet with poetic penetration and dancing with humorous irony." He was "in a sensitive way handsome, with dark, fine hair, flowing mustache, and fresh healthy color." Music was a common bond, although here, paradoxically, Mason was the classicist while Robinson's enthusiasm went to Wagner, in whose exuberance and exaggeration he probably found emotional and intellectual relief after the restraint of his literary standards. In poetry, to continue the paradox, Mason preferred to *The Children of the Night* the highly colored romanticism of Moody, Robinson's successful rival in student verse.

When Moody, who was teaching at the University of Chicago, came to Cambridge for a few weeks, Mason brought the poets much closer than they had been at college. Both were reticent—there was a Harvard saying that it took Moody "a pipeful to make a remark"—but Moody's silences had none of Robinson's tense self-consciousness. They were friendly, provocative, inviting. Robinson envied his practical talents. He had earned much of his way through Harvard and was now teaching successfully and writing poetry too, in spite of the "shiny taste of themes and literary drool" in his mouth. When he spoke, it was with a luxuriance of metaphor which was the natural tongue of his verse, and with exaggeration revealing the generosity of his character.

Another poet friend of Mason's Robinson had discovered for himself in Winthrop, whence he wrote Betts enthusiastically of *The Wayfarers* by Josephine Preston Peabody. Her lyrics moved him by their sincerity and idealism. In her diary she had called them "the far cry of youth inconsolable with homesickness" and suffering from "lack of true experience about the typically human events." Miss

Peabody had been born in New York of cultivated parents, but her father's death when she was only eight had brought financial difficulties banishing her to the Boston suburb of Dorchester, where she grew up depressed by her mother's widowed melancholy and by an exclusively feminine society of "good folks without any ideal save of worldly respectability." A poem she sent to *The Atlantic Monthly* had attracted the attention of the editor, Horace Scudder, who arranged that wealthy people send her to Radcliffe as a special student the year after Robinson had left Harvard. Frail and lonely, she had been "half afraid of dying" before publishing the volume which held Robinson's attention. Mason, whose sister-in-law was her intimate friend, could tell him of her trials, so like his own. Robinson wrote Miss Peabody of his admiration for her verse and she read his, but he could not visit her in Dorchester until late in March, when she recorded in her diary: "He was not at all what I expected. His biting strength of insight and expression were hidden somewhere behind a gentleness and quiet." Nevertheless, Robinson felt crass and blunt in her ultrafeminine and ecstatic presence, and was more at ease in their lively correspondence, full of frank criticism of each other's poems.

At the favorite Old Elm restaurant of his student days he was accosted by a poet of a far different quality, employed as salesman by Badger's publishing house, where he had heard *The Children of the Night* praised. Joseph Louis French, son of a wealthy New York importer who failed in the panic of 1873, at fourteen had run away to the West, where he had worked on various newspapers before returning to the East. He joined Robinson at five one afternoon, and it was midnight before his monologue ceased.

The composer of a poem about derelicts and failures listened with profit as well as patience to the melodramatic life story of the pudgy man of forty, with its flashes of genuine tragedy and of literary taste amid bombast and histrionic gestures. Here were comedy and tragedy inextricably mixed. Robinson was sufficiently attracted to accept frequent invitations to see French at the restaurant. That the poetaster admired *The Children of the Night* for the right reasons was cause enough to endure his most tedious declamations.

In the Harvard College Office, Robinson knew what it was to be a misfit. Release in June from thwarting duties there set poetry flowing. Remaining in his familiar student rooming house in Cambridge, he reported to Mason: "I am in ridiculously good spirits just now, sending the *Pauper* along at a rate that makes him red in the face . . . and feeling every morning the joy of a liberated idiot for the thought that I am no longer a 'necessity' in University 5." He toyed with the idea of a Civil Service post, but was not attracted by the offer of the literary editorship of *The Kansas City Star* procured for him by the sister of his Gardiner friend James Barstow. To Barstow, who accepted it, he confessed the handicap of his "damfool ambitions," adding humorously: "Today I am round shouldered; eventually I shall be an arch with my gray hairs dragging in the dust."

In September the death of his brother Dean called him to Gardiner. The two days he spent there were memory-haunted aeons. How could he ever trust life when a brother so brilliantly endowed had come to such an end?

For the poetry forming in his mind, akin to Shakespeare's in its ironic mingling of good and evil, of pain and laughter,

Boston seemed too refined, too confined, too much of a piece. "My conscience tells me that New York is the place for me. I must have the biggest conglomeration of humanity and inhumanity that America affords and I must throw two books off my brain, if not off my hands, before next June," he wrote Moody. "What comes after that will come. We shall see what we shall see. I can't be a motor man on account of my absent-mindedness."

He went to New York in October 1899. After leaving two cheap Washington Square lodgings on account of bedbugs, he settled down for a year at 71 Irving Place, where Burnham was living. His was a little box of a room, but fresh and clean. For decoration he bought a fifty-cent photograph of Beethoven as an encouraging reminder of "a fellow who did things without ears" (as he, too, might have to do if deafness progressed).

With "The Pauper" becoming more a portrait of Alfred Louis than he had intended, Robinson was stimulated by listening again to Louis discourse on literature, religion, and politics—Greek, Hebrew, and modern. There was intellectual triumph over material standards in the lordly gesture with which the schoolmate of an Archbishop of Canterbury borrowed money as if he were conferring a favor. And beneath lurked tragedy, for Robinson had reason to suspect that Louis had been confined in an institution for mental disease: some maggot in his brain had kept him from worldly success. One paid rather dearly in other terms than money for knowing him. He would rouse Robinson, exhausted by a night's writing, early in the morning to listen to his interminable monologues. And to be seen on the street with a companion so dirty and foul-smelling sorely tested the unconventional opinions of the fastidious poet, aware that his own clean clothes were getting shabby.

After he had introduced Louis to Thorne, the swash-buckling charlatan who edited *The Globe*, each confided to him the opinion that the other was crazy. Here was matter for comedy. Old Louis was best taken in the company of the Clan, where Betts would interrupt to recite poetry and Coan to criticize manuscripts he had been reading (his offer to blue-pencil Robinson's verse had to be tactfully resisted). As their convivial evenings wore on, alcohol would at length lift Robinson to equality with these formidable talkers. "Now I am up where you fellows are," he would say proudly, as he began to speak as he wrote.

In early May "The Pauper," rechristened "Captain Craig," was sent to the Scribner publishing firm, where Gardiner had a friend. After much hesitation, the poet had ventured to give the manuscript to Louis, sure that he would recognize himself. The old man returned it after a week, "with hands trembling and eyes full of tears, saying that perhaps now he knew why he was still in the world, and that it was his best justification for being."

Scribner's rejected the poem. Evidently it was too experimental for the taste of established firms, Robinson surmised. He accepted Mason's suggestion of the struggling Boston house of Small, Maynard, which had taken Moody's *Masque of Judgment*. "Captain Craig" traveled to Boston in July; and for months nothing was heard.

Meanwhile there was the encouraging word that the veteran broker-poet Edmund Clarence Stedman, who had received an inscribed copy of *The Torrent*, wanted to include in his comprehensive *American Anthology* "Luke

Havergal," "The Pity of the Leaves," "The House on the Hill," "The Clerks," and a ballade. Nor did Stedman stop at this. The shy young man was induced to come to dinner at the older poet's home in Bronxville. He presumed he would be the only guest, but Stedman had prepared a surprise in Ridgely Torrence, whose first volume of verse, *The House of a Hundred Lights,* had just appeared. The host's introductory words, "Torrence—and The Night After," wittily parodying Robinson's title, prepared the way for Torrence to tell of his delight in finding *The Children of the Night* among a pile of books he was cataloguing for the New York Public Library. The tall, slender Ohioan of twenty-four had the social ease Robinson envied—and much besides. Under a high, broad forehead were unforgettable eyes, penetrating, mystically withdrawn or sparkling with mischief as his mood shifted. He spoke slowly, choosing words with an artist's care, and the gravity of his manner could be a perfect screen until he was well launched into parody of irresistible drollery, from which in a twinkling he could resume seriousness. Robinson was strongly drawn to a nature so like his own though so different outwardly. On the way back to New York they became friends.

Divining Robinson's need, Stedman suggested there was ready money in journalism. His letters to *The Tribune* and *The Evening Post* procured for the poet commissions to write editorials. Robinson labored as meticulously as over his verse, but none was accepted. Nor was *The Literary Digest,* where Betts gave an opening, more hospitable. In September, Robinson confided to Mason: "The last smash in my western real estate has left me guessing a little." The next month he wrote sympathetically to his friend Ed

Moore of the League of Three, who was having a hard struggle on a New Hampshire farm: "I have been where S. E. Pope . . . calls 'on Hog Row' for the past six months, —and if I don't watch out I shall get used to being there. I think I always [had] a little of the aboriginal Hobo in me anyhow—though you may not have suspected it. Just at present I am toying with the arch-devil of journalism. . . . I have written a book of 'revolutionary' blank verse. . . . I eat two square meals a day with some apples or something for luncheon. I can't get along without apples. I could have baked beans for the same money but I shall change over when the cold weather sets in . . . the first duty of man is to like beans. . . . I wish you could get into some other sort of slavery, but don't for heaven's sake get into my sort unless you have a bean vineyard in your own name."

At this juncture Miss Peabody, who had a reputation as a magazine poet, intervened to break Small, Maynard's silence about "Craig." Inviting Maynard to dinner, she introduced Robinson into the conversation, saying that he was "a coming man." Maynard confessed there was a manuscript he hadn't time to read, and asked if she would read it. In the middle of December Robinson was elated by a letter of acceptance, although indignant at Maynard's fibbing statement that the high merit of "Captain Craig" had been the cause of the long delay. The news came just after he had been forced to rescue the unsold copies of *The Children of the Night* from a Badger bankruptcy. "I have good reason to suppose that my affairs will be in better shape before long," he informed Betts, who, when Robinson the month before had moved to Yonkers for cheaper living, had been immensely helpful, giving a hand in the packing and lending money.

Burnham had gone with his friend to the boarding-house at 91 Palisade Avenue. Fullerton Waldo, a Harvard acquaintance tutoring in a Riverdale family, walked over to find Robinson "living on an ignominious little street, atilt like a house roof, all of cobbles, opposite a factory." In "about the meanest house in the mean street," the poet worked at a table "draped with red-checked cloth" on a linoleum-covered floor, the landlady bustling in and out careless of disturbance.

Sustained in these drab surroundings by the thought that "Craig" would soon be in print, Robinson made excellent additions to the volume of shorter pieces he had been working on since early in 1898. He revised "The Old Maid," sketched in Gardiner two years before, refining its title to "Aunt Imogen," and took up again the story of George Annandale. Before going back to his New York boarding-house in March 1901, he had composed three new pieces: "Isaac and Archibald," "Sainte-Nitouche," and "The Return of Morgan and Fingal." The volume would be "a queer mixture," he told Moody.

What was discouraging was the persistent refusal of magazines to accept his verse. Since the seven dollars from *Lippincott's* in 1895, not a single penny had come from this source, the most profitable for poets. Showing Miss Peabody two "boomerang" sonnets, he remarked: "My poetry is rat poison to editors, but here and there a Philistine seems to like it."

Moody's "Ode in Time of Hesitation," in the columns of *The Atlantic Monthly*, had made a stir by its rebuke of imperialism as a betrayal of the American tradition of political idealism. The *Ode* was "big," he wrote Moody, but given to what Hays Gardiner called "an occasional affectation of the vocabulary." In objecting a few months later to archaisms like "lifteth," as giving neither melody nor strength, he prophesied: "I am pretty confident that in ten years from now this sort of thing will not be tolerated." His friend's acceptance of such frank criticism from an author without favor in the periodicals was support to Robinson's self-confidence. Moody's *Masque of Judgment*, coming to his hand the first week of 1901, moved him to enthusiasm. "It seems to me that he has written the greatest American verse since the best of Emerson," Robinson informed Mrs. Edmund P. Mason in a letter of January 7, "and he hasn't found himself yet, by any means." When Moody, in New York for several weeks that winter, visited him in Yonkers, they went for a walk, for a long time in silence. Turning to look at Moody, Robinson encountered Moody's eyes intent upon him. Each wanted to know, Robinson remembered with amusement, what the other was "up to."

Miss Peabody, another favorite of the magazines, also showed respect for his taste. Obviously hurt when he first advised her not to "dock the tail of her poetical horse," she soon recovered. Robinson's letters were freighted with painstaking criticism of her manuscripts, chiefly for diction. "When you tell me that you are going to keep 'sharpens' because it expresses just what you mean," he wrote from Yonkers, "you compel me to pound my critical pulpit again and to call your attention to what I believe to be an important fact in poetry: viz., that the word which seems to express the required meaning most clearly and concretely is very often the last word that metrical language—particularly song language—will tolerate." Her use, following Browning, of the contraction *o'* for *of* seemed "always bad." In her turn, she found "Sainte-Nitouche" vague and was among his friends who wanted "sweating blood" excised from "Isaac and Archibald." She wrote in her diary for April 1900: "E. A. Robinson exhorting me to drop 'philosophizing' and twittering about infinities to write about things objective. Want to, but how can I without being d——d pessimistic (pleasantness even of small decent things gone, because of M's [Mother's] continued depression, mental and physical)."

Visiting him soon after his return from Yonkers, Miss Peabody had found Robinson disgusted and bewildered anew by Small, Maynard's treatment of "Captain Craig." The firm, in financial difficulties, had gone under new management, which decided against publishing the poem. Still the manuscript did not come back, and there was no reply to his inquiry as to its whereabouts. Silence hid the embarrassment of acknowledging that diligent search failed to find "Captain Craig" in the office. At length the manuscript arrived, with a lame and vague apology. Robinson was more angry than hurt. The "sickening" theft of well on to a year's time was worse than the disappointment. The truth, which leaked out to him long after, was bizarre beyond his imagining. "Captain Craig" had lain for weeks in a Boston brothel, guarded by the proprietress until the return of her anonymous customer, a member of the publishing staff. As was so often the case in Robinson's life, tragedy was mingled with matter for laughter.

The Café Francis on West Thirty-sixth Street had succeeded Mouquin's as the favorite resort of artists and men of letters. Robinson occasionally allowed himself the luxury of a meal and drinks there. The proprietor, James Moore—grandson of that Columbia College trustee who had written "A Visit from St. Nicholas"—learned that the poet could not pay his room rent. Used to helping painters in distress (the salon of his house on West Twenty-third Street was hung with canvases that were their grateful gifts), he offered Robinson a room, to be paid for at convenience. In April 1901, while "Craig" was still missing, Robinson moved to one of the two topmost rooms at 450 West Twenty-third Street, looking upon that busy thoroughfare leading to a ferry; the painter Ernest Lawson occupied the other. Climbing four flights of stairs, he was often aware of the presence of women at the late parties his bachelor landlord gave; but Moore was discreet in vice, after the fashion of a time more hypocritical than ours, and the austere poet, in his sparsely furnished room above, was not unduly disturbed by hilarity, though one wonders about its effect upon his admiration of *Trilby*. In the basement of the neat brownstone house were a shooting gallery and a bowling alley. There Robinson met a friend of Lawson's, the young sculptor James Fraser, fresh from the West, in whose home he was to spend his last years.

By September "Craig," turned down by three houses more, was having his sixth inspection. "His trousers are pretty badly frayed, and his general appearance seems to be more and more disreputable on each return," his creator wrote bravely to Mason; "but perhaps that is all right. He is a sort of disreputable cuss, anyhow." Moody's *Gloucester Moors and Other Poems*, out this year with Houghton Mifflin's imprint, was already in a second edition. Robinson commended Moody's progress toward stylistic simplicity in "The Daguerreotype" and defended his experimentalism in "The Menagerie," which reversed Tennyson's "I the heir of all the ages" by permitting animals from their cages to despise as the end product of evolution "A little man in trousers, slightly jagged" (a line anticipating the taste of today).

Hays Gardiner offered to guarantee the publication of the volume of short poems, now ready, and to take charge of its marketing. Robinson gratefully accepted, sure the sales would save his friend from loss though candid as to marketing difficulty: "There is something in all my stuff that kills it in the eyes of the publishers. I don't know what it is; and as long as it appears to have the opposite effect with some rather intelligent people at large I don't know that I ought to worry much about it. Perhaps I can relieve you to a slight extent by assuring you that there is nothing in this new book that is half so 'modern' as C. C. [Captain Craig]. In fine, I fancy the whole thing is rather respectable, though I hope it is not so to the extent of being like some other books that I know." Barrett Wendell joined Gardiner in recommending the volume, then called *Isaac and Archibald*, to Scribner's. The reply came on November 21 over the signature of their friend Peter Duffield: "We could see, of course, readily enough, what enlisted you and Mr. Wendell in favor of the poems; we liked ourselves their quaint contemplative philosophy. The audience that awaited them, however—persons for the most part of the poet's own Brahmin class—would, we suspected, have been rather outside our reach here in New York. The poems were interesting, yet at once too simple and too sophisticated for the constituency that is ours."

Hays Gardiner must have smiled at Robinson's being

called a Brahmin, but he took the hint of trying Houghton Mifflin, the firm most responsive to Boston Brahmins and to Harvard, whose chief reader was a colleague, Bliss Perry. Moody, Lewis Gates, George Lyman Kittredge, and other Harvard men recommended the book to Perry. Moody, a popular Houghton Mifflin author, encouraged Robinson to send "Captain Craig" along with his other manuscript.

Bliss Perry replied for the publishers on March 14, 1902. In conferring with Kittredge he had gathered that "most of Mr. Robinson's friends recognize, as I think any critical reader must, the obscurity which characterizes a good deal of his work. Our readers have recognized his power of phrase, and the insight into character, as well as the humor and pathos, which his poems constantly display. I feel bound to add that their whimsicality, not to say perversity, of both mood and technique, could not escape our attention." The combined volume, in short, was a bad financial risk, yet distinguished enough in quality for Houghton Mifflin to undertake publication "on commission."

The money was put up by Gardiner, and in secret Mrs. Richards—for Robinson knew of her husband's loss of his mills, which obliged them to earn their living by the then novel expedient of a boys' camp. There would be an edition of five hundred, priced at one dollar to attract readers. Publicity copies were sent to editors and people of taste and influence, including William Dean Howells, R. H. Stoddard, Colonel T. W. Higginson (who had discovered Emily Dickinson), William Lyon Phelps, and in England Hall Caine and Alice Meynell, who had heard of the author through her protégé, Alfred Louis. One of Mrs. Richards' sisters would try to show it to Henry James.

Miss Peabody or the young Harvard teacher William Allan Neilson might do the important *Atlantic Monthly* review. So Robinson's Gardiner friends conspired.

The poet had an attack of conscience for having added "Craig" to the volume without consulting them, especially since it was too experimental for Gardiner's taste; he had to be assured that it was welcome. But he rejected Mrs. Richards' prudent suggestion that it be given last place in the book, after the more conventional short poems. "Craig" must give the volume its title and appear first, in order to show what "the book means." He was eager to have the English copyright in his own name, expecting four readers in England to one at home. "I hope to get over there for a few years before long," he added. "I've got to get out of this region for a while if I want to keep the machine going."

To keep the machine of his body going would be difficult enough between signing the contract for *Captain Craig* in June and its publication in October 1902. In May he declined a dinner invitation from Betts because his dress was "too seedy" for the Salmagundi Club. His unpaid rent weighed on his mind. But he was sanguine about "Captain Craig," which would announce and inaugurate the poetic manner of the new century, and as a basis for future work spent the summer trying to get "some Greek lymph into [his] system." He consulted Smith about interleaved translations of Homer and the dramatists, read with delight Mackail's versions of the *Greek Anthology*, and attacked the Greek original of Xenophon "like a schoolboy," with the intention of advancing to Homer. In sending an inscribed copy of *Captain Craig* to Torrence in October, he mentioned his project for a play, probably part of the trilogy of closet dramas in blank verse "with a spatter of rhyme here and there" described to Mrs. Richards earlier in the year.

With "Captain Craig," the title poem, Robinson had reached the stage in artistic development represented by Keats' *Endymion* and Shelley's *Revolt of Islam:* the stage in which a young poet wishes to test his inventive and constructive powers by a work of considerable length. The theme Robinson chose gave free play to experiment in style and taste. He had produced a medley of naturalistic frankness and soaring imagination, of sordidness and beauty, of pathos and humor, irony and high seriousness, scorn and pity. Except for passages in Whitman, there had been nothing like it in American verse, although in England Byron's *Don Juan*, which Robinson had admired before he went to Harvard, Burns' "Jolly Beggars," the Elizabethan dramatists, Browning, and lately Kipling, all in their various ways had triumphantly made poetry of such incongruous materials. There were parallels in French, with Rabelais, Villon, Hugo, and Verlaine. As bold in print as he was hesitant in speech, Robinson designed a twofold assault upon conventional conceptions of beauty and conventional ideas of worldly success. Overrefined friends like Miss Peabody, Hays Gardiner, and Mrs. Richards raised their eyebrows; but he looked ahead, characterizing his poem to Smith as "a rather particular kind of 20th century comedy."

Set going by the incongruous funeral of E. R. Protheroe, he transferred Alfred Louis, altered into an American Craig, to Tilbury and gave him auditors resembling the

Quadruped. To avoid monotony in a poem largely monologue, he built up a minor figure, the poetaster Killigrew,
to voice the suspicion that Craig is an impostor and a parasite, a suspicion which the narrator, who resembles Robinson, must struggle to overcome, and also to be the butt
of gibes against derivative versifying. A six months' absence
of the narrator from Tilbury slightly varies the monologues
by altering them into letters from Craig's pen.

The poem vindicates the principle, which Robinson
shared with poets in the Romantic tradition, that a man
should obey the child in himself and follow the logic of
his character, undeterred by social disapproval. Putting the
principle into action has brought Craig, whose "Captain"
is evidently an ironic title, to destitution; but he is so
aware of the richness it has given his character, superior to
the prudence and religiosity of a Tilbury willing to let him
starve, that he preaches it to the saving remnant of young
Tilbury men who succor him. He is a sun-worshiper, even
though light has to struggle through the dirt of his garret
window, an optimist who believes that the sages and saints,
the prophets and poets have the best even of this earthly
life upon which the materialist stakes his all. Optimism was
not easily won, for Craig knows of

> . . . men on stretchers or on beds
> Or on foul floors, things without shapes or names,
> Made human with paralysis and rags;
> Or some poor devil on a battlefield,
> Left undiscovered and without the strength
> To draw a maggot from his clotted mouth;
> Or women working where a man would fall—
> Flat-breasted miracles of cheerfulness
> Made neuter by the work that no man counts

Until it waits undone; children thrown out
To feed their veins and souls on offal.

Yet to be miserable

. . . because one half of human kind
Lives here in hell,

would only draw all down to a common darkness. Craig
carries conviction to his hearers by his countenance, "con-
clusive, shrewd" and "unendurable for sheer beneficence."
Bequeathing his philosophy as his last will and testament,
he dies happy in the garret, thinking himself Socrates. His
auditors carry out a joke he had suggested by hiring the
Tilbury brass band to lead Craig to his grave as triumphantly
as if he had been a leading citizen.

The poem is unique in Robinson's work for youthful
high spirits. The banter at "The Chrysalis" probably reflects actual meetings of the Quadruped. Killigrew's absurd
ballad, an early formal exercise Robinson happened to
preserve, takes off delightfully Rossetti's imitators; and the
dirge, "The toiling ocean thunders of unrest," is an equally
diverting parody of the current vogue of Neo-Elizabethan
verse. The aged Captain flavors his seriousness with face-
tious learned allusions and with droll similes, at least one
of which, "As a frog on a Passover-cake in a streamless
desert," must have come from Alfred Louis' lips. Craig
looks back on his own life with lighthearted detachment:

. . . I doubt not
The First Intelligence, which we have drawn
In our competitive humility
As if it went forever on two legs,
Had some diversion of it,

and forward to his imminent funeral as

> When I go riding, trimmed and shaved again,
> Consistent, adequate, respectable.

What Robinson characterized in his verse as "semi-intellectual humor" modulates into Chaucerian irony in the account of Tilbury's treatment of Craig:

> . . . there were no men to blame:
> There was just a false note in the Tilbury tune—
> A note that able-bodied men might sound
> Hosannas on while Captain Craig lay quiet.
> They might have made him sing by feeding him
> Till he should march again, but probably
> Such yielding would have jeopardized the rhythm;
> They found it more melodious to shout
> Right on, with unmolested adoration,
> To keep the tune as it had always been,
> To trust in God, and let the Captain starve.

Where the author himself suffered, in the attitude of America to the poet, there is surface lightness in the comment. In Colonial days,

> An admirable poet undertook
> With earnest fingers to graft asphodels
> And old-world cypress-plumes on apple-boughs

and from his life's endeavor left only "Six measured songs too beautiful to die." From such sparse beginnings has grown an America whose immensity and heterogeneity overtax a modern poet

> Who dreamed that he was Aeschylus, reborn
> To clutch, combine, compensate, and adjust
> The plunging and unfathomable chorus
> Wherein we catch, like a bacchanale through thunder,

The chanting of a new Eumenides,
Implacable, renascent, farcical,
Triumphant, and American. . . .

From his dream remained a single verse that

Went singing through the remnant of his life
Like a bagpipe through a madhouse.

He dies young, content that he has not overestimated his achievement, whispering: "Never mind . . . for I might have written Odes."

We see much of Robinson in the sympathetic narrator, whom Craig cannot bore:

. . . My friends got out,
Like brokers out of Arcady; but I—
May be for the fascination of the thing,
Or may be for the larger humor of it,
Stayed listening, unwearied and unstung.

His comprehension of the dying Captain's gratitude has a delicacy and a restraint learned in the school of suffering:

I stood before him and held out my hand,
He took it, pressed it; and I felt again
The sick soft closing on it. He would not
Let go, but lay there, looking up to me
With eyes that had a sheen of water on them
And a faint wet spark within them. So he clung,
Tenaciously, with fingers icy warm,
And eyes too full to keep the sheen unbroken.
I looked at him. The fingers closed hard once,
And then fell down.—I should have left him then.

The height of compassion lies in a sonnet composed by one of Craig's former companions,

A vagabond, a drunkard and a sponge,
But always a free creature with a soul,

concerning a certain Carmichael, whose bizarre humor
reveals that he is going insane:

Carmichael had a kind of joke-disease,
And he had queer things fastened on his wall.
There are three green china frogs that I recall
More potently than anything, for these
Three frogs have demonstrated, by degrees,
What curse was on the man to make him fall:
"They are not ordinary frogs at all,
They are the Frogs of Aristophanes."

God! how he laughed whenever he said that;
And how we caught from one another's eyes
The flash of what a tongue could never tell!
We always laughed at him, no matter what
The joke was worth. But when a man's brain dies,
We are not always glad . . . Poor Carmichael!

The sonnet form, of strict Italian construction, is a final
touch of incongruity in this miniature triumph of Gothic
art.

The short pieces bound with "Captain Craig" show
the poet's growth toward sympathetic understanding of
women. Hitherto his verse had been not only masculine
in tone, but almost entirely masculine in theme. The few
women were variants of a single enigmatic figure, alluring
and sinister like Manon Lescaut and seen always with men's
eyes, who appears in "The Night Before," "For Calderon,"
and "Her Eyes" of Robinson's first volume, and again in
"The Story of the Ashes and the Flame" in *The Children
of the Night*. What wrought the change? Probably his
admiration for Emma, Herman's devoted wife, heroic in

adversity. Probably too, his making friends among women: Miss Brower, whom he visited in Wilkes-Barre in 1898, Mrs. Richards, Miss Peabody. Women's ways were not men's ways, yet he saw that they were not less often right. The new insight possibly began with the conception of George Annandale early in 1898, although the figure of Aunt Imogen, created later that year, is still only a mask for the poet's own emotions. But the predominant theme of the verse composed at the same time with "Captain Craig" is love between the sexes, seen chiefly with women's eyes.

"The Book of Annandale" opens with the masculine point of view, but in the closing section Robinson enters into the mind of a young widow who has rashly promised her husband on his deathbed never to marry again, and follows the slow and delicate process of the breaking down of her scruples against remarriage. "The Woman and the Wife" and "The Wife of Palissy" (later called "Partnership") are wholly from women's lips. The former shatters the sentimental commonplace, more often uttered in 1900 than today, that a man should refuse to release a reluctant woman from her engagement because his devotion will teach her to love him after marriage. Palissy, the sixteenth-century French potter whom Robinson encountered in Longfellow's "Keramos" as a symbol of "the prophet's vision," has told in his autobiography of his sixteen-year search for the secret of white enamel, to which he sacrificed everything, even feeding his kiln with his household furniture as a last resort. Robinson lets Palissy's wife tell her side of the story, and defend, in the very moment of his triumph, her imperfect sharing of his faith while every amenity of her home—every necessity, even—was being sacrificed. These dramatic monologues suggest Robinson's self-questioning. What if he had pressed his suit too hard and known the unsatisfied hunger of loveless marriage? What if a wife had been obliged to share his sacrifices for the sake of poetry? His mind was telling his heart that there was worse suffering than loneliness.

Not that he underestimated women's capacity for self-sacrifice. That could go beyond male comprehension. In "As a World Would Have It" (his retelling of the ever-fresh Greek legend) Alcestis, restored from the grave, seems to Admetus so inhumanly strange because of her sacrifice of life for his sake that he greets her coldly. Even in the lower ranges of womankind were amazing possibilities of surrender to love, as "The Growth of 'Lorraine' " tells. Lorraine, unwilling to struggle against her temperamental inclination to promiscuity, refuses the marriage that might have saved her. Yet the memory of her lover's faith in her gives at length the courage which rescues her from degradation.

Granting equality to the sexes augmented the dramatic and objective qualities of Robinson's art and the subtlety of his psychological probings. To compare the sprawling "The Night Before" with the sure concentration of "The Wife of Palissy" is to measure his advance in the dramatic monologue. Both "The Woman and the Wife" and "The Growth of 'Lorraine' " condense drama into two sonnets, separated by the lapse of years. "The Book of Annandale" is almost a debate between the masculine and the feminine approaches to a problem of conduct, a debate lengthened by the overrefinement of feminine scruples. Here psychological complexity calls forth more intricate syntax than hitherto in Robinson's verse, unusual compound words, "upstarted," "under-thoughts," "brown-glimmered crimson," and polysyllabic effects: "Through deserts of unconscionable years." This poem foreshadows the long psychological narratives of his later work.

Plunging the reader into some action or situation already far advanced, and showing a zeal for concentration which may have been a reaction against the loose volubility of "Captain Craig" as well as against the diffuseness of contemporary American writing, Robinson has become for the first time a difficult poet, giving some color to the Scribner reader's reference to his "Brahmin class" and to Houghton Mifflin's hesitation over "obscurity" and "apparent perversity." He spot-lights psychological effects, but gives too little information as to their causes. What beautiful object Palissy holds triumphantly before the weary eyes of his wife, we are not told (and in the 1919 reprint Robinson even removed the name Palissy—which at least might have directed diligent readers to consult a biographical dictionary—by renaming the poem "Partnership"). That six years have passed since Annandale began to write his book and only five since the death of Damaris' husband—facts essential for the understanding of the relations of the man and the woman—are separated by one hundred and fifteen lines of subtle psychological analysis, taxing the memory of the closest reader. In remaining a mere uncharacterized name, although she has involved the clergyman Vanderberg in a *Scarlet Letter* situation, Sainte-Nitouche gives no help toward one's judgment of the poet's apparent reversal of Dimmesdale's experience in Hawthorne's novel. The making of poems into puzzles for the exercise of the intellect is scarcely a literary achievement. But lack of audience leads poets to opaqueness.

Fortunately, these gratuitously difficult poems are a minority in the volume, which contains their opposite in "Aunt Imogen," "Isaac and Archibald," and "The Return of Morgan and Fingal." Captain Craig's remark, "The ways of unimaginative men/Are singularly fierce," might have served as a motto for "Morgan and Fingal." Three hardened salts, gathered for a convivial night, are broken in upon by a woman crazed with grief and hardship who implores them to row out into the storm to bring a dead girl to land. With scarcely suppressed grumbling they do their duty, and return to drink and song as if nothing had happened to interrupt. The ballad stanza suits exactly the objective manner of the narrative, with its implied contrast of the callousness of the narrator and his convivial friends with the horrors they witness.

A poem with a Tilbury setting, "Isaac and Archibald," is idyllic remembrance. On the surface it is a humorous tale of two old farmers, lifelong friends, each of whom confides to a twelve-year-old boy, the narrator, his opinion that the other is obviously failing with the years (a transfer from New York of the situation in which Thorne and Louis each considered the other crazy). But of deeper significance is the contrast of the mellow wisdom and the melancholy of the old men with a boy whose mind shows exceptional possibilities of growth. In the boy, who in Wordsworthian fashion casts glory on everything about him, thinking of old Isaac as the wily, much-enduring Ulysses yet observing him and his friend with humorous realism, Robinson gives us a glimpse of the dawning of his own poetic powers. While Archibald was resting,

I know I lay and looked for a long time
Down the orchard and across the road,
Across the river and the sun-scorched hills
That ceased in a blue forest, where the world
Ceased with it. Now and then my fancy caught
A flying glimpse of a good life beyond—
Something of ships and sunlight, streets and singing,
Troy falling, and the ages coming back,
And ages coming forward . . .

In simplicity and naturalness of style and diction, in an unusual proportion of natural description, in the irradiation of the actual with the imagined, in the study of the awakening of the poetic mind, Robinson in this poem approaches closest to Wordsworth.

With "Isaac and Archibald," "Aunt Imogen," and "The Return of Morgan and Fingal," Robinson had achieved poems readily accessible to the general reader, yet with overtones of the highest subtlety. "The Growth of 'Lorraine' " combines tragedy with a colloquial ease which at a dramatic moment states a candid truth with the effect of humorous surprise: " 'I'm going to the devil.' And she went." The volume joining these pieces and "Captain Craig" was full of variety and experiment, of promise even more than achievement.

The critical response was dubious from the outset. The *Boston Evening Transcript*, first in the field with a greeting for a book issued by the most important local publisher, while commending its seriousness of purpose and "fine large sense of humor," protested against its "obscurity" for the "normal reader's mind," against its "perverse plainness" encouraged by the bad example of Browning and Meredith, which had brought "some lines near the level of prose." To show that the author "can write beautiful verse when he will," the anonymous reviewer proceeded to quote "Twilight Song" (in which Robinson had tried to do something "rather swagger" to give the volume a conventional uplifting close). In *The Book-Buyer* Frank Dempster Sherman, facile lyricist and Columbia Professor of Architecture, admitted Robinson's talent for narrative, but took him to task for "the rough, crude and altogether prosaic character of the blank verse," and suggested further use of the "file" upon the rhymed poems.

But *The Nation,* which had welcomed *The Children of the Night,* gave *Captain Craig* the most serious attention among sixteen volumes of verse noticed in its December 11 number. "One of the most promising of our younger poets," he had not yet "mastered his own powers." At his best bringing "marvellous color and music into his verse," he "sometimes draws near the unintelligible," like Browning losing "himself and his readers in regions of abstract thought," a fault probably arising from his "working too much alone." Perhaps it was better thus, for a young poet saying things "with more uniform melody" might be flattered away from his originality. "This book is likely to be passed unnoticed by all indolent readers, and with impatience by those a little more careful; but those more careful still will revert to it again and again. . . . There is not a trivial or meaningless thing in it; and when there is obscurity, it is often like that of Emily Dickinson when she piques your curiosity through half a dozen readings and suddenly makes all clear." Like the *Boston Transcript, The Nation* closed by quoting "Twilight Song" to show that the poet could write conventional verse when he wished. This perceptive review was reprinted in the New

York *Evening Post* two days later. William Morton Payne in *The Dial*, recalling his praise of the "earnestness and vitality" of *The Torrent*, put the new volume first among a group of twenty. Walt Whitman seemed "largely responsible" for its "philosophy of a free spirit that has given no hostages to the conventional life, and that seeks to divest from their adventitious trappings the fundamental verities of existence." In the character of Craig, who treats human problems with irony, Payne perceived traits of Socrates, Aristophanes, and Carlyle. It was Browning who had encouraged "the dramatic quality and the element of sardonic humor." The shorter poems, though not so interesting, were "impressive in their appeals to the fundamental emotions."

An anonymous writer for *The Independent*, even more clairvoyant than Payne about the origins and the direction of the title poem, found in it a menace. He introduced two pages of thoughtful consideration by contrasting contemporary French verse, based on "first-hand impressions of life" and a "well-set" conception of poetry, with British and American, "mainly derivative and vaguely reminiscent," venturing "nothing but what already has a place in letters and a following among the public." Robinson was an exception "symptomatic of certain tendencies of modern verse, the sum of which is making for what may be called the secularization of poetry." Craig is anomalous and ambiguous as the central figure in a poem—"whether he is a humbug or misfortune, failure or supersensible success you cannot tell for the life of you"—and "the language is no less diametrically opposed than the subject to all that we usually think of as poetic. There is absolutely nothing to distinguish it from prose, either in diction, imagery or

rhythm." The poem was a portent of "that modern formlessness of which Browning stands as a conspicuous example," a formlessness which was going to "allow anyone
to say anything in any kind of way,"—as the sonnet about
Carmichael, quoted entire, went to prove. "Here indeed is
poetry suited to all the uses of modern life—a sort of prose-
poetry or poetical prose, which by virtue of its amorphous-
ness strains out no jot of the welter of everyday things,
adaptable to the commonplace, not incapable perhaps of
rising to the usual degrees of emotional excitement, a
suitable medium in its own confusion for hasty, turbulent
thinking, unhampered by an ideal of beauty or literary
distinction, but compatible, like the present volume, with
a great deal of vigor, humor, caricature, even satire and
pathos." One already seems to hear the voice of Irving
Babbitt, of Paul Elmer More, of Santayana, raised against
"the poetry of barbarism." "Can the lesson be lost?" the
reviewer concluded. "Shall not the many merits of the
book—for it has many, as we have just tried to suggest—
rather emphasize than conceal the dangers to which poetry
is exposed at present?"

Robinson had not hidden his pleasure when *The Critic*
asked him to sit for his photograph, to accompany a review
in its March number (his first photograph to be published).
But the reviewer, Clinton Scollard—a facile versifier until
recently Professor of English in Hamilton College—expanded Sherman's strictures on the "disturbing volume,"
which, "with strength, and to spare," went "slovenly clad."
Blank verse which was little more than "prose chopped
into lines" constantly elbowed passages "shot through with
real poetic force." Scollard, who in the same general review
praised Edith Thomas' "very delightsome lyrics" and

Madison Cawein's "lovely nature effects," in Robinson found "real and sustained satisfaction" only with "The Sage" (a sonnet to Emerson) and "the swinging rhythm" of "Twilight Song." In *The Reader* the Canadian poet Bliss Carman pronounced "Captain Craig" "worse than Browning . . . a mistake rather than a failure and . . . only saved from being the most dreary of failures by the very marked power of the author."

These were the final notices by professional critics. The young poet Trumbull Stickney—recently called to teach Greek at Harvard after eight years in Europe, where he was the first American to win the degree of *docteur ès lettres* from the University of Paris—read the attacks on Robinson with gathering ire. The cry, This is not poetry, had been raised against original writers in every age. "The test of all forms of expression lies not in their resembling other forms, but in their proving adequate to the thought. Otherwise literature would be a long comment on the classics," he wrote in *The Harvard Monthly*. ". . . the fact that so much poetry past and present is written in what professors of rhetoric call an elevated style does not necessarily condemn authors who use plain Anglo-Saxon. The metrics of Milton and Browning do not banish loose and smooth versification. The English sonnet is not bound to be serious, lyric, and climactic—let me prove it to you" (and he quoted entire the controversial Carmichael sonnet). Stickney added a personal tribute to Robinson's exposure of the "brutality" of "material pursuits." "The honesty and simplicity of his mind, the pathos and kindness of his heart, above all the humor with which his imagination is lighted up continually, have made me begin life over again and feel once more that poetry is part of it, nay the truth of it."

Stickney's brilliantly phrased championship appeared in December 1903, when Robinson was at the nadir of his fortunes, so fatigued that he may not have read it for months. Stickney himself, the only American poet at the turn of the century besides Robinson, Frost, and Santayana to have achieved an individual style, was to die before another year was out, horribly, of a brain tumor. He was a loss to criticism as well as to poetry.

The first printing of *Captain Craig*, five hundred copies, had been sold in less than four months; but the publishers saw the need for only one hundred and fifty copies more, even though William James, who was convinced that Robinson had "an important future," had written them that "Isaac and Archibald" was already "fully as good as anything of the kind in Wordsworth." At Gardiner's insistence, the second printing was raised to two hundred and fifty, but it sold slowly. The Houghton Mifflin imprint and the sprinkling of favorable reviews made no impression on magazine editors. Between 1896 and 1905 Robinson's verse appeared in no commercial periodical. The editors obviously shared the taste of Sherman and Scollard, whose verse they printed liberally. By discouraging Robinson from further experiment, they delayed the advent of the twentieth-century style for over ten years. Otherwise, there might have been no gap between "Captain Craig" and *Spoon River Anthology* and *Prufrock*.

As the year 1903 wore into summer, it became clear even to a poet clinging to hope that his book had failed to lead poetry into new paths. His friends had done their best. The publishers, the publicity, the readable form of the book were all he could have wished. But they had not opened the way to the American public, which read magazines and newspapers. The poetry lay in print, to be discovered, perhaps after his death. The long delay in getting "Craig" printed, the hopes raised only to be dashed in the most irritating way, the creation of what he thought were among his best short pieces in bare lodgings as his last dollars slipped away, their disillusioning reception—accumulated strain and undernourishment took the youthful resilience out of Robinson before he was thirty-four. When "Captain Craig" had been five times rejected, he was already telling Mason that *Jude the Obscure* was Hardy's single "true" book, doubtless because he found Jude's fruitless knocking at the gates of Oxford a parallel to his own literary experience.

Once again, as during those years just after Harvard, he withdrew into himself, longed to get away from New York, with its now unhappy associations, to Europe, the impossible.

He was reduced to the humiliation of borrowing freely from friends. Stedman, past seventy, climbed the stairs on West Twenty-third Street to offer him a hundred dollars. Though he concealed his straits from Mrs. Richards, in his despondency he tried to break off their correspondence by declaring that they had little in common and were unlikely to meet again. Coming upon his landlord on the stairs, he stammered something about expecting rent money. Whereupon Jim Moore, who had been drinking, burst out with a violence that frightened him: "Robbie, you pay me that money when you get goddam good and ready."

Generous in his turn, he would give meals to French, Badger's former salesman, who in his downward course had become a fellow lodger at Moore's. The problem of food for himself was partially solved by free lunches in saloons, a recent state law having decreed that food must be served with liquor. Coarse dishes served unattractively were the fare of the connoisseur of delicacies like *pâté de foie gras* and roast mussels. And there was a snare in the free lunch: drink. Whiskey made him forget his ill-fated verse, his ill-fated family, turned him once more into a social being, in the convivial company of Lawson, or Burnham, again under the same roof with him, or of Torrence. But there were lonely days in his room and lonelier nights, when his neighbor Lawson could hear the creak of his rocking chair, a flat-footed man's substitute for pacing the floor, well into the morning. Torrence observed that he always sat facing the door, as if expecting someone to enter and change his luck. His whole life had been unfortunate, he was now sure. In an unguarded moment he mentioned his comfortable boyhood to Torrence, who ventured the remark that he had started out luckier than most men. "I guess the trouble was," he concluded after reflection, "that I was born with my skin inside out."

The Harvard Office had convinced him that he could not hold a job and write poetry; but now that he was too disheartened to compose, there was no reason why he should not work for a living, at any odd job. In the fall of 1903, when *Captain Craig* had been out for a year, Burnham remarked that his brother, one of the engineers constructing the first New York subway, could employ him as time-checker. This meant noting each worker's arrival and departure, and in the interval recording loads of material dumped at tunnel mouths. By no means an attractive job, ten hours a day, but paying two dollars. With debts on his conscience, the poet took it.

For a nearsighted man walking underground by the uncertain light of a lantern, the work had dangers. The first day he fell into a pit of water and injured his knees so badly that he decided to quit. But in the morning he gritted his teeth and went back. Unaccustomed to physical labor, he was utterly fagged at night. "Robinson is not much use for purposes of comradeship these days," Moody, now freed from teaching by a successful textbook, reported in December. "He is working at a very dreary job, poor chap, and is too tired after he gets through to do much but to roll into bed."

To Miss Peabody, who expressed alarm at the weary tone of his letters, Robinson replied that his working in "a hole in the ground" was quite in the fated course of his life: "I was a tragedy in the beginning, and it is hardly probable that I shall ever be anything else. What manner of cave I shall select for a time is of no real importance." She should reserve her sympathy for those friends of theirs whose minds were in servitude to magazine editors—for Torrence in the office of *The Critic* "under the eye of J. L. Gilder, reading bad manuscript from morning till night," for Mason, working for *The Outlook* and "trying to fit his immortal soul (in a cold room at that) into the mold approved by the sons of the Reverend Lyman Abbott —not to mention Hamilton W. Mabie." He reminded her that she herself had to submit to the arrogance of the actor-manager Sothern in trying to get her play, *Marlowe*, produced: "This utter lack of consideration for others goes far toward making this life of ours the rat-trap that it is. With the world so beautiful and life itself so hideous, I don't wonder the closing choruses of the Greek tragedies were all alike. With my freedom [from literary servitude] I feel that I have little to complain of."

He rejected Gardiner's offer of financial aid on the ground that the subway was good for his character. "If my mind is not large enough to include a few months of monotony and dirt, it is not large enough for you to think about. . . . If I were to come out of my hole now I should feel that I was making the mortal blunder of my life. Some time in the future, when my new book is ripe, I may humbly let you help me out, if that is necessary."

But the subway was not good for his character. He was too impressionable. The darkness and cold, the noise and confusion, the damp and the gas from exposed mains, a job that seemed spying on men he pitied as drudges for the callous rich, deepened his melancholy to despair. His life had gone down into a pit, and death was the only release. He began to drink for oblivion, as his brothers had done. One night before dinner he produced a bottle of whiskey, telling Burnham he had never brought one home before. His friend was horrified to see him swallow three-quarters of a glass as his first drink. Other friends urged Burnham to save him from self-destruction, but Burnham, with Oriental faith in the moral order of the universe, refused to act: "I know Robinson. When the time comes he will see the necessity and do the right thing."

French, the seasoned journalist, thought of a way of saving Robinson while filling his own purse. He offered to Pulitzer's Sunday *World* a feature story: "A Poet in the Subway." While the editor was exploring the idea by sending a reporter to consult Stedman, French told Robinson what he was doing. To his surprise, the poet was furious.

Such a story would be the ultimate humiliation. French had to promise to ask Stedman to quash it. The broker in Stedman replied, not the poet. The publicity couldn't harm Robinson, and might help him.

So on May 15, 1904, a photograph of Robinson with glasses and flowing mustache appeared between a miniature of the title page of *Captain Craig* and a representation of the poet, transformed by a mackintosh and a sombrero, holding a lantern beside two laborers and a car of dirt. Beneath was French's sensational copy: "Even the poet must have means to live. . . . His days are passed in the dark and damp recesses of the unfinished tunnels of upper Broadway. . . . He is a mystery even to his Friends," among whom were Miss Peabody and Stedman, who vouched for Robinson as "a true poet. . . . Such a poet gains at first a select audience, if any." In corroboration, French quoted from his verse, including the line, "What does it mean, this barren age of ours?" The feature closed on the note of "his hermit life," his resistance to the efforts of his friends to introduce him even to literary circles.

The publicity seared Robinson like hot iron. For once French had gone beyond the reach of his charity.

The completion of the section of the subway in which he was employed released him in August 1904, after about nine months. His humor survived the ordeal. After a ride over the familiar roadbed, he reported to Miss Peabody: "Dark and stuffy, but smooth and otherwise satisfactory. On the whole, I'm rather glad I built .it."

He resumed mental labor at once, plugging at Italian with a view to reading Dante. He managed to read the episode of Paolo and Francesca and a few other passages in the original, but for the rest leaned on John Carlyle's interleaved prose translation. Leopardi, recommended by Miss Peabody, was too hard. The tragic fate of Leopardi reminded him to tell her of the untimely death of Trumbull Stickney. "We could not afford to lose him."

Barely two months after his release from his own inferno, he informed Betts of his plan for a comedy in prose. "Sometimes I feel as if I ought to go and drown myself for cherishing the mere thought of succeeding in anything, but then I get over it."

Burnham had been justified in trusting his friend to work out his own salvation. The meaning of his subway experience Robinson told to Gardiner in a letter which rises from humorous self-analysis to accents of nobility. "I shall soon be at work again in my old unreasonable way. . . . Sometimes I am inclined to look with envy at any fellow who has an enthusiasm for anything so practical and immediately advantageous as running a peanut stand or swallowing swords. If I were to go into the peanut business I should burn more than I sold. If I were to swallow a sword the results might be more satisfying to some of my friends, though I might not enjoy the process any more than I did the subway. I write this in the greatest good humor, even in the face of all the things I know about myself. For among other things, I know that I can keep on waiting for some time longer in the dark. . . . The present day disregard of everything save dynamics and dollars does not worry me in the least. If I happen to be ground to pieces in the hopper, I still have faith in the pieces. One of the things that gives me faith is the knowledge that I have a few friends like you."

Another of these faithful friends, William Butler, intervened to soften the consequences of this stoic resolution by offering employment in writing advertisements for his department store that would leave two-thirds of Robinson's time free for writing. The salary would cover the bare necessities of life. Robinson accepted gladly, and reported for work in Boston early in January 1905.

Toward the end of that month a letter from R. W. Gilder, editor of *The Century Magazine*, dated January 24, was forwarded from his New York address. The poet-editor asked Robinson to have luncheon with him and enquired how his writing was getting on. Robinson replied frankly: "My getting on has consisted chiefly in the publication of one volume of verse (*Captain Craig*, Houghton Mifflin & Co.) and in tramping the New York subway, when uncompleted, for nine months. At present I am making a living by writing advertisements for a department store and inviting famine by writing more verse." Gilder's response, received in March, Robinson thought "kind and guarded." It invited him to send poems.

On March 16 he complied. On receipt of his manuscript, Gilder scribbled a few lines to his poetry editor, Robert Underwood Johnson: "Here is the Robinson in whom President Roosevelt is interested. He needs help—I learn from Moody—who admires him. Most of this is unuseful to us but 'Uncle Ananias' might do for *In Lighter Vein*— don't you think? & if so accept, send him the much needed check." On March 24, Robinson acknowledged payment for "Uncle Ananias," his first paid acceptance since the sonnet on Poe ten years back.

A week later, on returning from the department store to his drab lodgings at 1 Yarmouth Street, he found a letter bearing in vivid blue the sender's address: The White House. It was dated March 27 and was in the President's handwriting: "I have enjoyed your poems, especially 'The Children of the Night,' so much that I must write to tell you so. Will you permit me to ask you what you are doing and how you are getting along. I wish I could see you."

How had *The Children of the Night*, resigned to oblivion after seven years, come to a busy President's eyes? The answer went back to the town of Gardiner.

The Town Down the River

H ENRY RICHARDS, JR., of Gardiner, who taught at Groton, had *The Children of the Night* among his books. Kermit Roosevelt, aged fourteen, calling on his teacher for advice about reading, borrowed the volume. This was late in 1903, just as Robinson began work in the subway. The precocious representative of the taste of a new generation was so strongly attracted that he ordered copies from the Badger firm, and sent one to his father on January 19, 1904. In the fall of that year, when campaigning for election while filling out McKinley's term, the advocate of the strenuous life found time not only to read but to reread Robinson's verse.

A man of literary cultivation in the Presidential chair was then somewhat of a novelty. After the March 1905 inauguration, Richard Watson Gilder interviewed him for a *Century Magazine* article on "The President as a Reader." Before he could be questioned, Theodore Roosevelt asked, "What shall we do with Robinson?" Under prodding which had begun in January, the editor overcame his distaste for Robinson's verse to the extent of printing the humorous poem "Uncle Ananias"; but, aware that the

President was ready to do much more, he consulted Moody, whose verse he admired. Robinson's friend suggested a sinecure in the consular service, a long-established means of subsidizing authors, and mentioned England as especially to the poet's taste. Gilder transmitted the suggestion to Roosevelt. The President, who disliked sending a writer so far away from the American scene, was willing to offer a governmental post nearer home.

This plan had been implied in the President's letter to Robinson. Since he had no suitable clothing, the poet evaded the invitation to call at the White House. He did, however, confess his penury in terms similar to those of his January letter to Gilder. The reply came by wire. Would he accept an immigrant inspectorship at Montreal or in Mexico, with eventual transfer to something more congenial?

Robinson did not leap at the opportunity, even though his brother Herman's family sorely needed his help. Could the President, he inquired, offer something with more leisure, such as he enjoyed in Boston, but with better pay? Good-humoredly Roosevelt asked what sort of post would suit him, adding that in his opinion it should be within the United States. Robinson hinted broadly his preference for New York.

New York had become home to him. Three years before, he had informed Miss Peabody: "What little of New England was ever in me has been pretty much extirpated—though of course my arms and legs and nose music when I talk will always proclaim the state of my birth." Now while awaiting the President's decision he was writing to Betts: "Boston is a good town to write in—perhaps the best. Just as New York is the best town to live in."

By tactful persistence he got what he wanted. Early in June 1905 he was installed in the Custom House on Wall Street at a salary of two thousand dollars a year, riches to him. He had bought the conventional derby hat, he announced gaily to Betts, and then slipped into grave retrospect: "Sometimes I think the funniest thing in my whole life, and pretty much all of it is funny, is my staying alive since 1903—I mean since 1902. All I am afraid of is the empty hours in an office. I had five months of that at Cambridge."

The President's aid did not end with economic security: it went toward providing Robinson with what he desired still more, a hearing for his verse. He invited Robert Bridges, literary adviser for Scribner's, to meet the poet at Sagamore Hill. That firm, which had refused both "Captain Craig" and the shorter poems later published with it, saw the wisdom of pleasing the patron of letters by taking over *The Children of the Night* from Badger and reissuing it in October.

The President prepared the way by writing about it in *The Outlook* for August 12. Observing that "the 'twilight of the poets' has been especially gray in America," where they were not the equals of the sculptors and the painters, he adroitly commended Cawein, Scollard, and Carman before saying: "It is rather curious that Mr. Robinson's volume should not have attracted more attention." It had, he thought, an "undoubted touch of genius . . . just a little of the light that never was on land or sea." If Robinson was sometimes nebulous, the reader should remember it was "not always necessary in order to enjoy a poem that one should be able to translate it into terms of mathematic accuracy," as Browning's "Childe Roland"

and some of Turner's canvases proved. "I am not sure I understand 'Luke Havergal'; but I am entirely sure I like it." The President praised the "local touch": whoever had lived "in country America" knew "the gray, empty houses from which life has gone," such as Robinson's "house on the hill." Many of the poems "could have been written only by one to whom the most real of lives is the life of the American small town." Some of the images, like "The brown, thin leaves that on the stones outside / Skipped with a freezing whisper," fixed themselves in the memory. Roosevelt quoted "The Wilderness" as the work of "a man into whose heart there had entered the very spirit of the vast and melancholy northern forest." This statesmanlike appreciation, stressing the materials for poetry in the American people and the American landscape, closed quietly: "Mr. Robinson has written in this volume not verse but poetry. Whether he has the power of sustained flight remains to be seen."

The President broke the solid front of magazine resistance only to the extent of procuring for Robinson entry into *Scribner's Magazine*, which published twelve of his short pieces between 1906 and 1910, and of stirring *Lippincott's* to print the "Poe" paid for ten years before. After "Uncle Ananias," for which he gave graciously an extra five dollars on publishing it in August 1905, Gilder took nothing until 1910. The few reviewers who noticed the reissue of *The Children of the Night* resented the President's intrusion into their domain, where they were sure of Robinson's status as a decidedly minor poet. *The Bookman* wrote an ironic "Apology for Overlooking Mr. Robinson," which pointed out that the average literary editor had to dispose of about twelve bookshelf feet of poetry each year: "Three-fourths of this is tinged with the 'certain sad mysticism' detected by the President in Mr. Robinson's verse, and one half of it is almost if not quite Robinsonian in merit. The more anxious one is lest a genius may escape him, the more he will read, and from much reading he will, in spite of himself, grow callous. Hence, cold and routine methods of dealing with the program have developed in editorial offices." The New York *Evening Post,* Roosevelt's political enemy, produced an indignant editorial: ". . . there are few lovers of fair play who do not honestly regret to see a person in high authority turn from his course to puff a book mediocre in character and little distinguished from scores of similar volumes put out by a busy press." *The Literary Digest,* with a sniff at Badger, quoted the *Post's* blast beside a report of the President's activity as a reviewer of verse.

The mildest reproof, an allusion to "the calamities of injudicious praise," came from *The Nation,* which found *The Children of the Night* "a very pleasant little book" by a "minor poet" with refreshing freedom from poetic conventionalisms. A "haunting individuality pervades all of Mr. Robinson's work, and makes it, even when least poetic, of a curious vividness." The reviewer, Ferris Greenslet, went on to praise more highly Richard Watson Gilder, Whitcomb Riley, and Robinson's younger contemporaries George Cabot Lodge and Trumbull Stickney (whose verse had been posthumously collected by Lodge and Moody). Toward the close of this survey of recent verse, Greenslet indulged in a general reflection: "It is a fair question whether, after all, the chief business of a minor poet nowadays is not the production of magazine verse. It is certain that only in the magazines is he secure of a market and a hearing." In this situation lay the rub for Robinson, classed among the minors. Between that year, 1905, and 1913, his only acceptance, outside the realm of Roosevelt's personal influence with *Scribner's* and *The Century Magazine*, was by *The Atlantic Monthly*, which printed "Calverly's" in May 1907.

Out of habit as well as economy, Robinson had gone back to his bare room at Moore's. Fullerton Waldo observed what the Chelsea region meant to him: "I don't suppose Charles Lamb loved the tidal fullness of life along the Strand or O. Henry the uproar of the 'Four Million' any better than Robinson loved the ferry-seeking traffic before his door or the clack and clangor of the elevated trestles, in whose shadow, round the corner, he ate his frugal meals. In the crowd he found his freedom and his solitude, and in the noise his silence." Visiting his room, Waldo found it "blue with smoke from five Bohemians, three seated on the bed, one on the solitary chair, one on the window sill, all talking about poetry. Robinson, who knew more than all of them about it, only listened." French, after humiliating him by the feature article for the Sunday *World*, was back in favor for having written in *The New England Magazine* for December 1905 an article, "Younger Poets of New England," containing an estimate of Robinson as "more nearly a Greek than any singer of note whom we have with us today . . . one of the very few genuine poets that New England has produced within the generation and, in his stark affinity with the soil and tradition . . . perhaps the most important of all." Robinson tried to repay the favor by procuring for French, through Gilder, free treatment in S. Weir Mitchell's private sanatorium for nervous disorders. French remained only three days, returning, in a rage at having been spied on, to his life of alcohol and borrowing. Robinson lent what he could.

After what he called his "compulsory vacation" from verse for four years, he found it hard to return to composition, in which he retained his exacting standards. He confided to Betts his amusement at Madison Cawein, whom Gilder had invited him to meet. "His chief fault seems to consist in writing too much—rather on the touch him never so lightly principle. And I make a venture that he uses violet ink—against which there is no law." There was bitterness in his comment to Hays Gardiner about the praise given to the reissued Badger volume by his old idol, Charles Eliot Norton: "It was very good of him to go over the Children again after having forgotten them so comfortably. If he means what he says about C. C. [Captain Craig] his words mean a good deal to me."

In the fall of 1906 he was obliged to seek new lodgings, for the house was up for sale because Moore's partner had absconded with the assets of the Café Francis. Among the furnishings put up at auction were the canvases on the second floor, many of which, bought by Robinson's sculptor friend Fraser as agent for Mrs. Whitney, became the nucleus for the Whitney Museum.

Robinson consulted Torrence about where to go. They both moved into the Hotel Judson on Washington Square, frequented by literary people. Robinson took a room with a single window, facing the rear. His personal effects, which he boasted could always be packed into a suitcase, were readily transferred. The choice was happy, for Torrence helped him make acquaintances, including the free-lance writer Olivia Howard Dunbar (later Mrs. Torrence) and the magazine editor Lyman Beecher Stowe, who proved so agreeable that Robinson broke his habit of casual and mostly solitary eating in restaurants to become a regular boarder at the hotel. Occasionally he was joined by his old friends Moody and Mason, Moody's friend Percy MacKaye, a playwright, and a poet friend of Torrence's, Louis Ledoux. Robinson began to resume social habits.

Before going to the Judson, he had been sought out by a foreign author. May Sinclair, after having written a highly successful novel about poetic genius, *The Divine Fire*, on the basis of knowing only one very minor poet, repaired her lack of experience by meeting Moody, Torrence, and Robinson. In an article, "Three American Poets of Today," for the *Fortnightly Review*, September 1906, Miss Sinclair introduced Robinson, along with Moody and Torrence, to the British public as being completely free from the Whitmanesque formlessness and egoism expected from America after Whitman. Robinson was distinguished by his "psychological vision, his powerful human quality." He had it in him, she thought, "to write a great human drama, a drama of the soul from which all action proceeds and to which its results return." But the English sales of *Captain Craig*, upon which he had once counted so confidently to surpass the American, did not rise above thirty copies.

Years of privation and anxiety had left Robinson in imperative need of relaxation and good food. After struggles with his conscience about the vagueness of his responsibility to the Custom House, he reconciled himself to the idea that the President intended him to write rather than to serve the Government. He did not make his appearance at his empty office until afternoon, if at all. He slept until noon, and was back at the Judson in late afternoon to write letters or to read casually until dinner at seven. He would often linger after dinner in a friend's room for a couple of hours before suggesting that they go "shopping," as he called it, among saloons. "My only way of establishing warm relationships with my fellowman is by way of booze," he told his Gardiner friend James Barstow. Thus warmed, he would invite a companion to his room and continue sociable drinking, showing no more effects than glowing cheeks, a loosened tongue, and willingness to read poetry aloud. He knew he was a bad reader of verse and thought Torrence a worse, but in convivial evenings they enjoyed listening to one another. Robinson's taste ran to melancholy reflection, to Rossetti's "Lost Days," to Coleridge's "Youth and Age," to Lamb's "On an Infant Dying at Birth," with its arresting line, "The economy of heaven is dark."

The two played for many years a game of dramatic speculation concerning the facts of rustic life as presented by a country correspondent's column in a weekly newspaper. "We became," Mr. Torrence recalls, "extremely familiar with the names of all the residents of the countryside, but this was not all. Through a close attention to the names and their various activities we pretended to discover sensational facts about them amounting, in a number of instances, to outrageous scandals. There was, in particular, a man whom we will call Jonas Perkins, and a lady whom we will protect by the name of Mrs. Harry Gaveston. Both of these persons were evidently married and with large families, but it happened again and again that the two would be reported as having visited other places at the same time. Mr. Perkins would be on a business trip to Boston and inevitably Mrs. Gaveston would also be found

making a necessary journey to Boston. The poor unconscious figures in our sardonic drama must have been highly
respectable and innocent persons, but it was amazing the
precision with which our sensational make-believe was
supported. Unknown to the puppets we watched their
innocently suspicious movements with tireless attention.
For a number of years I doubt whether we missed a careful
examination of a single report from that vicinity. The
slightest detail sometimes assumed great importance in the
ironic game." When at length the names they played with
disappeared, Robinson wrote in the margin of the newspaper for January 1922 a line from Lamb: "All, all are
gone, the old familiar faces."

No one saw him writing verse, though an occasional
piece in *Scribner's* showed that the Muse had not deserted
him. Perhaps he composed during those invariable weekend disappearances even Torrence dared not ask about,
which prove to have been nothing more mysterious than
visits to his Gardiner friend Seth Pope, a commonplace
librarian whose merit was his devoted admiration of Robinson's verse, and his ability to read "Captain Craig" in
one sitting. Robinson described him to Moody as his "chief
laudator."

Robinson's reviving energies were largely diverted into
prose. He had been among the writers gathered in Moody's
room one evening in November 1905 to hear Percy
MacKaye read from manuscript his play, *Joan of Arc*. "He
hypnotized me with the first two acts," Robinson confessed
to Miss Peabody, so well had the flashing eyes and gestures
done their work. Whenever he saw a curtain rise, his
critical powers slumbered; from his Harvard days, he had
found something to enjoy in every play he saw. But he

read plays critically, and was a strong partisan of Ibsenite realism, which with Pinero, Jones, and Shaw had been conquering the London stage. He was eager to see it lift the American theater from Victorian sentimentalism and melodrama.

The success of Miss Peabody's *Marlowe* at Radcliffe in the summer of 1905, with Robinson's Harvard acquaintance George Pierce Baker in the title role, seemed evidence that American audiences were ready for something more serious. Moody and Torrence had been writing poetic dramas with no relation to the commercial theater. Now MacKaye, son of a successful actor and playwright, appeared as the providential link of literature with Broadway producers and the technique of the modern stage. His ambitions as a playwright did not exclude a generous zeal to advance American drama by encouraging and aiding the efforts of his friends. The gifted actress Nazimova, playing Ibsen to small audiences, was eager for promising American roles.

Moody was just completing a prose play, *The Great Divide*, based on the contrast between the New England and the Western temperaments, which had struck him immediately on his arrival at Harvard from Indiana. He rejected the suggestion of his admirer R. W. Gilder that it be performed by the MacDowell Club or by the Shakespearean actors Sothern and Marlowe, for the reason that it was "realism of a rather grim and uncompromising sort, without the romantic glamour which they effect." An actor friend of the author's brought it to the attention of Margaret Anglin, who saw sufficient possibilities for herself in the leading role to persuade the producer Henry Miller to try it out in Chicago, in April 1906. Its New York

opening in October was a resounding success. Critics hailed
Moody as the long-sought "great American playwright."
Robinson, going away from the first night in a fever of
enthusiasm, wrote a poem, "The White Lights," to celebrate the coming to America of classic popular drama on
native themes to parallel that of Greece and Elizabethan
England.

The translator of *Antigone* had already finished the first
draft of a tragicomedy in prose, *Ferguson's Ivory Tower*,
with its scene laid in Washington Square, and his hopes
were high when in the early summer of 1907 Wheeler, of
His Majesty's Theatre, London, asked to see the manuscript, rechristened *Van Zorn*. He wrote a second prose
drama, *The Porcupine*, a somber study of New England
village life, of which Moody thought so highly that he
volunteered to press it upon the veteran producer Charles
Frohman. Moody's opinion counted for much in that fall
of 1909, when *The Great Divide*, after a thousand American performances, was opening in London. But Frohman
kept the manuscript only forty-eight hours before returning it to Moody. It was an ordeal to break the news to
Robinson, who had toiled for almost four years in the
unfamiliar dramatic form, lured by the possibility of financial reward sorely needed by his brother's family.

Three days after Frohman's rebuff, Robinson dined with
Moody and Torrence on the opening night of MacKaye's
Sappho and Phaon, which the critics damned effectually.
Nazimova, after reading Torrence's three-act play, *The
Madstone*, with enthusiasm, lost interest. The next year,
with the failure of Moody's *Faith Healer*, the false dawn
of the new American drama was over.

The incursion into the most popular of the arts, where

to shun the obvious was a fatal handicap, had cost Robinson time better devoted to the poetry for which the President had given him the Custom post. The illusion that he could aid in a renascence of drama was shattered soon after Roosevelt's departure from the White House in March 1909 had made the post untenable. It seemed to him providential that the salary lasted just long enough to finish paying for the two years' illness of his brother Herman, who in 1909 died of tuberculosis in the Boston City Hospital. Pondering over the ways of destiny, he wrote "Vickery's Mountain," the portrait of a man who does not go where he knows gold lies, because "unseen hands" restrain him. "He still believes he will go for it, however, and is probably quite as happy as if he had it," the author explained when the editor of *The Century Magazine* found the poem obscure. Robinson's resentment of the elder brother who had been his parents' favorite and whose tastes had not been his had long ago dissolved in pity and understanding. In "Exit" he wrote with classic simplicity and compression a requiem for Herman and for others of like fate:

> For penance he would not confess,
> And for the fateful emptiness
> Of early triumph undermined,
> May we now venture to be kind.

In September he returned to Gardiner to advise his brother's widow, who since the sale of the Robinson house in 1903 had been living in her father's home across the Cobbossee, sewing to support herself. Her heroism gave him courage. While he was with her and her young daughters the habit of drink which had been impeding his writing could not be continued. He seized the moment to revise poems for the volume he felt he owed Roosevelt, and which was to be dedicated to him. Even coffee was rejected at night. He worked under pressure of the knowledge that he was approaching his fortieth birthday without recognition. "The lads coming home from school make me feel like an old [man]," he wrote Ledoux on September 30. "I have been out of school for twenty-one years and am not yet of age with publishers."

The problem of sustaining himself in New York after the loss of the Custom post had been solved for him by a friend he had come to know through Torrence. Mrs. Davidge, a daughter of Bishop Potter, had a genius for imaginative service. To Robinson's specifications she built a studio behind her house at 121 Washington Place, which was ready for occupancy before his birthday in December. Breakfast was brought to him there; the other meals he ate where he pleased. Soon after taking possession, he acknowledged the dedication of MacKaye's *Poems* jointly to himself, Moody, and Torrence: "I feel honored and puffed up—also chilly and grown old."

His own volume, *The Town Down the River*, was accepted by Scribner's, who were also ready to reprint *The Children of the Night.* But he needed more money than he could expect from verse. If his dramas could not attract producers, they might find readers by being turned into novels, so advised Hays Gardiner and other friends. While waiting for the publication of *The Town Down the River* in October 1910, he went back to the toil with prose fiction that had been fruitless in those Gardiner years after college. He worked all summer at Chocorua, New Hampshire, where he was the guest of T. H. Bartlett, with whom Moody and Mason had lived ten years before.

Bartlett, an aged sculptor, pensioner of Boston patrons, was an inspiring failure after the fashion of Captain Craig. A village stonecutter, he had been sent to study in Italy and France, and had produced creditable statuary before drifting away into teaching, into writing, and finally into nothing in particular. The example of Daumier, whom he had known in Paris, and of Walt Whitman, an intimate friend of later years, had encouraged his rustic independence, his contempt for mediocrity in the arts—contempt expressed in highly profane language shot through with poetic beauty. Believing that all creative work was done against heavy odds, he struck out against Robinson's first hint of self-pity, saying he "ought to wear out the knees of his trousers" in thankfulness that his lot had not been worse. What more he said in the same vein may be imagined from his reply to Mason's complaint that Hamilton W. Mabie blue-penciled his contributions to *The Outlook:* "This affair will teach you two good truths. First, that there is always some idiot attached to a popular publication, and second, what tribulation every decent soul has to go through in trying to do anything sincere and genuine. . . . You have worlds of practical life to learn; to find out why all the concentrated sentences of the best minds are based on blood, grief, and martyrdom. The literary charm of these sentences is pure mist in comparison to what *caused* them to be said. . . . Emerson is rotten with good things, but he nailed them with cold hands and an empty stomach. Think of his going lecturing in the wilderness of Illinois, in 1855, for fifty dollars a night, eating tough pork, sleeping in a cold room, and obliged to be pleasant with idiots. Every sentence of his cost Pain."

In the middle of October a telegram from Percy Mac-

Kaye brought to Chocorua the appalling news of the death of Moody at forty. Robinson tried to console MacKaye and himself by replying: "Well, he did enough to give him his place among the immortals, and I believe he did no man an injury while he lived." Sorrow cast a shadow over the appearance of Robinson's fourth volume that month.

Abandoning the experiments of *Captain Craig,* the collection of short poems called *The Town Down the River* develops chiefly two themes announced in *The Torrent:* individual character and the literary life. New York, the town down the river, had deepened and widened Robinson's understanding of both.

In the isolation of Gardiner, he had defended his high conception of the profession of letters. During his first New York years he had taken the offensive to pillory the poetaster Killigrew. Now in the wealth of his acquaintance among authors he is more tolerant. Only the sneering critic Momus merits castigation. He smiles at the impotent romantic longings of Miniver Cheevy and at the Broadway light-weight in "Bon Voyage," and pardons the imitative mediocrity of Atherton. O'Leary, a poetaster who wakes to his folly and renounces verse, wins his admiration. But the fine ironic sonnet, "The Sunken Crown," scorns the world's scorn for the idealist who risks his all.

In the general studies of character the men are mostly seen in retrospect as frequenters of Calverly's bar or restaurant, reminiscent of the Clan of his first New York years. There is something of Betts in Lingard, the incurable idealist, and a mingling of Louis and French in Leffingwell, fallen from high aspiration to be "a parasite and a sycophant," whose profane and vehement valedictory to life haunts his friends. The "Doctor of Billiards" betrays in his "false unhallowed laugh" a realization of the tragedy of his wasting high abilities on mere gaming. Among the failures Robinson counts himself, under the thin disguise of Clavering, the good listener, who "clung to phantoms and to friends/And never came to anything." A friend describes him as he appeared to the group, noting his defects of brooding on the past and tolerating bad men like Calverly, owner of the resort, and the snakelike Cubit. But ingeniously the poet inserts glimpses of Clavering as a man undeluded by mirages, who saw "Too far for guidance of to-day,/Too near for the eternities."

Among portraits of women, the most finished is given in the threnody "For a Dead Lady." The death of a beautiful woman, which Poe in his comment on "The Raven" called the supreme theme for poetry, Robinson meditates upon with a characteristic mingling of realism with wonder, lyric regret, and metaphysical questioning. Endowed with every beauty, every grace and subtlety, the lady is sensitive to applause and has a "laugh that love could not forgive." For all her worldliness Robinson cannot restrain regret for the passing of so perfect a work of nature and of art. Leonora, like Lorraine, death saves from an inevitable path of shame. "Leonora" is a poem of subtle overtones, in which the tripping of hexameter and the idyllic description of her grave do their best to disguise and soften her somber story.

For Leonora the grave is best, and so too for the deceived husband in "The Whip" and for Annandale, whom a physician mercifully puts out of the way when he is physically beyond repair. In years that had often been a weary burden, Robinson had come to defend the right of the individual to end his own life, and to approve of mercy killing. The world could be too horrible. There was the almost un-recognizable wreck out of his past who knocks at the poet's door in the powerful sonnet "Alma Mater."

The only poems in a new vein—"The Master," a tribute to Lincoln, and "The Revealer," a tribute to Theodore Roosevelt—open and close the volume. At length social sympathies have affected Robinson's political thinking, as they had affected Moody's a decade before. Lincoln, the homespun, wins posthumous recognition as a Titan by "the gentlemen who jeered." Roosevelt has battered open the doors privilege had built for its plunder of the people. It will be the people's fault if they have not the wit and the will to enter into their own:

> What You and I and Anderson
> Are still to do is his reward;
> If we go back when he is gone—
> There is an Angel with a Sword.

The poet has more than a shade of doubt as to whether his fellow Americans will deserve this second Titan:

> Down to our nose's very end
> We see, and are invincible,—
> Too vigilant to comprehend
> The scope of what we cannot sell.

Here appears for the first time in his verse Robinson's tortured love for his country, which was to engage a protracted battle between his heart and his head.

The poet was curious to learn from his friend Ledoux why the editor of *The Outlook* would not print "The Revealer": "Did Abbott seem to know what I am driving at in T.R. or did he disagree with it with some degree of intelligence? I have encountered so much rotten imbecility in the way of failure to get my meaning that I am beginning to wonder myself if it may not be vague. But I won't have it anything worse than obscure, which I meant it to be—up to a certain extent." The intentional opaqueness was part of the poet's playing with the literalness of the American political mind. Otherwise, with the notable exception of "The Whip," *The Town Down the River* is free from the obscurity and vagueness of some of the pieces in *Captain Craig*. Not every poem yields its meaning at first reading, but the meaning is precise. "Leonora" is momentarily a puzzle, until the reader observes that the lilting hexameter couplets and the decorative diction are in designed conflict with the somber situation, just as in Eliot's "The Hollow Men" the rhythm and associations of a child's game, "Here we go round the mulberry bush," convey the circling anxieties of an old man's sleepless early morning.

Where, on the contrary, rhythm is used to reinforce the mood and theme, Robinson is equally skilled; whether in the elegiac unrhymed hexameters of "Pasa Thalassa Thalassa" or in the trochaic trimeters tripping beside iambic dimeters to heighten the graceful frivolity of "Bon Voyage." Stanzas of invariable structure manage to convey, by variation of pauses, both Atherton's literal superficiality and the heights of poetry that loom above it. The other superb artist of Robinson's generation, Robert Frost, master among our critics of poetry, coming upon Robinson's work for the first time in this volume, was charmed by the placing of the fourth "thought" in

> Miniver thought, and thought, and thought,
> And thought about it.

"There is more to it than the number of 'thoughts,' " Frost pointed out a quarter of a century later: "There is the way the last one turns up by surprise around the corner, the way the shape of the stanza is played with, the easy way the obstacle of verse is turned to advantage." In the slow maturing of this volume, Robinson had become master of his medium.

Highly finished work with nothing to shock traditional aesthetic susceptibilities, *The Town Down the River* won respectful criticism. *The Outlook* found a good omen in its taking a middle ground, which would "comfort those who have been led to expect that new poetry must be as polished and lifeless as the statue of the 'Greek Slave,' or as noisy, violent and profane as a far Western barroom on a festive night: Mr. Robinson is quietly himself; he is neither a reactionary nor a rebel; he steers clear of the commonplace and escapes the strain of a deliberate and painful effort to be original." There remained a stumbling block in the demands the style made on the reader's imagination. The English poet Richard Le Gallienne, writing in *The Forum*, held the influence of Browning and Housman responsible for the "somewhat too stringent and tight-packed style," and for "too many dark sayings and drastic abbreviations of his meaning." *The Literary Digest* was more emphatic and less urbane to the same effect: "At times his style is too cryptic and occasionally the meaning dives into complete obscurity and does not reappear again for several stanzas." *The New York Times* warned its newspaper audience that the book was "esoteric . . . something expressive of a small group more than humanity at large." But his style was finding admirers. Payne in

The Dial praised discerningly its "quintessential purity of distillation," *The Outlook* its "strength of plain words and compressed experience." Robinson was a "reticent poet," Payne admitted, "but a few of his words will outweigh the fluent utterance of the more voluble . . . [with] its grave and measured discourse." Even Le Gallienne could not resist the pervasive "persimmon humor," the "cryptic mirth," sometimes concentrated in poems like "Miniver Cheevy."

Critics were unanimous in admiring the union of a sense of reality with a sense of beauty and of mystery. "There is always something in the lives—each person has a lyric secret" (*The Literary Digest*). "Mr. Robinson may be said to put what appeals to him into words, just before it escapes into the region beyond words" (*The New York Times*). "For a Dead Lady" was singled out for its beauty, "The Master" for its strength. *The Outlook* deplored "the disheartening silence about verse . . . which is neither academic nor journalistic, but fresh, human and alive." Le Gallienne, admiring Robinson for having "gone through the mill—in a man's way," blamed the false impression that "there are no poets nowadays" not upon publishers, for even established names did not pay the expense of publication, but upon the general reader: "The public only cares for poetry that has some national or moral or mawkishly sentimental theme; or maybe, makes some momentarily sensational appeal. The best of its great 'popular' poets it knows nothing of. It knows Tennyson by 'The Charge of the Light Brigade' and 'The May Queen,' but probably never heard of 'The Lotus Eaters' and 'Lucretius.'" The best of Longfellow was obscured by his "horrible popularity."

The meager sales of *The Town Down the River* must have underlined for Robinson, who had fairly conquered his critics, the public indifference to quality. Writing verse meant "starving in a hole." He was turned back anew upon prose.

The Man Against the Sky

THE CITIFIED AUTHOR of *The Town Down the River*, arriving at Chocorua not "at ease with nature," a month later was rising, to his surprise, before eight "a-sniffing of the mountain air," ready for seven hours' work by daylight. Eleven years earlier, before New York had become home to him, he had thought nostalgically of apple-picking: "The Virgilian *rusticus es* in me will not be killed. And on the whole I am not altogether certain I wish to kill it." His rustic self, appearing in "Isaac and Archibald," revived incredibly as he stayed on with Bartlett through the glory of autumn leaves and into the chill bareness of November. After another New York winter, he had found himself craving a country summer.

A summer neighbor in New Hampshire, Hermann Hagedorn, on a visit to New York suggested the Mac-Dowell Colony for workers in the arts among the pines at Peterborough. Hagedorn, Robinson's future biographer, who had helped George Pierce Baker prepare the pageant, accompanied by MacDowell's music, which had given the recently established Colony dignified publicity in the summer of 1910, had invited the poet to attend the performance. He had refused, scoffing at the idea of getting involved in a miscellaneous group of creative workers, with their clashing temperaments. He knew what colonies were like. But now hunger for the country made him listen more sympathetically to Hagedorn's explanation that the MacDowell Colony was exactly suited to his needs.

Edward MacDowell, composing music amid the distractions of teaching and New York noises, had alarmed his wife by his fatigue when summers came. Without his knowledge, she went to Peterborough and rented a cottage. The summer so rested him that he invested his savings of fifteen hundred dollars in a farm. A year later he built a log cabin at some distance from the farmhouse to insure absolute seclusion in the pine woods. A crumpled paper bearing a discarded exercise caught the eye of his musician wife when she was emptying the cabin wastebasket. Rescued, it attained enduring popularity as "To a Wild Rose," and carried financial relief with it. Before his tragic death the gifted composer had planned to share this seclusion with other creative artists, who should work in detached studios like his cabin and meet only at the end of the day. With vision and executive force Mrs. MacDowell at fifty-two had begun to put the plan into being.

Robinson was persuaded to give the Colony a trial. He arrived tardily in July 1911, carrying, out of characteristic caution and tact, the draft of a telegram which could call him away if his doubts were confirmed.

Too late to get a studio, he worked in his bedroom in the men's dormitory on the Dublin Road. A fellow colonist, Parker Fillmore, observed him with eyes sharpened by suffering. "It struck him," records Mr. Hagedorn's biography, "that this man, who seemed neither young nor old and appeared interested neither in himself nor in anyone else, was burdened with a sadness transcending discouragement." Robinson ate ravenously, like a starving man, and smoked Sweet Caporal cigarettes incessantly.

Undisturbed as never before in his life, in three weeks he quarried eight chapters of a novel out of *The Porcupine*. Then, written out, he sat brooding, letting cigarette butts and newspapers litter his room and neglecting the Colony duty of making his bed. If a window got closed, it remained so, even in stifling weather. He was helplessly indifferent to housekeeping, though scrupulously neat about his person. "Fillmore, seeing him in his evil-smelling room . . . smoking and sighing, had a sense that here was a sick soul."

The peace and freshness of the countryside, with now and then a social evening with music, insensibly wrought change. "The world was made in order and the atoms march in time." Mount Monadnock, which inspired the line from Emerson that he had found so consoling after his mother's death, overtopped the Colony grounds with its imposing serenity. After a month's stay he wrote to Ledoux: "I came down prejudiced against all 'colonies,' but I wish now that I were a millionaire in order to make it more of what it is. MacDowell knew what he was about."

Fillmore won his heart by sending for his volumes of verse and by telling him how much he liked them. By his own frankness about family obligations, which had worn him to nervous collapse and tuberculosis and were still on his shoulders, Fillmore drew Robinson to talk of his personal affairs and dubious prospects. Robinson's passion for music led to friendship with another colonist, Lewis M. Isaacs, a former pupil of MacDowell. Many years later, his legal knowledge was to guide Robinson's financial affairs. Mrs. Isaacs, associate editor of *The Drama Quarterly*, shared his love of the theater. In their cottage across the Nubanusit River music and good talk gave him relaxation.

Mrs. MacDowell had welcomed Robinson's request for admission to the Colony, for she had been attracted to his poetry by the enthusiasm of her old friend Miss Brower, who had written so intelligently about her husband's music that she respected her judgment of verse; but she had doubted whether he would like the Colony. When he came to call at Hillcrest before leaving, she confessed her initial doubts. He produced the telegram he had prepared, and they laughed together. Humor, often hiding grief and pain, was a bond between them. From Fillmore he knew of her suffering from an injured back as she jogged over wood roads in a buggy to select studio sites. She managed the Colony by remote control, never obtruding upon her guests. In gratitude for what the Colony had given him, Robinson resolved to give up drink.

The "woes of the wagon" were greater than he anticipated, and there were relapses to whiskey, which blotted out anxiety about his future. "The wolf is keeping quiet for the present," he wrote Ledoux from Peterborough, "but I know that the brute is licking his chops behind some stone wall, or, at the farthest, somewhere in the neighborhood of Sixth Avenue and Washington Place." Before his return to that neighborhood, the Ledoux invited him to enjoy the autumn coloring in their country home near Cornwall on the Hudson. Mrs. Ledoux steadied his resolution by suggesting that he report to her every time he took a drink, and he conscientiously fulfilled his promise. The wolf showed his head often this winter, but checks from

Ledoux, Butler, and Gardiner kept him at a distance. Roosevelt, fighting Taft for the Republican nomination, asked Robinson to tea, and Mrs. MacDowell invited him to return to Peterborough for the summer.

The novel made from *The Porcupine* found no better market than the play. By May 1912 he told Ledoux his thoughts were turning to poetry, though he felt "too stirred" by his struggle with drink to compose it. His second summer at the Colony was spent on a play which, he persuaded himself, had "a real odor of the stage." Again to no avail.

Ledoux encouraged his return to verse by a letter to *The New York Times* defending *The Town Down the River* from misinterpretations and giving it perceptive praise: it was curious, he wrote, "that work so strikingly original . . . should not yet have become more widely known." In this autumn of 1912, the market for serious verse was greatly expanded by the founding of the first American periodical completely devoted to verse and to the criticism of poetry: the well-endowed *Poetry*, edited in Chicago by Harriet Monroe. Mrs. Moody, one of its enthusiastic backers, invited her husband's old friend to contribute. Robinson replied sadly: "I haven't written a verse in two years. . . . It looks now as if I should have to waste a few more years over more or less experimental prose to pay for my venturing into that apparently forbidden country to which I was called and hauled."

Deprivation of drink was excruciating. At times, he told Torrence, he felt like "scratching down the stars." The Ledoux, the Isaacs, and the Hagedorns steadied him by invitations to their homes. His studio on Washington Place had been sold when Mrs. Davidge married an artist named

Taylor. In December he joined them on her estate of eighty wooded acres on Staten Island. Taylor and his wife conspired to keep Robinson's mind away from drink by never leaving him to his own thoughts in the evenings. Discovering his desire gone, he was amazed. "Call it suggestion or anything you like, but there it is."

The alcoholic obsession lifted, he recognized his vocation, as he had in reverting to poetry after two years' trial of prose fiction in Gardiner. "There are too many words in prose, and they take up altogether too much room," he had remarked in his second Peterborough summer. But he knew well where following his bent might lead. "The chief objection I have to poetry—after forty—is that it has a way of making Bellevue or Blackwell's Island appear unpleasantly democratic and adjacent," he told Kermit Roosevelt in February. ". . . I don't like to think where I should be now if it had not been for your astonishing father. He fished me out of hell by the hair of the head, and so enabled me to get my last book together, and in all probability to get it published."

Two weeks later he enclosed an unfavorable analysis of *The Porcupine* by the producer Winthrop Ames to buttress a decision announced to Hays Gardiner. "It isn't that I can't write a play, so far as the technique goes—in fact, I believe it is admitted that I can—but I cannot hit the popular chord, and for the simple reason that there is no immediately popular impulse in *me*. In poetry this is an advantage, but for commercial playwriting it is deadly. When I come out of myself and try to write for the crowd, I perpetrate the damnedest rubbish you ever heard of. . . . At last I can see light again, and I am going to write a book of poems. . . . I don't believe the human brain was ever constructed that could stand much more of the kind of wear and tear of conflicting activities that mine has undergone during the past three years. . . . I feel that I have given the thing a fair trial and it would be unfair to you as well as to myself to waste any more of my life in doing something for which I have come to see that I am not fitted." From this decision of March 9, 1913, there would be no wavering.

He had to call on Fraser, Ledoux, and Gardiner for money to get him to Peterborough, but in Boston, where he stopped on the way, he found his verse more in the public eye than it had been since Theodore Roosevelt's *Outlook* article eight years before. An English visitor was the cause.

In the course of a newspaper interview on arriving in Boston, Alfred Noyes, the acclaimed young poet of the moment, had remarked that Robinson was the foremost living American poet. Seizing the occasion for a loyal word in behalf of a friend, Carty Ranck, a journalist and playwright who had met Robinson at the Colony, used Noyes' statement as the text for a column, "An American Poet with a Message," in the *Boston Evening Transcript* for May 12 (Ranck was to receive his reward in the dedication of *Nicodemus*). The *Transcript's* poetry editor, William Stanley Braithwaite, followed two weeks later with the report of an interview in which Robinson, asked to define his "message," replied: ". . . a faint hope of making a few of us understand our fellow creatures a little better, and realize what a small difference there is after all between ourselves as we are and ourselves not only as we might have been but as we would have been if our physical and temperamental make-up and environment had been a little different."

The rival *Boston Post* thereupon sent a reporter, obviously less specialized, to Robinson's lodgings on St. Botolph Street. He began by asking if the poet shared Noyes' belief in the possibility of universal peace. Replying briefly in the negative, Robinson turned to literature, saying that he agreed with the English visitor that Emerson was the greatest American poet, even though what technical skill in verse he had was nearly "accidental." He regretted that, among contemporary English poets, Kipling was not known by his best pieces. Pressed to comment upon American contemporaries, he called Moody the ablest of his generation, and mentioned with catholic generosity Hagedorn, Miss Peabody, Miss Branch, Torrence, Ledoux, and Kilmer. He was irritated when the *Post* failed to print his further mention of Woodberry, Cawein, and Van Dyke. As to the prospects for poetry in America, he was hopeful: "It is the remnant that saves. . . . I have great faith in the younger men." Meeting Noyes, Robinson described the merits of these younger men and gave him a copy of Ledoux's poems.

"My work is going pretty well," he reported to Ledoux from Peterborough, "and I don't believe I have lost anything during my three years' chasing of false gods." Among the products of the summer was "Eros Turannos," the condensed drama he was born to write, outwardly impassive but tense within, the silent suffering of a patrician soul too proud to acknowledge a fatal mistake.

Another significant event was his coming to know Mr. and Mrs. Thomas Sergeant Perry, of the neighboring village of Hancock. Mr. Perry, one of the richest personalities of the time, author of *English Literature in the Eighteenth Century*, which Robinson had read at Harvard, in his mid-sixties was devoting himself to the fine art of friendship in correspondence with distinguished men all over the world. In his brilliant talk Robinson had intimate glimpses of the best of the elder generation of American writers and thinkers—of Henry and William James, Perry's friends from boyhood, of Howells, his close associate in journalism, of Henry Adams and John Fiske, his Harvard colleagues. He was more widely read than Robinson in the literatures of the world, and out of ten years' experience in Europe and three in Japan confirmed the ominous view of the world situation which had caused Robinson's dissent fr⌐m Noyes' optimism about universal peace, an optimism widespread in the United States. From his own thwarted effort to establish himself as a literary critic after the manner of Sainte-Beuve in a country where criticism fell between the stools of journalism and academicism, Perry understood what Robinson's poetry had to contend with. In sardonic realism, in wit, in seasoned humanism the elder and the younger writer were at one. Lilla Cabot Perry, a warm, outpouring nature, practiced the arts of painting and of poetry, and read verse beautifully. Robinson was soon scanning her verse with the severe yet encouraging criticism he had given Miss Peabody's and was listening to her read his own manuscripts aloud for them both to judge their effect upon the ear.

The return of his best powers in ideal conditions for work and for conversation seemed too fortunate to last. The Colony in its "sea of trees" was an island of illusory refuge, which he must steel himself to leave as September came. Throwing aside the masks he had worn for fifteen

years, for the first time since *The Children of the Night*
he spoke in his own person, addressing Mrs. MacDowell
in verses called "Hillcrest," after her home. Though the
peace she had given tempted him to console humanity, he
could
> . . . never dare again
> Say what awaits him, or be sure
> What sunlit labyrinth of pain
> He may not enter and endure.

Experience had taught him "to count no thing too strange"
and to pity those who take peace for granted, expecting the
soul to triumph without chastening, like

> . . . a child who sees the whole
> World radiant with his own delight.

The poem was no conventional thanks for hospitality, but
it was fully understood by a clear-sighted woman whose
gifted husband had been worn to an early grave. In the
somber reflections and dubieties of "Hillcrest" appears
Robinson the sage, ready at length to teach the meaning
of suffering, like him who had heard "The still, sad music
of humanity."

"Eros Turannos" went by way of Mrs. Moody to the
columns of *Poetry*, which later took "Bokardo." Accept-
ances by the more conventional magazines rose from a
single poem, "The Field of Glory," printed by *The
Outlook* in 1913, to five in 1914 and six in 1915. Why
periodicals like *The Outlook*, *The Atlantic*, and *Harper's*,
shut to his verse for so many years, should now be open
puzzled Robinson. He discussed the enigma with Robert
Frost, who reported a similar experience. American periodicals and publishers had been so cold toward the pieces
collected in *A Boy's Will* (1913) and *North of Boston*

(1914) that Frost had been obliged to go to England to find a publisher; but now they were welcoming his work. The poets agreed that since they had not altered the manner or the quality of their verse, the magazines must be changing their minds or their staffs. Apparently it was the staffs. A new generation of poetry editors, with a new set of values, was appearing with men like Harold Trowbridge Pulsifer, an admirer of Robinson, who had entered the *Outlook* office in 1913.

The rise in Robinson's reputation gave Louis Ledoux the opportunity to bring pressure on Scribner's to reissue *Captain Craig* and to publish *Van Zorn* and *The Porcupine* by mentioning the Macmillan Company's offer to do both. Scribner's, who had paid one hundred dollars of advance royalty toward a volume of new poems, were willing to do more for the verse, but balked at the plays. Robinson, insisting on all or none, went over to the Macmillan Company, which published *Van Zorn* in 1914, and in 1915 *Captain Craig*, augmented by "The Field of Glory" and eleven free translations from the *Greek Anthology*. The new publishers took a calculated risk of losing money on the plays with the prospect of gaining from the poetry to come.

In the spring of 1914 a legacy of four thousand dollars from Hays Gardiner dropped like manna. At last there was security for sustained effort.

But across the summer fell the shadow of war in Europe. "We're all going to be caught in this," Robinson said to Fillmore as they walked to the village of Peterborough for news. He feared for his country, unprepared because most Americans, blind to the consequences of their commitment to capitalism, imperialism, and the values of European civilization, thought it exempt from the logic of history. His anxiety was shared by Thomas Sergeant Perry, who from his wide knowledge of the world had written back to Boston from Tokyo in 1900: "Because in America we get rich easily, is it to be supposed that we can avoid all the troubles which have made the world? Not a bit of it: the old Devil is waiting for us yet." Robinson felt he must warn, even though his words would probably have the fate of Cassandra's.

The magazines would not print his "Cassandra." When it appeared in the *Boston Evening Transcript* in December, "few heard," as the poem predicted. Now we count it among the best of our patriotic literature; for he who loves, chastens. A shudder at disaster narrowly missed and at perils still to be mingles with our admiration of the lapidary form of stanzas baring the faults of the American mind:

> You laugh and answer, "We are young;
>   O leave us now and let us grow."—
> Not asking how much more of this
>   Will Time endure or Fate bestow.
>
> · · · · · · ·
>
> What lost eclipse of history,
>   What bivouac of the marching stars,
> Has given the sign for you to see
>   Millenniums and last great wars?
>
> · · · · · · ·
>
> The power is yours, but not the sight;
>   You see not upon what you tread;
> You have the ages for your guide,
>   But not the wisdom to be led.
>
> · · · · · · ·
>
> Are you to pay for what you are
>   With all you are? . . .

Western civilization, misled by the philosophy of materialistic determinism, of the dominance of impersonal economic forces and the fated struggle of races, was suffering once more the death and birth pangs which had produced human history. "The world has been made by upheavals, whether we like it or not. I have always told you it's a hell of a place," Robinson wrote Hagedorn.

Returning to Peterborough by way of Boston in the fall of 1914, Robinson renewed his discussion of the meaning of life with his old friend Lawrence Henderson, Assistant Professor of Biological Chemistry at Harvard. In the previous year, Henderson had published an amplification of his Lowell Lectures under the title of *The Fitness of the Environment: An Inquiry into the Biological Significance of the Properties of Matter.* He proposed to supplement Darwin, who had studied the adaptation of organisms to environment, by investigating the truth of the converse, that "in fundamental characteristics the actual environment is the fittest abode of life."

A survey of chemical and physical knowledge had led Henderson to conclude that "peculiar and unsuspected relationships exist between the properties of matter and the phenomena of life: that, logically, in some obscure manner, cosmic and biological evolution are one." The sciences of matter, more advanced than those of living organisms, had proved to his satisfaction that "the whole process of cosmic evolution from its earliest state to the present is pure mechanism," aided initially by chance. "If then," he asked, "cosmic evolution be pure mechanism and yet issue in fitness, why not organic evolution as well?" The objection that the perfect adaptation of life and matter to each other must have come about by purpose or design he countered by the hypothesis that the adaptation might be one of the properties of mechanism itself, that "matter and energy have an original property, assuredly not by chance, which organizes the universe in space and time." Of course this was merely hypothesis, since the best biologists, including Darwin and Liebig, had admitted that the problem of the existence of life may be insoluble. But probable insolubility did not haunt Henderson with a sense of mystery. The chemist, he remarked, "puts his mind at rest concerning the existence of life just as the physicist calms his concerning the existence of matter, simply by turning his back on the whole problem. Thereby he suffers nothing in his task as a man of science."

Robinson, to whose task as a poet that problem was central, listened attentively to his friend. Henderson was not dogmatic but willing to consider seriously the arguments for purpose in the universe put forth by Bergson and the Vitalists, by recent advocates of indeterminism in physics, by metaphysicians from Kant to Royce; and, as a man of artistic culture, was responsive to the magic of great poetry, painting, and music. Nevertheless, the poet remained unshaken in his conviction that life has a purpose, the conviction that issued from the intense suffering and compassion of his Gardiner years. Untrained to observe that the indeterminate behavior of electrons and the consequences of the theories of Relativity were already taking scientific ground from under Henderson's feet, he resisted all-embracing mechanistic materialism on the ground of its metaphysical and logical weakness, and still more because of its consequences for humanity. In the ironically titled "Field of Glory" he had already obliquely asked what justification materialism could offer for the duty-bound life of "a poor devil, totally miscast" as the only support of a widow. "If materialism is true," he said in explaining the poem to Hagedorn, "then parenthood is the greatest of all crimes, and the sooner the much advertised 'race' is annihilated, the better."

During the winter he relived the anguish and the illumination that had resulted in "Credo," "Two Sonnets," and "The Children of the Night." There was nothing in those poems he wished to change, after years of living by their light, except their form. What in them was individual and abstractly phrased, he must make universal and concrete. By using the language of metaphor and symbol and drawing upon deeper and wider human knowledge, he must establish the full horror of living in terms of a universe governed by "the properties of matter."

Early in March 1915, vivid recollection of sunset blazing on the bare peak of Monadnock, high above the great pines of Peterborough, gave a focus for these meditations. A man alone up there in the sun's fierce rays would be Everyman, representative of collective humanity at the summit or end of earthly experience, exposed to the searching light of wisdom a brief moment before beginning the dark descent from which no traveler has returned.

Here would be a poem drawing upon all he had written, yet demanding a new style. There was no avoiding the magisterial tone, the singing robes of the ode. Most of his work had pointed unconsciously to this ode, as Wordsworth's to his ode on the "Intimations of Immortality," which seemed to Robinson worth all the rest.

With a hand practiced in portraiture, he speculated upon the character and experience of the mysterious figure who loomed between him and the sunset. Was he heroic, or mediocre? insensitive, self-centered, cynical? Was he a failure, or what the world calls a success? Major human types filed past, to a common destination of death, which each man must face alone. None was to be envied, when he had passed through the ordeal of the poet's scrutiny. Failure was horrible, insensitivity ignoble, cynicism despicable, success illusory. And to what does death open the door? To Heaven, to Hell, or to oblivion? If to oblivion, life is a nightmare for the individual, however science may babble about the progress of the race, however communism may extol the coming benefits of equality. Those who invest all their treasure in the things of this world, those sure that man is a mechanical product in an accidental universe, have no logical reason to endure the ills of life:

> 'Twere sure but weaklings' vain distress
> To suffer dungeons where so many doors
> Will open on the cold eternal shores
> That look sheer down
> To the dark tideless floods of Nothingness
> Where all who know may drown.

Thus ends in recommended suicide a poem that began with the vision of a marvelous and inscrutable figure moving across a flamelit height

> As if he were the last god going home
> Unto his last desire.

But only apparently, for the close is ironic. Robinson had considered italicizing the final line, "Where all who know may drown," to make clear that only the presumption of scientific knowledge concerning man's nature and destiny ought to lead to self-slaughter; but characteristically he decided that such readers as accepted the materialist's premises should be left to face their consequences. For the others, he had scattered through the poem, which he called "The Man Against the Sky," glimpses of values transcending earthly experience and giving it meaning:

> . . . eternal, remote things
> That range across a man's imaginings
> When a sure music fills him and he knows
> What he may say thereafter to few men.

What makes life worth living points beyond life. Many years before, Robinson had protested: "The world is not a prison house, but a kind of spiritual kindergarten, where millions of bewildered infants are trying to spell God with the wrong blocks."

"The Man Against the Sky," completed at Peterborough in July, gave the title to the volume of poems which the Macmillan Company published in February 1916. Robinson, in his late forties, had reached the height of his creative powers, as he would later tacitly recognize in placing the volume first among his *Collected Poems*. In the twenty-five shorter pieces issued with the great title poem, old themes came to perfection and new were announced. The mystery of characters like Alfred Louis finds its most impressive embodiment in Flammonde,

> With news of nations in his talk
> And something royal in his walk,

who, through some "small satanic sort of kink" in his brain or some broken link in his destiny, has become a castaway, a parasite. Flammonde enlists our sympathy more fully than Craig because his beneficence is not in words only but in deeds that win the gratitude of Tilbury Town. His foil is the materialist Bewick Finzer, completely and pathetically ruined by an itch for speculation. The Poor Relation is Aunt Imogen grown older, and no longer a mask for the poet, but authentically feminine. Studies of mismating continue, the comedy of "Llewellyn and the Tree" and the declaration of independence by the ironically styled "Clinging Vine" setting off the tragedy of "The Unforgiven" and "Eros Turannos." Subtly Robinson studies masculine and feminine responses to identical situations: to mistaken union on the basis of a plausible exterior in "The Unforgiven" and "Eros Turannos," to children unworthy of their parents in "Old King Cole" and "The Gift of God." The poet's judgment of men and women has become less indulgent. The shifty Bokardo, too cowardly to kill himself after flinging his friends before swine, wears out his patience. Theophilus and the Dark Lady are irremediably evil.

Two short pieces open veins which Robinson was to explore in long poems. "Stafford's Cabin" outlines a melodramatic mystery of the order of "Avon's Harvest"; and "Fragment," suggesting the gradual self-annihilation of Briony, who "knew too much for the life he led," inaugurates the studies of neurosis including *Roman Bartholow*.

"Hillcrest" and other poems are autobiographical. "The Dark House" contemplates the miracle of salvation from drink. "The Burning Book" describes the peace which might come from renouncing the effort to find readers and enjoying spiritual vision as a private possession. Much of Robinson appears in the reflections on the paradoxes and the mystery of the life of the world's supreme poet in "Ben Jonson Entertains a Man from Stratford," originally published in *The Drama Quarterly* for the Shakespeare tercentenary. Shakespeare, the incomparable realist, regarding men with such unilluded eyes that he never was young and has become so alone in spirit,

> The full brain hammered hot from too much thinking,
> The vexed heart over-worn from too much aching,

that he yearns to be free from the world, exactly on this account elects to lead, outwardly and in humorous acquiescence, the life of the ordinary Englishman of his time. In the failure of Jonson, the Londoner, to understand the Stratford in Shakespeare, we may read Robinson's awareness that his roots in Maine were hidden from his New York friends. That the reader never questions his right to enter into Shakespeare's secret thoughts is a measure of Robinson's stature.

In this volume of 1916, Robinson's art has reached its sharpest focus. Briony utters only five words, "Sooner or later they strike," and his neurosis stands revealed. A contrasted adjective and noun give intensity to "sunlit labyrinth of pain." Decoration gains force by sparseness, as in the unexpected touch of color at the close of "The Gift of God":

> . . . upward through her dream he fares,
> Half clouded with a crimson fall
> Of roses thrown on marble stairs.

New York is flashed before the eye:

> . . . the lamps along the Avenue
> Bloomed white for miles above an iron floor,

but to the ear recalled by appropriate lingering:

> And like a giant harp that hums
> On always, and is always blending

> The coming of what never comes
> With what has past and has an ending,
> The City trembles, throbs, and pounds
> Outside, and through a thousand sounds
> The small intolerable drums
> Of Time are like slow drops descending.

Memorable phrases, "the stopped ears of the strong," "the lonely changelessness of dying," abound. Restraint and delicacy save the poet from pitfalls in expressing the deepest, the most primitive emotions. He ventures in "The Gift of God" to describe maternal love, proverbial for leading American writers into the maudlin, because his humor can temper his tenderness. The Poor Relation's heartbreak is the more poignant through her refusal to yield to self-pity. Robinson never mistakes a pathetic situation for a tragic. The wife in "Eros Turannos" is a character of high tragedy, but Bewick Finzer, though fallen from high economic estate, is merely pathetic.

The two latter poems are masterpieces of compression. "Bewick Finzer" opens with assured economy:

> Time was when his half million drew
> The breath of six per cent;
> But soon the worm of what-was-not
> Fed hard on his content;
> And something crumbled in his brain
> When his half million went.

After a stanza lingering to suggest the passage of time, Bewick reappears to represent, in carefully chosen details of physical description,

> The cleanliness of indigence,
> The brilliance of despair.

A fourth stanza permits sympathy for a man who now finds
it hard to look into the faces of those who might easily have
been in his place. But the fifth and last returns to objectivity:

> He comes unfailing for the loan
>   We give and then forget;
> He comes, and probably for years
>   Will he be coming yet,—
> Familiar as an old mistake,
>   And futile as regret.

The similes, reserved for the end, give the poem a finality
that sticks in the memory like Pope's couplets. "Eros
Turannos," the title suggesting Greek drama, is high tragedy in a little room. A woman of intellect, taste, and wealth
who has sorely blundered in marriage holds to her Judas
husband out of pride and out of fear of lonely old age. The
stanza imagining her winters shut with him in their house
in a small seacoast town is big with tension:

> And home, where passion lived and died,
> Becomes a place where she can hide,
> While all the town and harbor side
>   Vibrate with her seclusion.

The grand style makes plausible belief in the implacable
pagan god of love:

> . . . they
> That with a god have striven,
> Not hearing much of what we say,
> Take what the god has given;
> Though like waves breaking it may be,
> Or like a changed familiar tree,
> Or like a stairway to the sea
>   Where down the blind are driven.

"Eros Turannos" best prepares readers of the volume for the gigantic figures of the closing poem, "The Man Against the Sky." The summation and concentration of his poems of character and his reflections upon the meaning of life, the ode stands apart in atmosphere as well as in form. There had been no such perfect blending of symbols from nature with human significance since "Luke Havergal," no such consistent elevation of style since "The Chorus of Old Men," where pity had been intensified by a sunset vision of human potentialities thwarted by fate:

Better his end had been as the end of a cloudless day,
Bright, by the word of Zeus, with a golden star,
Wrought of a golden fame, and flung to the central sky,
To gleam on a stormless tomb for evermore.

Splendor, so long damped down by the harsh conditions of Robinson's life, bursts forth in the opening lines of "The Man Against the Sky" and remains through three verse paragraphs closing in a heroic portrait adorned with a resonant Biblical simile. This exordium of forty-six lines adds to the grand style of the Greeks and the Hebrews touches of Romantic suggestion:

As if there were to be no last thing left
Of a nameless unimaginable town.

A long defile of human types follows, rounded off with a second Old Testament simile. The pace is quickened by a summary of human motivations, unforgettable in condensation:

Whatever drove or lured or guided him,—
A vision answering a faith unshaken,
An easy trust assumed of easy trials,

A sick negation born of weak denials,
A crazed abhorrence of an old condition,
A blind attendance on a brief ambition,—

which introduces the central theme:

Whatever stayed him or derided him,
His way was even as ours;
And we, with all our wounds and all our powers,
Must each await alone at his own height
Another darkness or another light.

"Alone" echoes and stresses a passage in the exordium:

For whether lighted over ways that save,
Or lured from all repose,
If he go on too far to find a grave,
Mostly alone he goes.

As in the mediaeval play of *Everyman*, adventitious trappings fall away as the individual faces death.

But Christianity, which made life meaningful by Heaven and Hell, has been superseded, the twentieth century says, by science, which palliates Oblivion by promising to make earthly life its own reward. With fine irony, Robinson turns from glory and tragedy to examine the pretensions of this new gospel. The grandeur and warmth of his style change to incisive questioning and mockery. Imagery becomes increasingly somber:

. . . each racked empty day
That leads one more last human hope away,
As quiet fiends would lead past our crazed eyes
Our children to an unseen sacrifice,

as the poem plunges to its conclusion in ironic recommendation of mass suicide.

In its form "The Man Against the Sky" stands apart, not only from what Robinson had written, but also from what he was still to write. He never returned to the irregular strophes of the Cowleyan ode, to the extended similes, to the conspicuous use of alliteration to reinforce rhyme. In this sustained effort of 316 lines he packed his mature conclusions, and he saw no reason to repeat. The mastery of the form at first trial is sure. Although he had had abundant practice with the pentameter line—the metrical basis of the poem—he is equally skilled in variations, from dimeter to hexameter, which changes of pace and of tone recommend. The rhymes fit the pace and the meaning like a glove. Robinson uses triple rhyme, like Dryden, for emphasis, and leaves lines unrhymed with the boldness of Leopardi.

Though its form and tone are those of the ode, in thought the affinities of "The Man Against the Sky" are with the great English elegies of the nineteenth century, especially *In Memoriam*:

> Not only cunning casts in clay.
>   Let Science prove we are and then
>   What matter Science unto men,
> At least to me? I would not stay.

But here Tennyson is plaintive and on the defensive where Robinson is militantly aggressive, and the American poet's mysticism has no specific Christian coloring, the "orient Word" coming from the East in general. In his review of human types, he classes the dogmatic scientist along with rulers and military leaders among the presumptuous and the purblind:

> He may have built, unawed by fiery gules
> That in him no commotion stirred,

A living reason out of molecules
Why molecules occurred,
And one for smiling when he might have sighed
Had he seen far enough,
And in the same inevitable stuff
Discovered an odd reason too for pride
In being what he must have been by laws
Infrangible and for no kind of cause.
Deterred by no confusion or surprise
He may have seen with his mechanic eyes
A world without a meaning, and had room,
Alone amid magnificence and doom,
To build himself an airy monument
That should, or fail him in his vague intent,
Outlast an accidental universe—
To call it nothing worse.

In the sardonic closing section the scientist is bracketed
with the communist, content with a materialistic interpretation of history:

No soft evangel of equality,
Safe-cradled in a communal repose
That huddles into death and may at last
Be covered well with equatorial snows—
And all for what, the devil only knows—
Will aggregate an inkling to confirm
The credit of a sage or of a worm,
Or tell us why one man in five
Should have a care to stay alive
While in his heart he feels no violence
Laid on his humor and intelligence
When infant Science makes a pleasant face
And waves again that hollow toy, the Race.

It is only when the poet turns away from "humor and intelligence" to let his heart speak that he approaches Tennyson's tone with the lines:

What then were this great love of ours to say
For launching other lives to voyage again
A little farther into time and pain,
A little faster in a futile chase
For a kingdom and a power and a Race
That would have still in sight
A manifest end of ashes and eternal night?

In *The City of Dreadful Night*, a poem Robinson admired, there is an impressive review of ten human types as they pass into the City; but because of his repudiation of materialism he has not Thomson's unrelieved gloom.

A still closer affinity is with nineteenth-century music, which Robinson loved passionately. The "dark, marvelous, and inscrutable" figure, boldly mounting the height "flame-bitten and flame-cleft,"

> As if he were the last god going home
> Unto his last desire,

irresistibly recalls Wagner's Siegfried, about to break Brünnhilde's flame-guarded slumber. The ode is Robinson's *Eroica*, with its scherzo following a funeral march.

Yet the poem is inimitably his own, a mingling of laughter, scorn, and irony with pity and magnificence recognizably the mature work of the author of "Captain Craig." The irony and pity which Anatole France popularized from Daudet as a mode of regarding humanity was for Robinson incomplete without wonder. That wonder and pity should come first and the poem close in irony has disconcerted conventional readers. But more flexible minds recognize in it the characteristic temper of the twentieth century. Robinson placed the ode at the end of the volume to which it gave the name, as its summation and seal.

Experience restrained him from any sanguine expectation of critical welcome. In 1914 he had written Miss Peabody concerning the prospect before one of her plays in verse: "I don't mean to be egotistic, but at the same time I don't believe there is any one on earth who can tell me, since the publication of my two last books, anything about the chills and silences that appertain to the poetry business. For two years after the appearance of each of them, there was hardly as much as a patter of intelligent appreciation. . . . The one perfunctory skimming that a book of verse gets from the rank and file of reviewers is in most cases worse than nothing—as you must know from experience, since you have written books that are worth while."

Braithwaite of the *Boston Transcript* was the first to speak. He lauded Robinson as "the poet with the most individual art of any in America," an art achieved "by a process that is baffling because it is simple." With the opportunity for more careful consideration offered by a survey of "The Year in Poetry" for *The Bookman* in June 1917, he placed Robinson "at the head of our poetry to-day," a poetry recently enriched by the "inevitable, clear touch of genius" in Robert Frost's *Mountain Interval*. Robinson's new volume showed an advance beyond *The Town Down the River*, "from presenting the character of the individual to interpreting the destinies of mankind," as in the title poem. Braithwaite shrewdly observed that his art had its closest affinity in "the ironic comedy of Shakespeare . . . the humorous, the pathetic and the tragic become interpenetrated."

The *North American Review* found Robinson "one of the few moderns who have a sense for language, for power and beauty of idiom as well as for melody and for imagery.

. . . Each one of Mr. Robinson's cleanly sculptured phrases challenges attention; each melodious sentence rouses the mind to alertness by an appeal to the aesthetic sense . . . makes thought musical." Where there is obscurity, as in the title poem, it is "due to compactness of expression and swift transition of thought." With "real elevation" and "intellectual power" he almost, though not quite, attains to "greatness." *The Outlook*, proudly calling attention to its having published "Flammonde" and "The Poor Relation," concentrated upon the character studies. The poet's "curious attitude of impartiality toward his characters" has done much to give him "his peculiar and enviable position in American letters. . . . Yet, for all this aloofness, the reader of Mr. Robinson's poems is tremendously conscious of his own personality and his own point of view." He "describes his characters in words, and himself in the rhythm with which those words move. . . . Certainly the characteristic rhythm of his poetry; the inevitableness of its flow, the cool, dry and severe movement of his lines; the compactness of sound; the swift and adequate final accents, are all the expressions of a personality." Edward Bliss Read, in *The Yale Review*, praised his sturdy independence, without "concessions to prevailing tendencies and tastes," which made his verse "surcharged with thought." To read "Ben Jonson Entertains a Man from Stratford" and "The Man Against the Sky" was "to understand why Mr. Robinson stands in the foremost ranks of American poets."

Most discerning of the critics was his fellow poet Amy Lowell, in the *New Republic*. She found the poems "modern because they are universal" and "dynamic with experience and knowledge of life." The volume was "a jar of compressed air." The title poem, placed last because it was "a serious argument against a materialistic explanation of the universe and bears with it a sense of finality," had "the power of high seriousness" to a greater degree than any contemporary American poem. Robinson was "magnificently noble" with "a great pitying tenderness." His style was "astringent," pruned of every tendency to luxuriance. "He aims at the starkness of absolute truth." Miss Lowell deplored, however, his "profound melancholy," his distrust of joy as "a mere phantasmagoria," and his putting courage "in its place as the consoler of mankind." His poems "do not invigorate; they mellow and subdue." But "in our material day, the spirituality of Mr. Robinson's work is tonic and uplifting." For twenty years "quietly and unobtrusively" he had been "a force in present-day literature."

The reviewers, now unerring as to the qualities of his style and personality, were still incapable of coping with the force and subtlety of his thought, still hesitant to commit themselves to recognizing greatness. American verse had been mediocre so long that no critic ventured to measure Robinson and Frost against contemporary European poets or against the American classics. Still, the advance in perceptiveness was marked. Only Oscar Firkins in *The Nation* dismissed the volume as "languid narrative . . . attenuated drama—above all—famished intellectualism." *The New York Times*, playing safe with a rising reputation, blew both hot and cold.

The change of critical opinion from respect to enthusiasm since *The Town Down the River* had come about through the emergence of a new generation of reviewers. The young poet Joyce Kilmer, in *The New York Times Book Review* for September 8, 1912, had been the first to hail Robinson as "A Classic Poet." In an interview, adroitly leading him by way of his estimates of Kipling, Browning, Wordsworth, and Housman to the generalization, "All real poetry is going to give at some time or other a suggestion of finality," Kilmer interposed with a question, "Why isn't genuine poetry immediately recognized?" Robinson replied, "Finality seems always to have had a way of not obtruding itself to any great extent." Thus, "quietly and unobtrusively," as Miss Lowell had observed, Robinson's poetry had been reaching individuals who appreciated the neglected *Captain Craig* and *Children of the Night*. Another poet, Harold Pulsifer, on joining the staff of *The Outlook* in 1913, had printed "The Field of Glory," accompanied by a reproduced portrait of Robinson under the caption, "An American Poet Whose Work Is Attracting Increasing Attention," and a short editorial on his achievement naming him along with Browning and Francis Thompson among poets in revolt against the "consummately commonplace and sentimental verses of Tennyson" so widely popular. "The most individual of American poets, he combines intensity of thought and of feeling with a curious simplicity of actual expression. . . . The words he uses are the words of ordinary speech, put together sometimes in cadences that seem close to actual prose, yet so subtly combined that their half-hidden but characteristic rhythm conveys to the attentive ear much of the story and most of the underlying emotion." Robinson would "eventually receive the wider recognition he so richly deserves."

Otto Theis recorded in *The Forum* for February 1914 the tonic shock of discovering "Luke Havergal" among a mass of imitative American verse in a Philadelphia public library on "a damp gray afternoon when snow was in the air and dusk already falling." He went on to read "The Clerks," which seemed to translate into words the painting of Millet and Meunier, social criticism the more effective for being without bitter accusation, and "The Chorus of Old Men in 'Ægeus,'" "noble poetry and one of the finest expressions of the Greek spirit in English" (curiously, no critic, in an era in which Greek was still widely read, had been struck by this poem hitherto). *The Children of the Night* had led Theis to "Captain Craig," with its "mellow laughter . . . close to tears," and to *The Town Down the River*.

While fresh blood was entering the staffs of established periodicals, the founding of the weekly journal of opinion, the *New Republic*, in 1914 was almost as auspicious for the new taste as had been that of *Poetry* in 1912. In 1915 it had opened its columns for an appreciative survey of Robinson's work by Lincoln MacVeagh, who compared his method of "suggestion" to that of the French Symbolists, whose work was beginning to exert influence in the United States. Robinson's symbolism, MacVeagh pointed out, "is one degree refined over that of Mallarmé. It is no longer a progress from 'object' to 'state of soul,' but from one state of soul to that soul's complete individuality," as in the case of "Luke Havergal." His genius, "punctual and intense," is at a disadvantage in the dramatic monologues and in "Captain Craig," where it "surfeits by repetition." "Probably his limitations, his artistic conscience, his humanity, neither barbarous nor over-civilized but scarcely contemporary, will save him from becoming popular. But . . . here is still some ground left where such real artists as we have may train a small public to appreciate beauty."

The critical welcome of *The Man Against the Sky* was

now preparing this small public, but it was still so small as not to mean much to Robinson financially. To Kilmer's question, whether literature had lost something through the poverty of poets, he had replied: "I think it is good for a poet to be bumped and knocked about when he is young, but all the difficulties that are put in his way after he gets to be twenty-five or thirty are certain to take something out of his work. I don't see how they can do anything else." But a poet, he added, ought to be able to live on a thousand dollars a year. John Gould Fletcher, driven back by the war from his poetic apprenticeship in Europe, met Robinson, whom he had heard Ezra Pound praise in London, at the Perrys' after most of the reviews of *The Man Against the Sky* were out, and was impressed by his attitude of "lonely integrity in defeat." Robinson "realized that he had come into the period when poetry again became a matter of public interest, largely through accident. Under any circumstances he was and always would be one to pursue his chosen path alone."

His friends, knowing how little he had to live on, were preparing a surprise for his birthday, December 22, 1916. On that occasion he received notice from the New York Trust Company that an annual sum of $1,200 to begin on January 1, 1917, and possibly to be renewed for three years more, had been placed to his credit. The donors, who were anonymous, had been led by Isaacs and Ledoux. In 1920 there was an extra $600 from a single source, and for 1921 and 1922 the regular amount was raised to $1,500. The sum was modest, less than the salary of the lowest rank of teachers in good New York colleges at the time, but with royalties and the poet's frugal habits, it was comfortable.

Since 1913, Robinson had been living alone in a single

room at 129 West Eighty-third Street. In 1918 he joined
another lonely man, his old Gardiner friend Seth Pope
the librarian, in his apartment at 810 Washington Avenue,
Brooklyn. The neighborhood, at considerable distance
from the theaters and from Robinson's other New York
friends, was not attractive; but the poet had a protective
feeling toward Pope, whom he had saved from bullying in
high school. In other ways, his life assumed a more regular
pattern. Every spring, on the way to the MacDowell
Colony, where he wrote the first draft of poems, he would
stop a month or two in Boston to see Harvard friends,
including Burnham, now employed in a railroad office, and
relatives and friends from Gardiner, and would return there
for a month or two on leaving the Colony in September.
In New York, the strenuous labor of revising poems for
publication and planning new work was relieved by the
theater and the concert hall and by visits to the country
homes of the Ledoux, the Isaacs, and the Hagedorns.

In acknowledging the annual gift he had expressed
gratitude for its permitting him "to go on with a rather
exacting piece of literary work without worry or inter-
ruption." The work was a comment on the war in Europe,
at a stalemate since the failure of the British offensive on
the Somme. The crumbling of the feudal and capitalistic
foundations of European society was so evident, the behavior of nations so true to pattern, that Robinson knew
prophecy about world affairs need never have been a super-
natural gift. Casting about for a well-known legend to
illustrate what he saw facing Western civilization, he
decided upon the Arthurian as most familiar to Americans
through Tennyson and Malory, and proceeded to mold it

to his purpose after the free and easy fashion of the Greek dramatists with heroic myth.

Robinson's Merlin, no wizard though wise beyond his time, conceives the experiment of letting Arthur build a kingdom on rotten foundations, so that its collapse may be a mirror in which ages to come may read the doom of every society so based. But the years during which Camelot totters to its fall convince him that he has been too sanguine, for few men are reasonable enough to be able to read from the mirror. He consoles himself with a vision, beyond centuries of more unsubstantial Camelots, of the world's salvation through the instinct of women to abhor war and even more through the slow lesson of other-worldliness, symbolized by the quest for the Grail. Arthur, who adumbrates the tradition-bound British Empire, and the light-minded, materialistic Gawain, who corresponds to the America of "Cassandra," perish; but Lancelot, though tarred by the same brush as Arthur, is slowly drawn to the spiritual life by the Grail and by Guinevere's conversion, and survives to typify the saving remnant of mankind. Robinson, who had smiled at Moody's taste for world allegory, found himself in its grasp, and unable, if he were to make his characters human, to do it up in his usual small package. Confronted with the probability of a poem twice the size of "Captain Craig," he divided it into a *Merlin* and a *Lancelot*. *Merlin*, published in 1917, less than a month before the United States entered the war, sold so badly that the Macmillan Company refused to risk *Lancelot*, which had to wait until after the Peace to appear with Thomas Seltzer's imprint. To promote advance sales, the Lyric Society announced the award to *Lancelot* of a five-hundred-dollar prize in a competition set by *The*

Lyric, which Seltzer published; but neither Seltzer nor the Macmillan Company would accept Robinson's proposal for a Tristram poem, for which passages in *Lancelot* prepare. *Lancelot* was published in 1920 with a dedication to Lewis M. Isaacs.

The two long poems, following the withering analysis of complacent materialism in "Cassandra" and "The Man Against the Sky," are constructive, describing the growth of spirituality. *Merlin,* dedicated to George Burnham, who had renounced worldly success for principle, reveals the insufficiency of the wisdom which is wise only in the world's lore. A towering figure, like those of Robinson's ode, Merlin goes "too far to find a grave" and must go "mostly alone," separated, by reason of his superiority, from the multitude he hopes to save. Robinson's blank verse was never to surpass in sustained elevation Merlin's musing on his future as he is separated from Vivien, the only human being who understands him:

> "The man who sees
> May see too far, and he may see too late
> The path he takes unseen," he told himself
> When he found thought again. "The man who sees
> May go on seeing till the immortal flame
> That lights and lures him folds him in its heart,
> And leaves of what there was of him to die
> An item of inhospitable dust
> That love and hate alike must hide away;
> Or there may still be charted for his feet
> A dimmer faring, where the touch of time
> Were like the passing of a twilight moth
> From flower to flower into oblivion,
> If there were not somewhere a barren end
> Of moths and flowers, and glimmering far away

Beyond a desert where the flowerless days
Are told in slow defeats and agonies,
The guiding of a nameless light that once
Had made him see too much—and has by now
Revealed in death, to the undying child
Of Lancelot, the Grail."

Loneliness is the ultimate human pang of Lancelot as he
resigns Guinevere to follow the Grail:

. . . Gradually,
In one long wave it whelmed him, and then broke—
Leaving him like a lone man on a reef
Staring for what had been with him, but now
Was gone and was a white face under the sea,
Alive there, and alone—always alone.

The poems are filled with Robinson's suffering at the
spectacle of war. There is terrifying wisdom in the allegory
when Merlin says, with obvious reference to the United
States,

. . . You are young,
Gawaine, and may one day hold the world
Between your fingers, knowing not what it is
That you are holding,

and when before Arthur's British eyes

A vision of a peace that humbled him,
And yet might save the world that he had won,
Came slowly into view like something soft
And ominous on all-fours, without a spirit
To make it stand upright.

In spite of many fine passages, neither *Merlin* nor
Lancelot is likely to be among Robinson's enduring achieve-
ments. *Merlin* is poorly constructed narrative, too often
static, and its Vivien section is dated by outmoded gal-

lantries. *Lancelot,* better told and freshly realistic in the treatment of Guinevere, is too long drawn out. Readers are most likely to return to the figure of Merlin, suffering from isolation from mankind by reason of his highest qualities, into whom the poet has put much of himself.

Robinson's mastery of his craft returned with short pieces published by Macmillan in *The Three Taverns* (1920) and *Avon's Harvest* (1921). The finest of these have a rural setting. "Monadnock Through the Trees," inspired by the view from his studio, rejoices that the mountain, there before the Pyramids were built, will remain after mankind has exhausted its possibilities for good and ill. Stopping beside an abandoned mill in West Peterborough, the poet thought of the hundreds of others in New England which had shared its fate when water ceased to be the chief motive power and when individual millers could no longer compete with great companies. He built about a confession of defeat, "There are no millers any more," a poem of twenty-four perfect lines, "The Mill." Into that compass are packed two suicides which the reader accepts as inevitable. Sensuous impressions intensify the tragedy by contrast:

> And in the mill there was a warm
> And mealy fragrance of the past.
>
> .   .   .   .
>
> Black water, smooth above the weir
>   Like starry velvet in the night,
> Though ruffled once, would soon appear
>   The same as ever to the sight.

The unobtrusive appearance of the significant word "yet" in the lines,

> And there might yet be nothing wrong
> In how he went and what he said,

is beyond praise. Immediately after "The Mill" in *The Three Taverns* Robinson placed "The Dark Hills," a moment of full-voiced lyrical music inspired by landscape, enriched by glorious and melancholy association with man. Natural background plays a conspicuous part in "Avon's Harvest," a blank-verse narrative of considerable length, in which a physician studies an obsessive fear. The climax arrives when a city man, never alone since birth, is left to spend a solitary night by a pine-fringed lake in a wilderness.

Landscape, dramatic narrative, lyricism, irony, humor, and pathos blend harmoniously in "Mr. Flood's Party," the short poem which perhaps best represents the quality of Robinson's personality and art. The poem arose from a visitation from his youth, a recollection of Harry Smith's father's story of a Maine eccentric who used to propose and drink toasts to himself. The humorous anecdote had become enriched in Robinson's mind by association with old things, happy and unhappy, and with the frailty of human hopes. In the background of the poem is a homestead in the hills, soon to be deserted like "The House on the Hill." The present occupant, an old man who has seen better days, on his way back to his solitary life there after a walk to Tilbury to replenish his liquor jug, his last remaining consolation, pauses on the road to exchange toasts with his dead friends in the town below. The language of the imaginary convivial party is appropriately banal, but the gestures of Mr. Flood have tragic and universal reverberations:

Alone, as if enduring to the end
A valiant armor of scarred hopes outworn,
He stood there in the middle of the road
Like Roland's ghost winding a silent horn.
Below him, in the town among the trees,
Where friends of other days had honored him,
A phantom salutation of the dead
Rang thinly till old Eben's eyes were dim.

Then, as a mother lays her sleeping child
Down tenderly, fearing it may awake,
He set the jug down slowly at his feet
With trembling care, knowing that most things break.

The poet's long experience of the vanity of human wishes,
beginning with those of his father for his sons, was concentrated in the final phrase. A stanza delicately modulates
to humor and melody:

> . . . soon amid the silver loneliness
> Of night he lifted up his voice and sang,
> Secure, with only two moons listening,
> Until the whole harmonious landscape rang.

Four lines more, and the poem returns to its somber key-
note, "alone," sounded in its opening line and repeated as
the first word in the third stanza. The art is perfect in
unobtrusiveness. In diction, style, and meaning the poem
is accessible to the most unsophisticated reader. The fine
sonnet, "Many Are Called," with its implication that few
are chosen by Apollo, is Robinson's disclaimer of personal
credit for such poems as this, "The Mill," and "The Dark
Hills." They came as inexplicable visitations, as the Poe
sonnet had come so many years before.

Four short pieces continue the political thinking of the
Arthurian poems. "Demos," directed against the vague

enthusiasm for democracy engendered by wartime slogans, warns against confusing it with leveling down:

> See not the great among you for the small,
> But hear their silence; for the few shall save
> The many, or the many are to fall.

The warning is reinforced from American history by "On the Way," a dialogue between Hamilton and Burr, and the monologue "John Brown," with its arresting final line: "I shall have more to say when I am dead." "The Old King's New Jester" mingles humor with gravity in chastening the opposite extreme of stubborn conservatism, even when adorned with the "injured glamour" of "the old wrong." Robinson wrote this fine poem, Carl Van Doren observes, "with the stern seriousness of a poet and the whimsical grace of a man of the world." It appeared in a volume appropriately dedicated to Thomas Sergeant Perry and Lilla Cabot Perry. The interest in Alexander Hamilton went back to Robinson's undergraduate years at Harvard, when Latham had almost forced him to read his biography. In politics as in poetry he stood aloof from parties.

Returning with "The False Gods" to the topic of the literary life untouched since *The Town Down the River*, he rebukes those taking the cult of free verse as a pretext for shoddy workmanship. "Tasker Norcross," the portrait of a materialist who suffers from vague awareness of what he is losing from insensitivity to the arts, augments its effect of pity and terror by the contrasted conversational ease of its style. The price true art exacts is the theme of "Rembrandt to Rembrandt," which Robinson ranked with "The Man Against the Sky" as his best work. The soliloquy is uttered at the decisive moment when the unconventional grouping and color of "The Night Watch" has destroyed the great painter's popularity. Shall he persist in painting what the Dutch people cannot, or will not, see? Were his wife Saskia alive, Rembrandt muses, decision might be more difficult. Though she had laughed at his critics, would mere faith in her husband have sustained her through poverty and obscurity? It was the old problem of Henry James' "The Lesson of the Master," of Palissy's wife, of Lancelot and Guinevere:

> A woman waiting on a man's avouch
> Of the invisible, may not wait always
> Without a word betweenwhiles, or a dash
> Of poison on his faith.

Conceivably Saskia might have won him to pander to popular taste, even though that for him was

> The taste of death in life—which is the food
> Of art that has betrayed itself alive
> And is a food of hell.

He had doubts enough without adding hers, and needed to look at his self-portrait and at his reflection in a mirror, to be reassured by the "fight and fire" in the jaws and eyes. An insidious tempter whispered, Of what avail recognition that would come, if at all, when he was dust and ashes? But all these doubts assumed that he had power of choice, when really he had none:

> . . . I am but a living instrument
> Played on by powers that are invisible.
>
> .   .   .   .
>
> One of the few that are so fortunate
> As to be told their task and to be given

> A skill to do it with a tool too keen
> For timid safety . . .

With a glint of humor, Rembrandt observes from history that

> Oblivion heretofore has done some running
> Away from graves, and will do more of it.

The soliloquy was really Robinson to Robinson, and along with "Hillcrest" was the most intimate self-revelation since *The Children of the Night*. It was written in mid-summer, 1920, six months after his fiftieth birthday had been greeted by a remarkable tribute from his fellow crafts-men. *The New York Times Book Review* for December 21, 1919, had carried a feature, "Poets Celebrate E. A. Robinson's Birthday." Introduced by Professor Bliss Perry, who remarked with exactitude: "Since he will never blow his own trumpet, strangers to him will join his friends in sounding all the trumpets for him," fourteen poets uttered their esteem for the man and for his work. Said Amy Lowell: "E. A. R. is poetry. I can think of no other living writer who has so consistently dedicated his life to his work. He is a poet for poets." Arthur Davison Ficke lauded his "scrupulous artistic integrity . . . beyond the reach of fad or fashion." Edgar Lee Masters, born in the same year with Robinson, testified: "Mr. Robinson was producing poetry in one of the most sterile periods of American poetry." For Vachel Lindsay, he was "a novelist distilled into a poet." Ledoux told of his "tense sympathy with those who have suffered misfortune." Torrence prophesied: "His poetry is one of the most valuable yields which this time shall leave to other times."

Kermit Roosevelt, whose schoolboy enthusiasm had

rescued *The Children of the Night* from ·apparent oblivion, added a personal word of appraisal in *Scribner's Magazine:* "He is essentially and above all else American, and at the same time cosmopolitan and of every country and age, as all great poets must be. The influences of Greece, of Elizabethan England, of France, and of modern England may all be felt in his verse." *The Outlook,* reprinting for the occasion Theodore Roosevelt's estimate of Robinson which had appeared in its columns, commented on his role as a "pioneer in the movement to break away from those worn-out symbols of expression which have lost the power to transmit thought and emotion to the modern mind." His career was a "gratifying indication that work of the first order will find its way to the front, no matter how devoid it may be of the superficial advantage of popular appeal." He had received "no applause which has not been deserved, nor published a single line which was not wrought with a devotion comparable to the devotion of those who builded in stone the faith and hopes of the Middle Ages."

Robinson's publishers were impressed. When he carried out a promise exacted by Braithwaite and asked them for a Collected Edition of his poems, they welcomed the proposal.

With the publication of the *Collected Poems* set for the fall of 1921, Robinson was thankful for the "early grilling exercises" which had prepared him for the exacting labor of revising his less mature poems for inclusion. "I am now more than inclined to believe," he had stated in a letter of 1917, "that the technical flabbiness of many writers is due to the lack in earlier years of just such grilling—in the years when one is not conscious of how hard he is working and of how much time he is wasting—unless he is ready to gamble his life away for the sake of winning the possible conjunction of a few inevitable words." The final process of proofreading had its hazards: "I'm still afraid of a proof-reader who insists for a third time on changing 'scared' to 'sacred.' Whenever this demon finds any poetry . . . he puts a query on the margin." When the *Collected Poems* appeared, he was horrified to find that, in spite of his vigilance, the meaning of "Reuben Bright" had been travestied by the insertion of "to" in the final line, so that it read: . . . "and tore down to the slaughter-house."

Robinson's revisions reveal the advance of his mature style over that of his early volumes. "Luke Havergal," after passing through six reprintings with changes only in punctuation and spelling, now received felicitous verbal alteration in part of the first stanza, which since 1896 had read:

> The wind will moan, the leaves will whisper some—
> Whisper of her, and strike you as they fall;
> But go, and if you trust her she will call,—

The Collected version becomes:

> The leaves will whisper there of her, and some,
> Like flying words, will strike you as they fall;
> But go, and if you listen she will call.

The improvement in tempo, in suggestive sound, in vigor is obvious. "Captain Craig," shorn of otiose lines in the 1915 reprinting, was reduced still further, and fumbling passages were remolded and concentrated into impressive assurance, as the following verses will reveal, the first text being that of 1902.

> There was a time
> When he had fancied, if worst came to worst
> And he could work no more, that he might beg
> Nor be the less for it; but when it came
> To practice he found that he had not
> The genius. It was that, and that was all:
> Experience had made him to detect
> The blunder for his own like all the rest
> Of him. There were no other men to blame.
> He was himself, and he had lost the speed
> He started with, and he was left behind.
>
> . . . .
>
> There was a time
> When he had fancied, if worst came to worst,
> And he could do no more, that he might ask
> Of whom he would. But once had been enough,
> And soon there would be nothing more to ask.
> He was himself, and he had lost the speed
> He started with, and he was left behind.

Presented with the opportunity to survey Robinson's entire work so far, almost six hundred printed pages, American newspapers and periodicals responded widely and with no dissent as to the impressiveness of his achievement. Notable appraisals were made by Carl Van Doren in *The Nation,* Amy Lowell in *The Dial,* and Edward Sapir in *The Freeman.* Van Doren, who had been delighted by the chance to publish "Mr. Flood's Party" the year before, accurately defined the poet's relation to American life and letters and his contributions to poetic technique: ". . . he has no more frittered away his powers in a trivial contemporaneousness than he has buried them under a recluse abstention from actualities; he has, rather, with his gaze always upon the facts before him, habitually seen through

and behind them to the truths which give them significance
and coherence . . . he is another Hawthorne, disciplined
by a larger learning, a more vigorous intellect, and a stricter
medium. . . . He has employed the sonnet as a vehicle for
dramatic portraiture until he has almost created a new
type: he has evolved an octosyllabic eight-line stanza which
is unmistakably, inimitably his; he has achieved a blank
verse which flawlessly fits his peculiar combination of
Greek dignity and Yankee ease; he has, for all his taste for
stricter measures, taught his verses, when they wanted, to
lilt in a fashion that has put despair in many a lighter bard."
Amy Lowell generously praised the man who had initiated,
single-handed and long alone, the revival of American
poetry of which she was among the doughtiest champions:
"Mr. Robinson is a sort of temporal Colossus of Rhodes;
he straddles a period. . . . He found his voice when
America was given over to pretty-prettiness of all kinds"
and was "twenty years ahead of his time. . . . He began
to see life with a touch of irony because it was not his life."
In his astonishing first volume he "started fully fledged
and fully armed," and his solitary course was maintained
"with a wistful nobility of purpose which our literature
has not seen before." For Edward Sapir, he was "the one
American poet who compels, rather than invites, consideration." Nowhere among contemporary writers was there
another "spirit which, for the moment, annihilates."

Since the failure of Robinson's expectation of more
readers for "Captain Craig" abroad than at home, there had
been no English edition of his verse; since Miss Sinclair's in
1906, almost no British critical notice. Now the influential
dramatist and poet John Drinkwater, to whom he had
presented in 1920 *The Children of the Night* as repre-

sentative of "some of the worst and some of the best of the sort of thing I have to do," wrote the Introduction to a British edition of the *Collected Poems* in 1922, presenting Robinson as the foremost poet in American critical estimation. From the Chair of Poetry, Drinkwater read before the Royal Society of Literature an address placing him in "the true Greek tradition" for seeing "man beset by his own character, which is fate."

At home, Robinson became a national figure with the award of the Pulitzer Prize for poetry in 1921 and the conferring of the degree of Doctor of Letters by Yale in 1922. Before the Yale Commencement crowd the retiring poet heard himself presented for the honor in words of the utmost appropriateness: "In an age of self-advertising, where many prefer notoriety to obscurity and would rather draw attention by any means than remain unknown, Mr. Robinson has invariably permitted his poems to speak for themselves." Five thousand copies of the *Collected Poems* were sold the first year. After 1922 Robinson lived by his pen, with no further need of subsidy.

It might be a "neat finish," he had written when the *Collected Poems* were ready for the press, "if I were to be struck by lightning this summer in Peterborough." So far as his poetry was concerned, there was truth in this surmise of a man almost fifty-two, wearied by years of creativeness. Nothing he was to write in the fourteen years that lay ahead would increase the esteem of the judicious, though nothing would lower that esteem. But death at that time would have robbed him of his greatest satisfactions as a man.

Afterglow

ONE MORNING in 1922, James and Laura Fraser were surprised to find Robinson, a late sleeper, at their door at seven o'clock. Greatly agitated, he told them that Seth Pope had dropped dead in the street. Would the Frasers take him in for a night or two, until he found lodgings?

Fortunately the studio on the upper floor of their house at 28 West Eighth Street was vacant. The three found living together so pleasant that Robinson had a home for the rest of his life. The husband and wife, both sculptors, understood a creative artist's need of independence and of sympathy. Their frank Western cordiality and their informal way of living put him completely at ease. They had a standing engagement with him one night a week for the theater, one night for poker at home. In 1927 he moved with the Frasers to 328 East Forty-second Street, his last New York address. In the Fraser country house near Westport, Connecticut, he had his room and bath under the eaves, an entire floor to himself. He could never quite believe his good fortune in having a permanent home. Each summer he would write from Peterborough to the Frasers, offering to go elsewhere; always he was assured of a warm welcome. The one exception to his quiet habits was the noise he made closing the outside door and on the stairs as he entered or left the house. It was his signal to his friends that there was another person in their home.

The summer after the *Collected Poems* he began *Roman Bartholow*, a dramatic narrative of materialism in modern life which he had had in mind for eleven years. Bartholow, the son and grandson of hard-fisted money-makers, is represented as living as a gentleman of leisure in his ivy-covered mansion in the midst of ample acres by a river, like Oaklands by the Kennebec. He has retired there out of jealousy for his wife, Gabrielle. Accustomed to the best of everything, he had chosen her because she seemed to unite "beauty, mind, and fire." In urban society she had altogether too many admirers. Gabrielle, a worldling who accepted him for his money and social position while caring so little for him that she went to sleep again after the sun wakened her on her wedding morning, has taken mute revenge for being removed from her natural environment by refusing to bear an heir to the estate. Finding in her no fire and a mind purely negative, Bartholow is tormented by her inaccessible and useless beauty. Like Briony in "Fragment" too intelligent for the life of idle seclusion he is leading, he falls into a neurosis such as blighted Briony's days. Friends send to his aid Penn-Raven, who has a reputation for healing soul-sickness.

When the poem opens Penn-Raven, with antecedents as obscure as Flammonde's and a philosophy like Craig's, has been Bartholow's house guest for a year. By diagnosing his host's illness as arising from illusions concerning his

wife's character and from incompatibility with his ancestral traditions, he has become more than a friend, almost
a god to him. Bartholow, his health and relish for life
restored by learning to follow his own nature and to face
unpleasant truths, regrets only that the beautiful Gabrielle
cannot understand and share his rejuvenation. Actually,
his cure is incomplete, for he has transferred his habit of
idealizing from his wife to Penn-Raven (one wonders if
this transference to his analyst reflects Freud or is the poet's
intuition), and has not completely broken the bonds of
convention. Robinson, with economy of means, reveals
this double insufficiency by a single incident. When Bartholow discovers that his friend has betrayed him by seducing Gabrielle, he springs at his throat, according to the
traditional role of the husband. Penn-Raven, physically the
stronger, pins his host down and obliges him to listen to a
discourse on the irrationality of jealousy, a remnant of the
cave man which modern man should be ashamed of.
Gabrielle undergoes a similar ordeal of facing truth, for
Penn-Raven, although yielding to physical passion, has
never had illusions about her character. In anger at her
playing with him, he so convicts her of the cold negation
of her nature that in self-abhorrence she takes literally his
parting words: "You are too beautiful to be alive." Nevertheless, all three have been mistaken about her absolute
coldness; for she drowns herself only because she thinks
that knowledge of her infidelity has destroyed the last
vestige of her husband's regard.

His wife dead and his friend driven away, Bartholow,
alone in his ancestral mansion, broods on the enigmas of a
false friend who has given wise counsel and a cold wife
who had kissed him on the forehead, saying, "You will

remember this," before slipping away to the river. (The parallel with "the kiss That flames upon your forehead" in "Luke Havergal" suggests that something similar in the poet's experience had engraved itself in his memory.) In bewilderment and grief Bartholow asks counsel of a neighbor, Umfraville, who has been observing the strange complication of the *ménage à trois*. As he tells his story, guided by tactful questions, it dawns upon Bartholow that he had rejected his wife's proffer of affection out of pride, because it had come late and with her lover still in the house, and that Penn-Raven's repentance had been sincere. Umfraville, a classical scholar acquainted with the behavior of man throughout the ages, comments that Bartholow and his wife had acted according to "the poisoning inertia of custom," which is "the arch-enemy of nature." As for Penn-Raven, the ambiguities of his character were neither unique nor rare:

> What wreckage has the gentlest of us left
> Among those who have smiled and are forgotten?
> What untold inward searing of the strong
> Has been the jest of innocence and weakness?

Liberated by these final insights into human nature, Bartholow resolutely leaves his ancestral home to lead a life according to his real inclinations.

Two of the characters in the long poem are familiar Robinson types: Umfraville, "doomed and irremediably defeated" by a grotesquely ugly face, and Penn-Raven, a parasite philosopher who like Flammonde played so well that observers were "half afraid To say for certain that he played." The others, Bartholow and Gabrielle, owe a great debt to the author of *Modern Love* and *The Ordeal of*

Richard Feverel. The ordeal of frankness which both fear
to pass through, the dead hand of convention which forces
Bartholow to act the role of injured husband to the end
and drives Gabrielle to unnecessary suicide, are Meredithian conceptions, and Meredithian also the style, as in
the aphoristic lines:

> Our souls are foreign in us till our fears
> Attest them and they clamor to be known
> And owned; they are our slayers and our saviours,
> And we more slain than saved,

which are easily distinguishable from the abstract manner
native to Robinson:

> Less to remembering an obscure monition
> Than to confessing an assured renascence.

From Meredith, too, comes the emphasis upon environment
and especially upon heredity: the ridicule of "atavistic
behavior," the fancies that Bartholow's idealism may come
from some unknown maternal line and that Gabrielle's
coldness may be a far throw-back to the fish stage in
evolution (Karen in *Talifer* was to be an "ivory fish").
As in *The Egoist*, characters tend to become abstractions,
like those in a morality play, and preaching goes on in
unrealistic situations. Penn-Raven, after releasing Bartholow's clutch from his throat, holds him down in a chair
while he discourses for over sixty lines of blank verse on
atavism and the futility of jealous revenge: a lapse of
visualization and of humor rare in Robinson, who in smaller
compass can moralize in a telling phrase:

> How much of easy death in life there is
> Where life is easy.

While he was composing *Lancelot* friends had dissuaded him from having Gawain talk in Meredithian epigrams; but now the "philosophy and sharp sayings" he had admired ever since he read *Diana of the Crossways* in his inarticulate college days found vent at last.

Not only is *Roman Bartholow* the most imitative of Robinson's major efforts, but it is also the most difficult, demanding an effort of imagination and memory that overtaxes the most seasoned reader of verse on first reading. Yet even with imperfect understanding, the central scenes leading to Gabrielle's suicide, attended by the repeated symbolic sound at the window of

> . . . clumsy moths indignantly
> Refusing to be free,

are tensely dramatic. Two or more readings are required to uncover the drama of the opening scene at breakfast, and on almost every page there is baffling indirection. But indirection and suggestion have their peculiar triumph in building up the character of Penn-Raven, the most mysterious of Robinson's parasites, whose eyes, like those of Amaranth to come, have superhuman power. Supernally wise about others, himself he cannot save, and his tears as he departs remorsefully to resume his nomadic existence move even the injured Bartholow. Intellectualized talk admirably suits Gabrielle, one of the most repellently negative and destructive minds in American verse, even though Robinson gives her a final moment of piteousness like that of Tasker Norcross.

Built like a puzzle, *Roman Bartholow* required extraordinary intellectual effort, and left the poet exhausted beyond his wont. It appeared in 1923 with a dedication to

Percy MacKaye, the most dramatic temperament among his friends. With the encouragement and financial aid of friends he took his first vacation in many years, sailing for England on April 18, 1923.

England meant more than satisfaction of his need of change. Of British descent, he wanted to see the country of his origins, a country that reconciled order with individual liberty, a country rich in literary associations. He would have gone on to France, where he owed almost as great a literary debt, had he been younger and not so bad a traveler and if there had not been the language barrier to circulation of his poems there. For most of all he wanted readers in Europe, where appreciation of the finer shades of literary art was greater. The publication of the English edition of his *Collected Poems* the previous October seemed to offer a likelihood of finding such readers.

He went directly to London, where he sought out "old ghosts," with John Gould Fletcher as guide to Cheapside, where Shakespeare had lived and the Mermaid Tavern stood, and with John Drinkwater for an afternoon in the Tower of London. Quaint place names, like Wapping Old Stairs, stirred his imagination. Mrs. St. John Irvine drove him about the West End; in passing the Serpentine he remarked that it looked like "a good place to commit suicide," reminded no doubt of Harriet Shelley. Alfred Noyes showed him the Roman antiquities of St. Albans. Oxford and Cambridge, where King's College Chapel seemed as miraculous as once to Wordsworth, were his farthest reach. Contemporary England, hard hit by the war, disquieted him by its need to break with its past.

He renewed acquaintance with Miss Sinclair, sought out

Gosse, who had welcomed *The Torrent,* and made a good friend of J. C. Squire, editor of *The London Mercury,* which had recently published a high estimate of the *Collected Poems* by the American poet Conrad Aiken. But Arnold Bennett, living in luxury by diluting his quality (like St. George in James' "Lesson of the Master"), roused his dislike. At a meeting of P.E.N. he was disappointed to find that few writers knew his poetry. He was inclined to think the English grudging toward American work. But what he had counted on most, his maturity of outlook and his adherence to traditional verse technique with a strong dash of French style, really cost him English readers, who expected from America something in the order of Whitman's "barbaric yawp." The work of Masters, Sandburg, Lindsay, and even Frost was preferred, as exotic, to verse which at first glance seemed not unlike that of a cultivated Englishman. Robinson should have been warned by Middleton Murry's comment on the *Collected Poems* the preceding November: "It is strange that a thing so old as Mr. Robinson's poetry should have come out of a country so new." His presence in England could scarcely enlarge his audience, for unlike Frost he was no illuminating and magnetic reader of his own verse. Nor was lecturing on literary topics possible for him. His verse, he concluded, must be left to make its way by the printed page. (A young man named Auden, unknown to Robinson, would soon be reading him with enthusiasm.)

In planning his journey, Robinson had sketched to Drinkwater the possibility of burying himself "in some quiet place with an inn and a cathedral," to write or not to write, as he pleased; but to Mrs. Richards he had confessed:

"I have a notion that New England beans and stone walls will get me in the end." They did, sooner than he expected. Before he had been abroad two months, the need to write returned; and no place seemed so attractive as Peterborough. England he had found "a strangely foreign sort of place that was strangely like home," where he could do no work, since "Old England and New England would be forever fighting for the upper hold." But travel had done him good: "Without any change of air there would never have been any peace for my troubled soul." However, "three months of unproductive change" would be "as good as three years." On July 26, one day short of three months from arrival, he sailed for home. He was at Peterborough early in August, ready for two months' work.

With *The Man Who Died Twice* (1924) Robinson returned to the theme of the artist's life, now in terms of music. This long poem reverses the situation of "Rembrandt to Rembrandt," where the painter triumphs by force of character. In Fernando Nash, Robinson has created a composer who cannot sufficiently control the lusts of the flesh, which are part of his endowment of genius, to wait for inspiration. Having built by twenty-five a style fit to bear his music to the heights, he lets it rust during twenty years of drink and women, when he should

> . . . have waited with his inner doors
> Unbarred to the celestial messengers
> Who may have come and gone a score of times.

Ironically he sees those messengers descend when his body is too much wasted by excesses to bear their message. Patience, constant attention to his art, would have put him in the immortal company of Bach, whose face so often rebuked him from the wall of his room. Incapable of self-deception, Nash acknowledges his death to art as deliberate sin against the spirit, and beats a drum for the Salvation Army until his ravaged body brings mercifully an early second death.

Like "Rembrandt to Rembrandt," *The Man Who Died Twice* brings us close to Robinson. He shudders at what drink so nearly did to his verse ("My poetry is not such a slow distillation as you think," he told a correspondent. "At the time of which you wrote, I was giving so much of my attention to other distillations that poetry really didn't have a chance"), while congratulating himself on the patient devotion to art that had saved him. Nash's "barren" room, "not much larger than the iron bed/On which he sat," reached by "four forbidding stairways," reproduces almost photographically the room at Jim Moore's.

Although Nash can only pity

> . . . the sanguine ordinary
> That has no devil and so controls himself,
> Having nothing in especial to control,

he spurns the facile excuse that he was made "mostly out of living brimstone" and set in "a somewhat fiery world." His clear-sightedness concerning himself is one of the marks of "inviolable distinction" that give him

> A giant's privacy of lone communion
> With older giants.

Since Nash is a fictitious character, there was an artistic problem absent from "Rembrandt to Rembrandt," where the reader accepts the fact of genius. If Nash were to speak entirely for himself, how distinguish him from thousands of failures who have made extravagant claims? Robinson surmounts the difficulty by reporting his confessions through an observer who has known his early promise and can recognize him in his Salvation Army metamorphosis. Himself a composer of music, he has his doubts; but these vanish at length before the personality of Nash, with its immense capacity for good and evil, its aura of nobility:

> . . . there was in him always,
> Unqualified by guile and unsubdued
> By failure and remorse, or by redemption,
> The grim nostalgic passion of the great
> For glory all but theirs.
> . . . I believe him
> To-day as I believed him while he died,
> And while I sank his ashes in the sea.

After the epigrams and the overrefined allusiveness of *Roman Bartholow*, Robinson's blank verse has returned to colloquial ease, which on occasion rises to nobility and beauty. The symphony that descends to Nash's bed of debauch is introduced by haunting cadences:

> . . . Smiling and still,
> He listened gratefully. It had come at last;
> And those far sent celestial messengers
> That he had for so long a time denied
> Had found him now. He had offended them,
> He had insulted and forsaken them,
> And he was not forsaken. They had come,
> And in their coming had remembered only
> That they were messengers, who like himself
> Had now no choice; and they were telling him this
> In the last language of mortality,
> Which has no native barrier but the grave.

This fine poem won its author a second Pulitzer Prize.

Dionysus in Doubt (1925) contains less of note than previous collections of short pieces. Artistically inferior to "Cassandra," the title poem and the dialogue, "Demos and Dionysus," which closes the volume reflect Robinson's increased uneasiness over the political immaturity of his countrymen after observing English maturity, and his indignation at the egregious expression of it in National Prohibition. He was disgusted at the supine cynicism of prominent people who limited their protest to a furtive breaking of the law when their duty was to eradicate it from the statute books. Where were the leaders in the democracy? he asked in these poems and, more picturesquely, in his letters: "One hundred men, who have all they want stored away in their cellars, could probably put an end to the whole business if they dared to open their mouths except to take a drink." In a more relaxed mood he informed Mrs. Richards, a supporter of the Amendment: "All human beings who are not made of putty are going to stimulate themselves in one way or another; and alcohol, in spite of its dangers, is the least harmful of all the active demons. Everything is dangerous which is worth having. For example, think of poetry and music, not to mention fried onions and cucumbers. Dr. Schumann was a fairly successful and contented local doctor until poetry got him at the age of thirty. The rest of his life was a slow débâcle, if there is such a thing, and he would have died poor, without the aid of rum (which he never 'abused') if he hadn't married some money. . . . If you need any further example of a life wrecked on the foaming reefs of song, consider the worldly voyage of

Your most obedient

E.A.R."

In the midst of clamor against the Versailles peace settlement, the farsighted sonnet, "The Garden of Nations," suggests that the younger generations, so sure of superior wisdom, may bring forth, instead of stunted plants, "more numerous weeds and weevils."

As poetry, the political pieces, which Robinson emphasized by position, are inferior to several sonnets of character, two fine sonnets on natural beauty, "The Sheaves" and "As It Looked Then," the dialogue, "Genevieve and Alexandra," a revelation of pitiful mismating, and "Mortmain," a dramatic narrative of cross-purposes in love, discovered too late to save a man's life from waste. "Mortmain" is one of the most moving portrayals of New England reticence, whereby speech is only a surface indication of passion and despair.

Aware that reticence had become unpopular with a younger generation of writers bent on displaying emancipation from Puritanism, Robinson included in this volume an ironic sonnet, "New England," caricaturing their disdain. When published in *The Gardiner Journal* for January 31, 1924, it wounded the local patriotism of a subscriber, who retorted with a letter and with a poem charging Robinson with infidelity to his birthplace. Grieved by the misinterpretation, the poet wrote to the editor that he had intended "an oblique attack upon all those who are forever throwing dead cats at New England for its alleged emotional and moral frigidity." In republishing the sonnet in *Dionysus in Doubt* he made his meaning obvious by removing a word of personal reference, "born," and substituting "we're told" for "it seems." Such are the trials of an ironist among the literal-minded American people, who blindly ridicule other peoples for their deficiency in humor.

Unconsciously Robinson was on the verge of closing the gap between himself and the American public by producing a long poem innocent of irony and giving full vent to passion in words. "I came down here with every intention of writing some short things for a new book," he reported from Peterborough in June 1925; "but my old friend Tristram, whom I have been fighting off for some five years, finally got me by the throat and refused to let go."

That month he had seen Maine for the first time in over fifteen years. The occasion of the visit was a Doctorate of Letters from Bowdoin College, which saluted him as "son of Maine, brought up by the shores of the lovely Kennebec; recognized at home and abroad as without a living peer in his own special field of verse." No doubt he had thought of that Bowdoin week end with Harry Smith which had brought his momentous decision to go to college. On the way back to Peterborough he had seen for the first time his birthplace at Head Tide, and spent a few days with relatives and friends, including Ed Moore, in Gardiner. The town gave him "the creeps," he wrote Harry Smith, now Professor of Greek at Amherst, so haunted was it with vanished faces. The memory of what sorrow and passion could lie beneath impassive manners may have had its influence upon him as he sat down again in Peterborough to let Tristram utter the bitterness of his self-reproach and jealousy alone on a Tintagel parapet while the wedding music for King Mark and Isolt of Ireland floats down from the castle. "The key and color of the thing are altogether different from those of *Merlin* and *Lancelot*," he wrote Mrs. Ledoux on August 3, "and may cause some readers to suspect that I'm getting a little tired of hearing too much about my New England reticence—which may be pretty true."

Using the freedom won by postwar writers, a freedom he had long known in French literature, he expressed Tristram's jealous imaginings with a naturalism unequalled in his verse since "Captain Craig" and broke the sex taboo observed even there. Tristram curses himself as one of the "pimps" of the "man-shaped goat" Mark, who soon will hold Isolt

> . . . in his vicious arms
> And crush the bloom of her resisting life
> On his hot, watery mouth, and overcome
> The protest of her suffering silk skin
> With his crude senile claws.

Recoil fills his mind with images of vomiting:

> . . . a cold soul-retching wave
> Of recognition . . .
>
> .   .   .   .
>
> . . . I'd feed a sick toad to my brother
> If in my place he were not sick without it.

In impotent rage at Mark he could

> . . . tear all the cords out of his neck
> To make a rope, and hang the rest of him.

But there is equal strength in the reticence of Isolt's cry of horror:

> . . . Tristram! Tristram!
> With you in the same house!

Fleeing the abominable castle, obsessed by

> A flame-lit picture of Isolt alone
> With Mark, in his embrace . . .

Tristram is waylaid by Queen Morgan le Fay, bent on seducing him, and after

> . . . long chagrin
> Of long imprisonment, and long prisoned hate,

he seizes her "like an animal."

Jealousy, self-reproach, thwarted sexuality, and the ideal longing of Isolt of Brittany, Robinson imagined powerfully; but requited passion lay outside his experience. So for the idyll of Tristram's union with Isolt of Ireland he chose as guide Wagner's music, which mingles passion with the tossing of the sea, with danger, and the swooning, delicious thought of death. For over four hundred lines Robinson's lovers discourse of love, while the reader's mind and imagination yawn. No doubt it was good for the poet to release long-pent emotion; but he forgot that words cannot do all that music can. For the first and the last time he was verbose and ineffectively repetitious.

Obsessed by his theme, he wrote with unusual rapidity, and paid by aggravation of his old plague, insomnia, and by the need to whip his morning sluggishness by cold baths. "I simply tried to do too much," he confessed near the end of the summer, "and Father Time shook his scythe at me." Dipping into Morris' *Life and Death of Jason* and finding it intolerably "long-winded," he was struck with fear that his own long poems would not endure, since Tennyson's *Idylls* "are strangely thin nowadays and Swinburne's *Tristram of Lyonesse* is strikingly prolix and saccharine." He reassured himself by the thought that long poems were not his "only stock in trade. . . . I like to believe that even without them there will be enough to justify— to me at any rate—a rather scrappy and not especially iniquitous existence." Exhaustion lasted into the winter, for at fifty-six he had lost much of his resilience.

Returning to Peterborough to complete the poem, he wrote with more caution and skill. "For some reason or other," he informed Esther Bates, "I am having more trouble with the catastrophe part than anything else— chiefly, I fancy, out of a possibly too acute fear of letting it run over into sentimentality—which is far worse than death. I have already killed them [the lovers] three times, but they are like cats with nine lives." Humor, hitherto absent from the poem, twinkled for a fleeting moment in the mocking letter from Morgan le Fay. Isolt's quiet assurance, "I shall hear all you do not say to me," speaks the language of perfect union more surely than the verbose protestations at Joyous Gard. King Mark's belated discovery of the "needlessness" of revenge and Isolt of Brittany's drawing wisdom from bereavement end *Tristram* in the best Robinson manner.

In structure, the poem binds together Matthew Arnold's "Tristram and Iseult" and Wagner. By representing Isolt of Brittany, left to suffer, as more pitiable than the tragic lovers, it begins and ends quietly, like Arnold's poem, in the manner of Greek drama. Within this frame of peace at the price of resignation lies tempestuous Wagnerian lyricism with recurring motifs: the sea in many moods and the stars as symbols of passion, time, insecurity, fear, and death as the gate to peace. Although Robinson's rejection of the legendary love potion humanizes the characters, they are not dramatic and growing, but lyric, simple, and static in comparison with Robinson's Merlin and Vivien, Lancelot·and Guinevere. Growth is reserved for the contrasted minor figures, the self-bound Mark and the almost selfless

Isolt of Brittany. The development of Mark from sadistic greed to perplexed tolerance: "I do not know . . . I am not sure," is Robinson's characteristic contribution to the legend.

The longest of Robinson's poems, *Tristram* was finally completed in September 1926, and polished with unremitting care. He felt he could never write another; "but probably I shall, for some diseases are incurable. In centuries to come, when there may not be any more art, perhaps poetry will be treated and cured, and the victim be converted into a useful bricklayer. Sometimes the future looks like that. Especially when one has just written 4400 lines that only the heroic few will read."

But this time readers had no need to be heroic, and they were not few. *Tristram* offered no character enigmas and emotional complexities like *Roman Bartholow*, demanded no special interest in the artist and his problems like *The Man Who Died Twice*, did not double back upon itself like *Merlin*, had none of "Captain Craig's" confusing mixture of straightforwardness and irony, humor and seriousness, and was not so highly concentrated as the short poems. A wider audience awaited it. That it became very wide was the result of commercial accident and the faith of one of the poet's most intelligent admirers.

The Literary Guild, just launched, was meeting so much opposition from bookstores because of the reduced prices at which its choices were offered, that it was considering means of mollifying them. In the decision of the Macmillan Company to sell *Tristram* to the bookstores at the Guild rate, Carl Van Doren saw the opportunity of a conciliatory gesture which would also give the Guild "a reputation for taste and courage" by aiding a poet he had long admired.

He proposed *Tristram* as the Guild's third offering to its subscribers, and found Joseph Wood Krutch and other members of its board of judges in hearty agreement. The enthusiasm of its advertising manager, a former promoter of automobile sales, for the poem after an overnight reading seemed a good omen for its popularity. To fulfill the engagement to provide subscribers with books at below market price, the Guild asked Mark Van Doren to write a biographical and critical introduction to Robinson to accompany *Tristram*.

The Guild gave the public a taste of what was coming by arranging a reading in the Little Theater of passages from the poem by Mrs. August Belmont (the actress, Eleanor Robson). Robinson feared that no one would come, and refused to appear. His utmost concession was to wait for his friends in the theater lounge. To his astonishment and relief he found the theater full to overflowing. While he waited nervously, out of sight, Carl Van Doren praised "the finest Tristram poem in the English language" and introduced Mrs. Belmont. After the reading, the poet's admirers crowded into the lounge to shake his hand. With red spots of excitement in his cheeks and his tongue loosened by the stimulus of success, he was for once almost at ease.

When he learned that the Guild was ordering 12,000 copies from his publishers, who had hitherto sold only two or three thousand of each of his long poems, he said to Carl Van Doren: "I hope you don't have too many left." Not only was the entire number distributed by the Guild, but the regular trade edition sold several times more, the total sales for the year being 57,475 copies. The author's royalties, including small sums from anthologies and similar sources, amounted to $14,535: "which isn't so bad for blank verse," he remarked to his friend Isaacs, who became his business adviser. A third Pulitzer Prize brought another thousand. But he was assailed by a novel anxiety. The popularity of the poem might indicate that the quality of his work had fallen off. Friends had to reassure him. *Tristram* went on selling; even in the trough of the depression, 1932, when the *Collected Poems* dropped to 723 copies, it sold 1,846. Still better, it raised the circulation of his later volumes to over three times the average of their predecessors.

There was no further reason for financial insecurity, and the last of his debts could be paid, but so deeply had poverty eaten into his soul that he did not slacken his labor of writing. When one of the many hopeful spirits of the late 1920's proposed to show him how to make one hundred per cent on his money, he said he "would rather keep what he had." In renewing correspondence with his old friend Gledhill in 1930, he remarked: "I have been over a more or less rough road, but on the whole haven't much to growl about. A fellow in my trade mustn't expect too much attention from a hard-boiled, child-minded world, and the wonder is that I haven't been exterminated long before now." He lived simply and continued his generosity to those who seemed down and out, even to French, now so insanely jealous that Robinson feared for his life. In vain Isaacs tried to protect him from panhandlers. Chief among his public benefactions was a diagnostic laboratory for the Gardiner Hospital in memory of his brother, Dr. Dean Robinson.

In his Introduction to the *Letters* (1929) of his friend Thomas Sergeant Perry, who died the year after the publication of *Tristram*, Robinson said: "As I have no personal acquaintance with Mr. T. S. Eliot and Mr. Van Wyck Brooks, it will do no harm to mention here his lively and especial interest in their work." By such scrupulousness he stood apart from the debased literary ethics of the period, which did not discourage logrolling or unblushing public laudation of close friends and connections. He did nothing to exploit his own success. The poems that followed were not catchpenny replicas of *Tristram*. They were not launched by literary "teas" or advertised by his appearance on the program of some department store "literary week." He continued to refuse to address women's clubs or to read publicly from his verse. After the informal reception in the Little Theater lounge, he never permitted himself to be lionized. To avoid persistent tufthunters, he spent more of each year in Boston, where Mrs. Perry provided him with the refuge of a studio. He accepted no more honorary degrees, though he would have made an exception of Harvard, toward which he felt a strong loyalty. It was not the fault of the Harvard faculty, where he had had admirers from the first, that no invitation came.

Before the postwar bubble burst, he composed *Cavender's House*, a long poem exposing the weakness of the idol of the moment, the big businessman. With Ibsen on his desk, Robinson plunged the reader into the last scene of the last act of a domestic tragedy. The setting, an unlighted, deserted manor house at midnight, misled some reviewers and many readers into interpreting as a dialogue with a ghost what was a monologue, a colloquy of the businessman with a projection of his own imagination. The situation had antecedents in Browning's "My Last Duchess" and Meredith's *Egoist*. Cavender, a dynamic captain of industry accustomed to obedience and to absolute material possession, marries Laramie for her beauty and apparent lack of mind and individuality. She has a mind, nevertheless, though it works unlike his, by subtle indirection; and she retaliates on his masterfulness by arousing his jealousy, replying to his accusations with an enigmatic smile. At length he goads her to a scornful response; whereupon he throws her over a cliff. But this exercise of his power only reveals its limits. With Laramie dead, he can never learn whether she was really false. She is accounted a suicide, and he is free to leave their home for restless travel, obsessed by his unanswered and unanswerable question.

The poem opens with his stealthy return to his house after ten years' absence, during which it has gradually dawned upon him that his wife had an individuality he should have respected and that the universe has laws stronger than he, stronger than all the laws of man. The beauty of the poem lies in the subtle progression of the debate within his mind with the image of his dead Laramie, now his implacable judge, toward relinquishment of the last vestige of his possessiveness and surrender to human law, the earthly representative of the moral law of the universe. Unexpectedly, the surrender is not an ultimate anguish, but release from all anguish:

> . . . He was afraid
> Only of peace. He had not asked for that;
> He had not earned or contemplated it;
> And this could not be peace that frightened him
> With wonder, coming like a stranger, slowly,
> Without shape or name, and unannounced—
> As if a door behind him in the dark,

And once not there, had opened silently,
Or as if Laramie had answered him.

In *The Glory of the Nightingales* (1930) the fullness of
Robinson's powers appeared for the last time in a long
poem, dedicated appropriately to the memory of Alfred
Louis, who had inspired his first poem of length. Again it
was a study of an egoist, an egoist more cultivated and
intelligent than Cavender. Nightingale, living on inherited
wealth and accustomed to easy conquest of all that lay
about him in Sharon, a New England city of fifty thousand, first met defeat when Agatha refused him, preferring
the poor and idealistic Malory, for whom he had a warm
youthful friendship such as Robinson had felt for Smith
and Gledhill, and whom his money had aided to become a
bacteriologist. Concealing resentment, Nightingale had
bided his time, which came when he learned that a mine, in
which he had invested and in which Malory had sunk an
entire legacy, was worthless. He withdrew his own money
without warning Malory, at a moment suited to kill
Agatha by the shock. Nightingale secretly rejoiced at her
grave, for she was the only thing he wanted which someone
else had acquired.

These events have taken place before the beginning of
the poem, which introduces Malory, a broken man, passing
through Sharon on his way to shoot Nightingale, who has
built a magnificent house on the seacoast, and then to end
his own misery. Finding the house, he nerves himself to
hear the voice he had loved in youth. He is unprepared for
the sight of Nightingale in a wheel chair, to his practiced
eye doomed to death by disease. Nature has beaten him to
the revenge, or God. Both Malory and Nightingale recog-

nize the futility of revenge in a world governed by Emersonian laws of compensation. In mocking possession of the "house/Which he had always wanted, by the sea," Nightingale confesses his vanity and his lust, and then fills the void of Malory's life with the vision of what a bacteriologist could do for suffering humanity. Bequeathing his house and his fortune to his boyhood friend for a hospital, he sends him off for a drive, during which he shoots himself. Commending Nightingale's courage, Malory finds himself left with no escape "From the long sentence of his usefulness."

With more naturalness and clarity than Robinson's other poems of comparable length, *The Glory of the Nightingales* employs his favorite device of plunging into an action far advanced and letting past events appear bit by bit. Each of its six sections is a poem in itself, and yet cumulative and forward-looking. The two characters are admirably individualized in thought and speech. The desperate Malory sees the sun rise

> Like a fire to burn the world, with all its anguish,
> And all its evil evidence of man,

and as a bacteriologist thinks of the human body as "This treacherous and imperfect house of man." The shrewd reprobate Nightingale dismisses Malory's ill-placed sympathy for his fellow victims, Absolom Spinner and his seduced wife:

> . . . She was not a wife;
> She was a fruity sort of Cyprian fungus,
> With arms and legs, the brain-pan of a chicken,
> And all the morals of a pleasant monkey.

. . . .

> . . . His only currency
> Worth counting in his triumph was a freedom
> To be a fool: and he had more of it
> Than he could use. Spinner had everything,
> And had it for three years in tropic bloom.
> Before it might have faded, or become
> Only an occupation, or a duty,
> Spinner died. He fell down under a dray,
> And died.

The same withering ridicule Nightingale turns on himself in recalling his days of blind vanity. Robinson's comments as narrator have characteristic edge:

> . . . How many a one we meet
> Would somewhat rather see us in a coffin,
> Is not a thought for any far pursuit
> On our part.

Nothing moved Robinson more than the sadness of broken friendship. In feeling it he is intimate with both the idealist Malory and the repentant realist Nightingale. Sudden remembrance of the attractive young Nightingale unnerves Malory at the pitch of his resolve to kill,

> Like a desolating cry of an old music,
> Long unheard, and falling strange in a new place.

Lacerated love turns to reluctant admiration as he feels the charm of Nightingale's candid, humorous, and wise confession of the degeneration of his character, ruined by a single flaw; and the courage of suicide after restitution wins back his old esteem. The style heightens to a threnody as he gazes on the body:

> You were blind, Nightingale, but never afraid
>
> .   .   .   .
>
> And your dark glass is broken.

There are still larger issues than the tragic relations of friends. Both see that Malory has duties transcending his personal misfortune. Nightingale, enlightened by incurable disease, repeats the theme of "The Man Against the Sky," the unimaginable horror, in terms of materialism, of millions hopelessly ill, condemned to

> . . . indignant uselessness,
> And misery too merciless and too harsh,
> And undeserved, to be explainable
> To eyes of earth.

(In the year of the poem's publication Robinson made the gift to the Gardiner Hospital.)

Consciousness of the natural world, far older than man, is stronger here than elsewhere in Robinson. Malory's conviction of having reached his last day on earth makes him cling to every familiar object:

> . . . a blank vision of oblivion
> Chilled him with an irrelevance of regret
> That he should never see that elm again—
> As if a landmark had a language older
> Than his, and a long eloquence that only
> Ruin could understand. . . .

> .   .   .   .   .

> [Malory] stood looking at the ocean, which he saw
> As men had seen it who were not yet men.

Both he and Nightingale read the fate of man in the moods of the sea, of which Robinson had abiding impressions from his Maine youth. In their different ways, they have to learn humility, and it is the immensity of the ocean that helps them accept it. The ocean writes the last words of Nightingale's epitaph:

There was nothing left of Nightingale but silence,
And a cold weight of mystery that was man,
And was no longer man—as waves outside
Were cold and still, and were no longer waves.

With *The Glory of the Nightingales* Robinson is in autumnal glory, his lordship of language unimpaired, his wisdom growing in his sixtieth year. But *Matthias at the Door* falls off decidedly. It repeats the chastening of the businessman who thinks himself perfect; but Matthias is by no means so complex or interesting as Cavender or Nightingale, and the means of his chastening—the successive suicides of two friends and his wife in the same spot—hovers between symbol and realistic improbability to a degree that somehow escaped the author's vigilant sense of humor. Yet Matthias' discovery that he must be born again inspired the fine poem "Nicodemus," which Robinson used as the title for his last collection of short pieces, published in 1932.

Short poems demand a wire-drawn concentration, a fusion of thought and emotion, which taxes the strength of advancing age. Robinson had taken it as happy evidence of vigor that the sardonic "Hector Kane," a practical joke of nature's on human presumption in the vein of Thomas Hardy, should have come to him immediately after *Cavender's House*. Of the ten short poems in *Nicodemus*, two—the title poem and "Sisera"—are admirable instances of the flexibility of his style. The colloquy of Nicodemus and Caiaphas, representatives of State and Church, introduce us to high politics. From his furtive night visit to Jesus, a black robe still hiding his brilliant costume of the potentate, Nicodemus has come to tell the High Priest that the new prophet has made dead men live and convinced

him that men like himself are spiritually dead. With a sneer
at the lowly carpenter, the High Priest maintains his satisfaction with the religious laws of Judea and the civil laws
of Caesar, which the "charlatan" will meddle with at his
peril. When Nicodemus interprets this threat as concealing
fear, Caiaphas, though graver, is unmoved. Finding pro-
traction of their conversation useless, the noble rises to say
he will not come again. The High Priest, noting the black
robe and knowing his visitor's antecedents, has the last
word:

>   . . . You are one of us,
> And you will save yourself at the last hour.

Nicodemus departs in tears at the vision of courage and
renunciation beyond his capacity.

From the suavity and complacency of high Jewish
society under the Romans, "Sisera" takes us back to the
heroism, the fanaticism, and the savagery of early Hebrew
history. "I have also been reading the Old Testament, a
most bloodthirsty and perilous book for the young,"
Robinson had written to Mrs. Richards. "Jehovah is beyond doubt the worst character in fiction." His retelling
of the famous story of Jael and Sisera emphasizes the
lengths to which a servant of the tribal god would go if
she were a woman. We follow Sisera's desperate flight
from the battle that has destroyed his army toward the
supposedly neutral tent of Heber the Kenite, and listen to
Jael's crooning voice as with maternal care she lulls the
weary warrior to the sleep that will know no waking. The
Hebrew general Barak arrives, describing with cruel
laughter how his troops stopped to watch Sisera's flight,
sure he would be caught in Jael's trap. But the hard pro-

fessional soldier is not prepared for what he sees: the
Philistine murdered in his sleep.

> . . . He stared at Sisera's head,
> Where the nail was, and slowly shook his own
> Before he spoke: "I am not sure of this,"
> He said, and looked at her uncertainly,
> As if to ask, for the first time, perhaps—
> Whose hand held death for him. She who did this
> Might one day flout her fealty to Jehovah
> And lust for Baal. She might do anything.

Jael is unmoved by the reproof. The poem ends upon her
song of triumph, meant for the ears of Deborah, who has
prophesied Sisera's overthrow and, being a woman, will
understand.

The speed and fire of "Sisera" are in the best tradition
of heroic verse. How surely Robinson could vary blank
verse for effects poles apart may be seen from comparison
of the conclusion of "Nicodemus" with the resonant and
triumphant opening of "Sisera" that followed on the next
page of the volume.

> Caiaphas rubbed his hands together slowly,
> Smiling at Nicodemus, who was holding
> A black robe close to him and feeling it
> Only as darkness that he could not see.
> All he could see through tears that blinded him
> To Caiaphas, to himself, and to all men
> Save one, was one that he had left alone,
> Alone in a bare room, and not afraid.

We turn the page to find:

> From Taanach to Harosheth, by the river,
> Barak had driven Sisera and his thousands
> Till there were only a last few of them

Alive to feel, while there was time to feel,
Jehovah's hand and Israel's together,
Smiting invincibly.

Robinson wrote no more short poems. When asked why, he would reply: "I am over sixty."

Long poems he could still create, although he felt increasingly the strain of holding for months incidents and ideas in a certain order in his mind. When he returned from the Veltin Studio to Colony Hall on summer afternoons, striking at mosquitoes that pursued him over the meadow, his feet dragged and there were ominous patches of red on his cheek bones. At dinner he smoked many Sweet Caporals. He played pool, with boyish eagerness to win, before he retired to his room upstairs with a detective story (any would do so long as it had no literary merit) to woo sleep by distracting his mind from the creative effort of the day. He slept badly and reappeared weary-eyed and without appetite. "I wish my breakfast had more sparkles in it," he would sigh.

Swaying gently in his studio rocker and gazing through a long avenue of tall pines at Monadnock, he would resume the search for elusive words. The best ideas and images often came just as he must leave for dinner. Once a word he had striven for all day flashed upon him when his hand was on the door. Turning back, he scribbled it hastily. The next morning he found in dismay that he could not read what he had written. "And it never would come back," he said, musing on the mysteries of the human mind. Final drafts of the poems, in minute penciled handwriting, offered difficulties even for the myopic eyes of the playwright Esther Bates, who for many years had prepared his typescripts. "When" and "where" were indistinguishable and marks of punctuation faint, although he was a stickler for the exact notation of pauses. Indications of revision were chiefly cuts. Apparently he pondered long before setting anything upon paper.

After *Tristram* he indulged his taste in red neckties, but fame in no way altered his habits or manner. "His face is very thin," reported a newcomer to the Colony, "and his expression a mixture of timidity and aloofness. His eyes are so mysterious that one doesn't make up one's mind about them at first meeting. He is so retiring that he wouldn't ask to join the two youngsters who were playing pool last night. They both were embryonic poets and of course would think it the height of presumption to invite him. Isn't it pathetic that a man of his fame should be so shy? It means that modest people are afraid to bother him, and he gets bothered by the bold and insensitive." One morning at breakfast he presented a case of conscience. How could he return a postage stamp enclosed in a request for his autograph without giving the autograph at least on the envelope or else troubling someone to answer for him?

Although he never thought of asking special privileges, the Colonists left free the first chair at the first table as one entered the dining room, which he had formed the habit of dropping into so as to be least observed; and they passed about the word that he should be included in the first pool game after dinner. When newcomers one summer, inspired by the Youth Movement before Hitler had made it odious, rushed to monopolize the pool table as a protest against respect for age and achievement, fellow Colonists were indignant, but not Robinson. The pronoun "I," prominent in the letters to Smith, Gledhill, and Latham, had long ago almost disappeared from his correspondence, and his conversation, still laconic, baffled Boswells by its impersonality. His struggles and sorrows, which few suspected, came out only when one avoided leading questions and let him ruminate until he forgot he had hearers. Once he drifted into mentioning traits he had observed among Italian laborers while working in the subway, and then fell silent, lost in memories. A young woman of conventional social habits broke what she thought an awkward pause in the conversation by exclaiming, "How interesting, Mr. Robinson! You must have enjoyed studying them!" Startled, he replied passionately, "On the contrary, I despised myself because I couldn't get a better job," and changed the subject.

Although a stimulating listener, reflecting every shade of meaning in his dark eyes, he still agonized over his incapacity to express himself accurately in conversation. What speech cost him, he revealed in an apologetic letter to a close friend: "Please don't worry over what I say and don't mean, and remember that it is with the greatest difficulty and by the most careful study and enunciation of every syllable that I can make myself understood at all." Nevertheless, the wisdom of his dry humor had become legendary, as in the story of advice he had given. A courtly Frenchman had begun kissing a fellow Colonist, an American spinster of sixty, on the forehead as a morning greeting. Pleased at first, she soon developed misgivings, and consulted Robinson as to whether it would be prudent to let the homage continue. "Does he ever kiss you at any other time than at breakfast?" the poet inquired. When the reply was "No," he decided: "Well, I think it's all right." His silence could be devastating. A practitioner of one of the other arts, finding him alone, thought to compliment him by saying he had heard him called "the American Browning." There was no reply for what seemed five minutes, then the drawl, "Well, people are likely to call you anything."

But usually he listened without comment to the most naïve literary judgments or to the proffered information that *The Faerie Queene* was written in Ireland and that Verlaine was a poet he ought to read. It was puzzling to see among his intimates not only distinguished writers but also some decidedly on the dull side or boisterous, until one learned that such a one had praised his verse when there were few to praise or had lent him money, and that he was tolerating a loquacious bore because the poor man was recovering from a nervous breakdown and needed constant society to escape from melancholia. The dependence of authors on the caprices of popular taste weighed on his mind. "Poor X," he would muse aloud, "I don't know what he is going to live on, now the kind of writing he does has gone out of fashion."

Pity for the weak made him stern toward the presumptuous. "Y thinks himself a great man, now the reviewers are praising his new book," he could remark with acid amusement. When a writer of mediocre verse who had made money by a lucky plunge into flashy fiction alighted from an immoderately large car to patronize the Colony, Robinson met him with ironic aloofness. Apparently without social defenses, he adroitly shook off lion-hunters and froze impertinent familiarities. Loving his country with a jealous love, he suffered from the spectacle of brashness and folly among his countrymen. Newspaper stories of Marathon dancing or tree-sitting provoked him to say, "That's peculiarly American foolishness." Permitting the small farmer to be ruined seemed the greatest national calamity of his time. Yet ignorant and tactless people could hurt him sorely by unfavorable comment on his verse. "It seems that some of my best work is in it," he wrote to a Colonist of *The Glory of the Nightingales,* "but it is apparently too much for the newspaper critics. At any rate they are writing some surpassing nonsense about it, which the publishers won't like."

Even in his semipublic situation at Peterborough, where every visitor wanted him pointed out, he managed to have a private life. There were disappearances over Sunday with old friends; there was frank discussion of literature at table or by the Colony Hall fireplace when he found himself in a group that seemed to deserve his opinions. He did some serious reading even while under the stress of composing. Among contemporary writers he preferred those who viewed life with somber realism, like Dean Inge, or produced highly finished art, like Isak Dinesen in her *Seven Gothic Tales* and Virginia Woolf. He was visibly pleased when one of his hearers reported that Robert Frost, lecturing at Amherst, said that "Robinson knew the art of poetry." The pretentious striving for greatness in the later dramas of O'Neill amused him, but the cult of Gertrude Stein seemed a bad omen for literature. Most he enjoyed rereading favorites of his youth: Wordsworth, Cowper's *Task, Wuthering Heights* (the amazing work of "a mere child"), Dickens, and Thackeray. Major Pendennis was the greatest character creation in English fiction and *Pendennis* an ideal novel, with real people in an interesting social scene and little plot to get in their way. But Thackeray's great weakness, in fiction as in life, was women. Robinson would have respected him more if he had either run away with Mrs. Brookfield or renounced her.

Although his vein of poetry ran thin after *Nicodemus,* his final narratives, *Talifer* (1933), *Amaranth* (1934), and the posthumous *King Jasper* (1935) are absorbing documents in the history of his mind, which, no longer feeling the necessity of veiling its opinions, pours itself out on paper.

In *Talifer* humor gets the upper hand and solves the *Roman Bartholow* triangle as pure comedy. When Talifer, a stiffer, less intelligent variation of the ancestor-dominated Bartholow, makes the mistake of jilting Althea for an "ivory fish," the beautiful, pedantic, and cold Karen, Doctor Quick (Penn-Raven without mystery) releases him by running off with her to England. Karen soon tires of Quick, who returns after two years to receive a joyful "home-breaker's welcome" from Talifer and his new wife, the thoroughly normal and gay Althea. Quick's comment on the situation, addressed to their infant son in his pram, is that of the Shavian hero who has found "a moral in his immorality."

Amaranth concludes the series of poems on the life of the artist. Although the theme of mistaken vocation is generalized to include medicine, law, invention, and the church, stress is upon misfit writers, composers, and painters. The dedication of this poem to the memory of Dr. Dean Robinson has led astray commentators who have not reflected upon the fact that Dean did not choose unsuitable work of his own volition, and that he did not lack intellectual qualifications for medicine. What set Robinson to writing *Amaranth* was his long observation of men and women with the urge for artistic creation but without the talent, who were temporarily encouraged by the boom of the nineteen-twenties. "The late twenties," Carl Van Doren has recorded in *Three Worlds*, "were a golden age for writers. . . . Volume after volume of minor poetry appeared, as much because there were more publishers as because there were more poets. . . . Newspapers and magazines, with an eye to book advertisements, gave space to book reviews. The leading reviewers had influence, or were thought to have it, and were courted by publishers. Most of the reviewers were honest enough, though they might not know much about literature, and might fall into loose enthusiasms over books that were better than the daily run." Then came the depression of the 'thirties, hitting writers and artists possibly even harder than it hit businessmen. Until W.P.A. projects got under way with a change of administration, the plight of the less competent was desperate. Robinson, meeting many of them at the MacDowell Colony and elsewhere, pitied them as only he could pity. He saw their situation as worse than that of genius struggling against popular incomprehension, for Rembrandt and his like had been sustained by consciousness of their high vocation. But consider the case of those mistaken in their estimate of themselves, like the classic example of the painter Benjamin Haydon or of the many obscure, including Robinson's old acquaintance Joseph French. Or Robinson himself, had he, and not the magazine editors, been mistaken about the quality of his verse. What anguish might be saved if men made no false judgment of their vocation, or admitted their error before too many years were wasted! Some indeed, like Robinson's O'Leary, a "Shadrach of the Gleam," were wise enough to escape the fiery furnace of art before it scorched them to cinders. But others far more numerous were martyrs to illusion.

Amaranth, "the flower that never fades," is Robinson's symbol for reality. Some of the misfits who steel themselves to face him are thereby cured of illusion and find useful work; others, feeling life unbearable without it, put an end to themselves. Miss Watchman, who preferred writing to truth or life, crumbles into dust. Throughout the narrative, appropriately a nightmare because concerned with the stuff of dreams, appears Robinson's conviction that art must have "roots" in life and truth. "Sinners in art" splash color about without learning to draw, in the belief that "there are short roads To glory without form." After ridiculing the cult of "pure poetry" in the account of Pink:

> . . . He cuts and sets his words
> With an exotic skill so scintillating
> That no two neophytes that worship them
> Are mystified in the same way exactly.
> All who believe themselves at one with him
> Will have a private and a personal Pink
> And their unshared interpretation of him—

Robinson reaffirms his conviction that poetry should illuminate life:

> . . . Poets, whatever the end,
> Should know a little more than most of us
> Of our obscurities.

His last work, *King Jasper*, which he playfully called his "treatise on economics," concludes the poems on material success. The decision to write it had come on the announcement of the bank holiday in 1933, which published to the world the incompetence and cowardice of the captains of industry and finance who had ruled the United

States for so long. The poem was an allegory, for signs of the approaching collapse of capitalism seemed universal. With consciousness of personal triumph he called it *King Jasper*, after the Jasper County Mine in which the last of his father's money had been lost.

Jasper, who has built up an industrial kingdom by exploiting the brains of the inventor Hebron, has for his queen Honoria—convention and good form. The kingdom is threatened with destruction by Hebron's son, who in eagerness to avenge his father, whom Jasper has let die in poverty, has become a communist, and with reform from within by Jasper's son, who has fallen under the influence of Zoë, knowledge which sustains life. Reared by a mysterious "wise one" who resembles Robinson's Merlin, Zoë is the poet's mouthpiece. She hates Hebron's

> Assurance of his power to serve the world
> When he is doing his villainous worst in it,

yet she finds Jasper too complacently ignorant and Honoria too inflexible to save their kingdom by reform. Frightened by the shape of things to come, Honoria kills herself; her son is shot dead in the revolt of Jasper's workers stirred up by young Hebron; Jasper dies of grief and defeat. Zoë, stabbing Hebron with her knife of knowledge, escapes the ruin of the kingdom, to remain

> . . . sorry for man
> Always and for the curse of time on man
> That shrieks to him unheard from history.
> .   .   .   .
> . . . It's well for folly
> That centuries are so many, and far to count.
> Fools against fools have a long time to fight.

Nevertheless, there must be some meaning in the world:

> . . . No God,
> No Law, no purpose, could have hatched for sport
> Out of warm water and slime, a war for life
> That was unnecessary, and far better
> Had never been—if man, as we behold him,
> Is all it means.

All who meditate must acknowledge God:

> I don't say what God is, but it's a name
> That somehow answers us when we are driven
> To feel and think how little we have to do
> With what we are.

From *Merlin*, "Cassandra," and "The Man Against the Sky," Robinson had gathered his final words on the riddle of the universe.

The summer before his sixty-fourth birthday, he said to Esther Bates: "Most of the poetic fellows have curled up before coming to my age—excepting the Greek tragedians, who kept themselves healthy and happy by writing about nothing but murder and worse." Labor over *Amaranth* the following year brought a succession of severe headaches. But the idea of *King Jasper* took hold, and he drove himself another summer. Returning to New York, he confessed severe abdominal pain.

On Christmas Day, he wrote to the present writer's wife: "Poetry is likely to be expensive in one way or another." Late in January 1935 he underwent an explorative operation at the New York Hospital, which revealed cancer too far developed to be removed. He seemed to accept a report that hid the truth, but he had not sufficient energy to leave his bed. Among many visitors, French slipped in under an assumed name, demanding money. Robinson gave him twenty-five dollars.

Looking over the typescript of *King Jasper* in March, he was disturbed to find an error which had escaped both Torrence and Ledoux. For the perfection he sought, he insisted on re-examining the entire text. Too weak to work alone, he listened and corrected while Isaacs read. Once he interrupted to change the name of the Queen from Hermione to Honoria. On April 3, *King Jasper* was ready for the printer. Three days later its author was dead.

I Shall Have More to Say When
I Am Dead

E A. R. is poetry." In the perspective of three decades Amy Lowell's tribute of 1919 has taken on wider meaning. The authenticity of Robinson's gift, his single-minded devotion to it and complete dependence upon it for a livelihood made him a test of the ability of American poetry to survive the two decades before 1912, when the odds against it were tremendous. The only other poets of significant achievement then writing, Santayana and Frost, had other strings to their bow. For Robinson it was poetry or nothing.

The first anthology in which his verse appeared, Stedman's *American Anthology* of 1901, accurately characterized the turn of the century as a "twilight interval, with minor voices and their tentative modes and tones." Except for Robinson, whose stature Stedman failed to measure, Santayana, whom he virtually ignored, and Frost, whom he did not mention, the judgment holds today. Poetry failed to compete for the attention of the American male against the claims of a continent to be exploited industrially and against materialistic science, which after Darwin seemed to show mankind wholly under the sway of the mechanical laws of matter and motion. The humanities, the soil of which poetry is the flower, persisted on condition of dehumanizing themselves. History and philosophy ceased to count themselves among the arts. Greek and Latin, on the defensive against the charge of uselessness, tried to justify themselves as "scientific" philology and "scientific" literary history; and the study of modern languages and literatures followed their example. It was the fashion to explain even literary creation in mechanical terms. Science and business were sacrosanct. The life of action and the life of intellect alike drew virile Americans away from poetry, leaving it to women and the intermediate sex as an elegant accomplishment, an outdated ornament.

As the main stream of American life turned away from poetry, poets withdrew from life. The periodicals, which chiefly sustained them, had three-fourths of their circulation among women, according to William Dean Howells. Women of the comfortable classes, cushioned from the rude shocks of the competitive struggle in which their husbands and sons were engaged, shrank from verse that touched upon that struggle or its results. The poetry that appealed to them spoke of ideals, not "sordid reality," dwelt wholly in the realm of beauty, expurgating its language as well as its themes. The feminization of poetry, of which Byron and Keats had foreboding, was almost complete.

Robinson, whose mind was neither historical nor philosophical, suffered from this plight of poetry for a long time before he understood its causes. From the first he was acutely aware of his difference from other boys and young men in liking poetry and preferring writing it to a life of action. When he tried to publish, he found the kind of verse he wrote unacceptable to editors, who knew the taste of their feminine readers. In his humor, in his irony, in his facing facts he was close to his male contemporaries in Maine, who did not like the poetry they saw because it had no relation to life as they knew it. Now and then women, like Emily Dickinson, admired intellectual values in poetry, and their number was increasing with better education and greater liberty; but at the outset his potential audience was masculine. By restoring intellectual virtues to poetry and by enlarging its province to include every aspect of life, he slowly won back the male readers it had had in all preceding centuries. But the process was almost unbearably slow to a man who had staked his life on it.

With a normal youth's gusto for the fullness of experience, Robinson found poetic utterance, once universal in Shakespeare, restricted to an area whose narrowness few now under fifty can conceive. There was not only the taboo which had bowdlerized Shakespeare; there was renunciation of the medieval freedom, reasserted by the Romanticists, to mix comedy and tragedy, ugliness and beauty, as they are mingled in daily life. After Byron and Keats had come the finicky aestheticism of Tennyson, against which Browning, Whitman, and Kipling were still unsuccessful protests. Why Kipling's vocabulary was a breath of fresh air to Robinson, it now requires exercise of the historical imagination to comprehend. In 1898 Thomas Bailey Aldrich could write of it thus to Richard Watson Gilder: "At a time when it is supposed to be poetical to write 'Gawd' instead of God and otherwise to mutilate God's choicest language, perhaps silence is the best poem for a man who respects his art." He went on to express his disgust that a theater audience should be deeply moved by such "rot" as the words, "Her body's in the baggage car."

Under such restrictions American verse had spoken less and less of man, and more and more of nature, particularly in her tamer moods. Robinson's gibe about the absence from *The Torrent* of "nightingales and roses" or a "red-bellied robin" shows his conscious return to man as the proper study of mankind, even when men like Aaron Stark and John Evereldown are slaves to an evil passion. In the turning of late nineteenth-century prose fiction toward realism and naturalism he foresaw consequences for the poetic style of the twentieth century. To become once more coextensive with reality, poetry must be willing to set off beauty by ugliness, tragedy by humor, high seriousness by irony; be willing, where the matter required, to descend to apparent prosiness in following the speech of modern man. Hardy, Carlyle, Daudet, George Moore, and Kipling's prose (as well as his verse), Byron's *Don Juan*, Browning's monologues, and Aristophanes encouraged the innovations of "Captain Craig," culminating in the lines about Carmichael, which put the sonnet to a use incongruous with its previous associations, like those waltz tunes distorted by the agony of the dying man who recalls them in Richard Strauss' tone poem, *Death and Transfiguration*. For a parallel to the audacity of that sonnet, American poetry had to wait for the implied contrasts between form and content in *The Waste Land* (1922). Had critics and public been ready to accept the aesthetic innovations of "Captain Craig," there need have been no break in the development of American poetry between it and the appearance of *Prufrock and Other Observations* in 1917.

The fate of Craig took the youthful audacity out of Robinson. For a quarter of a century he withdrew to the comparatively safer ground of *The Children of the Night*, still in advance of critics and public in its intellectual demands. Only after younger writers had won the battle against taboo did he give himself the freedom in expressing the jealous imaginings of Tristram which Shakespeare had with those of Othello.

Rescue of poetry from feminization was but part of what Robinson was obliged to achieve if he were to find an audience. Even more difficult was the task of convincing the American male of the importance of poetry as interpretation of life. Back of his dismissal of the poet as "impractical" and "dreamy" was not only preference of the active life to the contemplative, but also the loss of the religious sense. The Bible, synonymous with religion in a Protestant country, had lost its authority when an unimaginative and rigid literal interpretation had brought it into collision with scientific fact and with history (in the form of the "higher criticism"). The intelligent American who heard from the pulpit of a hell of actual brimstone, an exact six days of special creation, and a whale with a gullet large enough to admit Jonah could hardly be blamed for "having his religion in his wife's name," especially if he were uneasy about the relation of his business practices to some of the Ten Commandments. "Our religion has materialized itself in the fact, in the supposed fact; it has attached its emotion to the fact; and now the fact is failing it." Matthew Arnold, who thus described the situation with luminous brevity, saw the wide extent of its perils. If the literal habit of mind persisted, the moral authority of the Bible would be undermined, its beauty and greatness as literature forgotten, and poetry might cease to exist. For poetry could not thrive where symbol, allegory, myth, and legend were not understood.

Robinson, repelled like so many of his contemporaries by popular religion, had to rediscover religion for himself, guided by his poet's sense of mystery in the universe and in the heart of man. Before going to Harvard, he found help in his search from Carlyle, whose *Sartor Resartus* told of passage by the same route to a creedless spirituality. Carlyle's picturesque assertion, "Faith is the one thing needful; without it worldlings, in the midst of plenty, puke up their sick existence," by striking at materialism as a way of life, led toward the creation of Richard Cory. In his second Harvard year, the poet heard of philosophic idealism in Royce's course, and, more important for the moment, felt the influence of Norton, a friend of Ruskin and Carlyle, and caught from him their scorn of a civilization whose "Hell is not making money."

His nascent faith, tested in the years when he had to justify his poetic vocation while misfortunes were descending on his family, grew almost independently of the Scriptures. It was their value as literature which first impressed him. The way back to their spiritual value was through acquaintance with the Christian Scientist Jones, whom he met when "Luke Havergal" was already written. The poems of *The Torrent* declaring faith in the "Light" were off to the printer before he discovered that Epictetus and Socrates, Emerson and Carlyle, Paul and Jesus were essentially at one in denying matter otherwise than as "manifestation of thought." At length, after the crowning sorrow of his mother's death, he found in the Gospel according to St. John a meaning utterly different from its interpretation by the popular Christianity against which he had revolted, and wrote "Calvary."

Thereafter he turned from the defense of poetry and the spiritual life to an attack upon materialism. Richard Cory is the first of a portrait gallery of men of property corroded from within. Briony, too intelligent for his life of selfish retirement, is destroyed by the neurosis which would also have destroyed Roman Bartholow, had not Penn-Raven taught him that he had a soul. Finzer's greed, overreaching itself, leaves him a pitiable wreck. Tasker Norcross suffers from impotent awareness that he is dead to the world of art and of the spirit; a stronger sense of her negativeness makes life intolerable for Gabrielle Bartholow. Cavender, masterful captain of industry, discovers that there is something he cannot possess and surrenders to the moral law he has flouted. When the great depression, striking a few months after the publication of *Cavender's House* in April 1929, brought a spate of suicides, Robinson was human enough to exult in private. "There's a joke somewhere," he told Rollo Brown. "These birds used to refer to me as 'a mere poet'; and now they are going off and blowing their brains out and I am making a living writing poetry." There was no personal vanity in the statement. The triumph was not his; it was poetry's.

Defense of poetry had led him into realms which at first held no interest: economics, politics, science, philosophy. The young man who wondered at Harry Smith's reading Goldwin Smith and smiled when Moody wrote odes against imperialism, was succeeded by the author of "The Master," "The Revealer," "Cassandra," poems on Demos, and an acknowledged "treatise on economics," *King Jasper*. Robinson had begun, like the Thackeray of *Pendennis* and

The Newcomes, by presenting to a society ruled by money the opposite ideal of the free though impecunious spirit of literary, artistic, and intellectual Bohemia in "Captain Craig" and in the character portraits of *The Town Down the River.* But by middle life he perceived that he must strike at the intellectual roots of materialism in current science and philosophy, especially since Marxian communism, looming as capitalism's most serious rival, drew sustenance from the same roots. He struck with all his might in "The Man Against the Sky." Twenty years later, having read Eddington and seen the approach of a second world war, he returned to the theme with the apocalyptic *King Jasper,* which leaves humanity, among the ruins of a world in which both capitalism and communism have been destroyed, to continue its slow evolution toward wisdom, guided by something beyond itself which it calls God.

In a literary career bridging the interval between William McKinley and Franklin D. Roosevelt, between Herbert Spencer and the revolution in physics which has outmoded materialism, between years in which poetry was a pariah and years in which it had indiscriminate praise, Robinson wrote poems that are a journal of the vicissitudes of the literary life. The sonnets of *The Torrent* are cries of a lonely soul who knows that poetry has fallen on evil days and needs to "prop" his mind, in the manner of Matthew Arnold, by poets who have kept the true faith of art. In "Captain Craig" is a vision, alluring but overpowering, of the materials American life would offer to a new Aeschylus. The disastrous years which followed associated Robinson with a great variety of artists in their common struggle for existence. Anyone not a charlatan who wrote verse, however feebly, had claims on the friendship of the author of

The Town Down the River; whoever was indifferent or hostile to poetry was his enemy. When better days began to dawn, he deplored in "Old Trails" the playwright who forgot, when at length he "sauntered into fame," his bare room on Eleventh Street, his ten lonely years of European exile, and five more of lean toil in Yonkers. Robinson never forgot, when fame came to test him. Patiently and conscientiously he read the manuscript of any writer who asked his criticism, and, where he saw talent, did all he could to encourage. He never forgot the critics who praised his work when there were few to praise, even newspaper hacks whose comments were lame, vague, or flowery. In the 'twenties poets fell victim to the American tendency to extremes; after long neglect, they were pampered. The reaction against Puritanism romanticized debauch; the reaction against traditional versification condoned formless and slipshod work. The poet who in "Captain Craig" had defended Bohemianism and broken down artificiality in blank verse now warned in *The Man Who Died Twice* against the perils to genius in drink and women, and in "The False Gods" against the ephemeral nature of writing that flouted organic form and stored wisdom in art. Standing apart from schools with exclusive programs, Robinson had centrality of vision for the abiding qualities of poetry. "Rembrandt to Rembrandt" presents his ideal genius, neither spoiled by acclaim nor daunted by unpopularity.

"*The Man Against the Sky* indicated very clearly the place of the poet," observed Samuel Roth in 1920; "it was very high—how high we had not the standards with which to measure." In 1916, American critics, although aware that they were in the presence of a creative revival by Robinson, Frost, Masters, Lindsay, Amy Lowell, and others, fought shy of measuring these against their best American predecessors or against European poets of the past or present. Too recently, recalled Stark Young, American poetry had been content to be "a mild imitation of English importations that had grown a trifle stale at home. You thought of poetry as a manly man was to think of a lady, to be honored and revered but not to be held too responsible in grave issues." Robinson's *Collected Poems* restored confidence in the international significance of American poetry. In 1921, the year of their appearance, John Gould Fletcher compared "The Man Against the Sky" with Wordsworth's greatest ode, and Conrad Aiken proclaimed his American contemporaries "The New Elizabethans," with the vigor and daring twentieth-century English verse had lost.

At present writing in 1948, when the emergence of the United States as the strongest world power is exposing American poets to the opposite danger of more than their meed of attention and praise, Robinson, although recognized as foremost in the decisive effort to free American poetry from a lingering colonial sense of inferiority, is not likely to suffer from patriotic overestimate; for his national and local qualities are never exaggerated and his art does not break with European tradition. While the time is not yet to pronounce upon his place among American poets, there is agreement as to his salient qualities. To find his peer as an artist we must turn aside from Poe, and even Frost and Eliot, to the prose masters Hawthorne and Henry James. He is the greatest intellectual force in our poetry, bringing to it the new virtues of irony and wit, surpassing Emerson in consistency and subtlety of thought, Eliot in constructive skill. His insight into the human heart is of the order of Frost's and Dickinson's. Although not primarily a lyricist, he has written "Luke Havergal," which Allen Tate calls "one of the great lyrics in modern times . . . a poem in which the hard images glow with a fierce intensity of light." His series of poems on the artist's life, his compressed character studies, are unique in our literature; no American poet has used the sonnet for so many purposes or with such skill. "Cassandra," probing deeply into the weaknesses of our national character and phrasing them unforgettably, is the finest of our political poems. "The Man Against the Sky," bringing to bear upon the supreme problem of human destiny consummate qualities of intellect, human understanding, and art, towers above any other poem written upon American soil. Among other poems apparently secure as American classics are: "Mr. Flood's Party," "Bewick Finzer," "Miniver Cheevy," "The Mill," "The Poor Relation," "Flammonde," "Eros Turannos," "The Dark Hills," "For a Dead Lady," "Richard Cory." As with the passage of time their quality stands out from the bulky later work that tends to hide them, as the nation, in maturing, gains in respect for the intellectual and contemplative virtues and sees behind material satisfactions the tragedy of our human condition and feels the glory of art that in accepting tragedy transcends it, Robinson's figure will grow.

A distinguished Italian man of letters, engaged in translating American verse, recently asked the present writer for a representative Robinson poem. He listened attentively to "Mr. Flood's Party," then shook his head: "It is fine but it won't do for Italy. Too much like our Italian classics." J. C. Squire, in a series of appraisals of American poets in 1925, found a similar obstacle between Robinson and the

British public in his appeal to mature rather than youthful readers and his demand for the close and repeated reading the English give their own national classics. Thus he is among the American authors most likely to gain from the spread of the conception of world literature, a corollary of the political and economic conception of one world.

It is significant that he should have found his most appreciative foreign critic at the University of Paris, which has hitherto led in international literary studies. Professor Charles Cestre's survey of Robinson's achievement in *La Revue anglo-américaine* for April 1923 found in it "all that American culture has in common with the continent" of Europe. His genius, unlike that of most American writers, ripened early. With *The Children of the Night*, "already at twenty-eight he was in full possession of the qualities of content and of form which put him in the first rank of American poets and in a distinguished position among contemporary poets writing in English." "Captain Craig" was in direct line of descent from Shakespeare's wise fools and from Diogenes Teufelsdröckh. The deliberate breaking of unity of tone in "The Man Against the Sky" was in the vein of Carlyle and of Shaw. In other poems Robinson resembled the Metaphysicals Herbert and Donne. His "mastery of language" permitted him "to give an arabesque beauty to passages where intellectuality outweighs color or visual suggestion, to spread a harmonious tone over certain designs which in themselves would be too severe. Skillful antitheses, subtle symmetry, not of words only but also of ideas, raise such passages to an artistic plane enchanting to the intelligence." Professor Cestre's Bryn Mawr lectures, published in 1930 as *An Introduction to Edwin Arlington Robinson*, although suffering from being addressed to immature young women and from defining Robinson, "a modern classic," too much in terms of academic French classicism, delighted the poet by precise interpretation of what he intended to say. They remain the fullest analysis of his work and excel, where French criticism is wont to excel, in analysis of dramatic motivation and of qualities of style. Professor Cestre stresses Robinson's modernity in his use of the subconscious, of dormant overtones and undertones, and at the same time his deep roots in the humanistic tradition: "his occasional adaptations and variations of Greek themes fit in so exactly with his own work that they seem a spontaneous retrospect of his thought towards the past."

The threat of the extinction of humanism as a result of the Second World War, by turning Europeans to America for its support, is probably increasing the number of serious readers who seek in American literature what binds men together. No longer will it seem a paradox that old souls like Hawthorne, Emerson, Henry Adams, Henry James, and Robinson should appear in a new land. Frenchmen will admire in Robinson a poet steeped in Montaigne, in Voltaire, in Daudet, a poet who has affinities with Vigny and Leconte de Lisle yet is distinguished from them by his humor, his flexibility, his variety. Italians will find something Dantean in his style, something Leopardian in his conquest for classical form of the apparent commonplaces of common life, in his superb equipoise of mind with heart, in his unilluded but compassionate view of humanity; and yet they will discover novelty in his capacity for gaiety and his triumph over the nightmare of mechanistic materialism from which Leopardi saw no escape.

Englishmen will savor a poet who knew their classics as

well as they, who combined Wordsworthian qualities with that very un-Wordsworthian mingling of humor with tragedy which distinguishes English literature from French and is rare in German outside of Heine. In Robinson's variety they will perceive more flavor of wit than in Hardy. Closely akin to Housman in reconciling a Romantic theory of poetry with classical concision and polish, he has none of Housman's immaturity or narrowness of interest. A subtler and more sophisticated mind than Hardy and a more careful artist, he has no peer among his British contemporaries except Yeats. Beginning poles apart, the Irishman in Celtic myth and legend, the American in realistic study of the contemporary scene, they come close together in the utterance of late-acquired political convictions in a style of athletic sparseness and vigor. To say that Robinson has written the best Tristram poem in English, while true, is not his best introduction to British readers; for its rivals, *Tristram of Lyonesse* and "Tristram and Iseult," are no more the best Swinburne and the best Arnold than *Tristram* is the best Robinson. The choice of portions of "The Man Against the Sky" for reading over the B.B.C. in 1947 indicates that Robinson has English admirers with a sense of where his greatness lies.

The poetry is the world's; the poet is America's. Ours the blame for the long discouragement, ours the praise that there were individuals among us who permitted him to live by poetry. If we had seen his major importance when he gave us *The Torrent* and *The Children of the Night*, if we had encouraged his pioneering in "Captain Craig," Robinson might have gone directly, without strength-sapping years of prose, to the maturity of *The Man Against the Sky* and to something still better. It is our fault that the world must see him as a maimed giant.

Yet these were Americans who helped him cling to poetry: friends in Gardiner, at Harvard, in New York. An American President, patron of letters in the tradition of enlightened rulers, saved him at a critical moment. One of our most distinguished women provided him with ideal conditions for writing. His critical success and his popular success were American. In a nation supposedly given over to commercialism was found a saving remnant of admirers of a poet of austere professional ethics, who has left poems on the literary life which are the inspiration of writers with ideals. Robinson's life was a poem of courage, of genius for friendship, of devotion to art and to the best self of our nation.

"Why hadn't we heard of him before?" inquired a host of readers of *Tristram*. Scattered over a continent, they and their like are a potential audience for poetry vaster than the world has known. Robinson was himself among the thousands in our small towns, with nothing provincial in the quality of their minds, who must grope their way towards the best in literature. If their way as readers could be made easier, writers of his stature would be spared his ordeal.

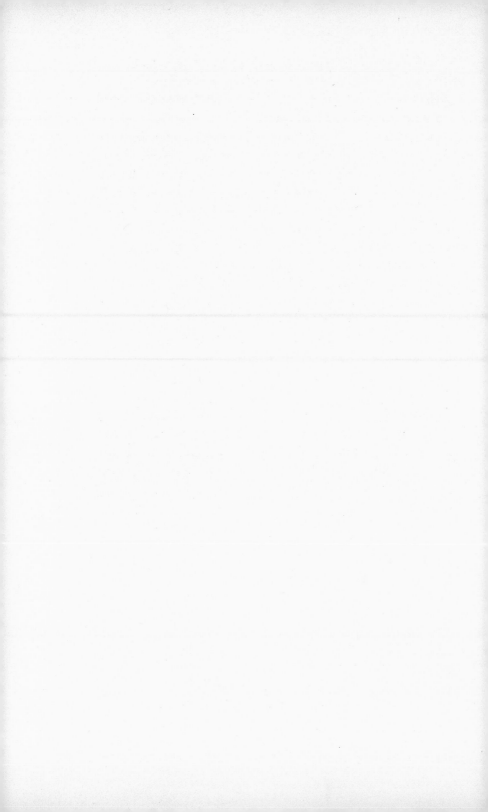

Selected References

Full information in regard to Robinson's publications and their critical reception may be found in *A Bibliography of Edwin Arlington Robinson,* by Charles Beecher Hogan (New Haven, Yale University Press, 1936), and its periodically issued supplements. The *Collected Poems of Edwin Arlington Robinson* are published by The Macmillan Company (New York, various dates).

The chief published sources for Robinson's life, besides the biography by Hermann Hagedorn, *Edwin Arlington Robinson* (New York, The Macmillan Company, 1939), are the following: *E. A. R.,* by Laura E. Richards (Cambridge, Mass., Harvard University Press, 1936), *Next Door to a Poet,* by Rollo Walter Brown (New York, The Appleton-Century Company, 1937), *Selected Letters of Edwin Arlington Robinson* (New York, The Macmillan Company, 1940), *Edwin Arlington Robinson and His Manuscripts,* by Esther Willard Bates (Waterville, Maine, The Colby College Library, 1944), and *Untriangulated Stars: Letters of Edwin Arlington Robinson to Harry de Forest Smith,* edited by Denham Sutcliffe (Cambridge, Mass., Harvard University Press, 1947). Interesting reminiscences of Robinson may also be found in *Three Worlds,* by Carl Van Doren (New York, Harper, 1936), *Life is My Song: The Autobiography of John Gould Fletcher* (New York, Farrar & Rinehart, 1937) and *Music in My Time, and Other Reminiscences,* by Daniel Gregory Mason (New York, The Macmillan Company, 1938). Robinson's account of his artistic apprenticeship, "The First Seven Years" (*The Colophon,* December 1930, reprinted in *Breaking Into Print,* edited by Elmer Adler, New York, Simon & Schuster, 1937) is illuminating.

The chief critical monographs have been the following: *The Poetry of Edwin Arlington Robinson,* by Lloyd Morris (New York, The George H. Doran Company, 1923), *Edwin Arlington Robinson,* by Ben Ray Redman (New York, Robert M. McBride & Company, 1926), *Edwin Arlington Robinson,* by Mark Van Doren (New York, The Literary Guild, 1927), *An Introduction to Edwin Arlington Robinson,* by Charles Cestre (New York, The Macmillan Company, 1930), and *Edwin Arlington Robinson,* by Yvor Winters (Norfolk, Connecticut, New Directions Books, 1946). Robert Frost's Introduction to Robinson's *King Jasper* (New York, The Macmillan Company, 1935) is indispensable. Discerning comment may be found in the following general studies of American literature: *Tendencies in Modern American Poetry,* by Amy Lowell (New York, The Macmillan Company, 1917), *American Poetry Since 1900,* by Louis Untermeyer (New York, Henry Holt & Company, 1923), *American and British Literature Since 1890,* by Carl Van Doren and Mark Van Doren (New York, The Century Company, 1925), *Poets and Their Art,* by Harriet Monroe (New York, The Macmillan Company, 1926), *Contemporary*

American Authors, by J. C. Squire (New York, Henry
Holt & Company, 1928), *Our Singing Strength: An Out-
line of Contemporary Poetry (1620-1930),* by Alfred
Kreymborg (New York, Coward-McCann, Inc., 1929),
Reactionary Essays on Poetry and Ideas, by Allen Tate
(New York, Charles Scribner's Sons, 1936), *New England:
Indian Summer,* by Van Wyck Brooks (New York, Dut-
ton, 1940), and *A History of American Poetry* (1900-
1940), by Horace Gregory and Marya Zaturenska (New
York, Harcourt, Brace & Company, 1946). Excellent criti-
cism remains uncollected from periodicals (see Charles
Beecher Hogan, *A Bibliography of Edwin Arlington
Robinson,* and its supplements).

Index I

Index II

THE WORKS OF EDWIN ARLINGTON ROBINSON